STEAMBOATS
on the St. Croix

Anita Albrecht Buck

NORTH STAR PRESS OF ST. CLOUD, INC.

*I dedicate this book
to my husband
Gene
who has always given me
the encouragement and the freedom
to write.*

Acknowledgements

No book, particularly a research project, may be written without the help of many people. I thank all those from whose material, written and oral, I gleaned information. The sources are listed in the bibliography.

Special thanks are extended to those who made photographs available to me: Dick Anderson, Durant Blanding, William D. Bowell, Debra Chial, James Taylor Dunn, A. Carr Griffith, Jim Johnson, Jim Miller, Dick Muller, Bill Murray, the Stillwater *Gazette*, and the Washington County Historical Society.

In particular, my sincere thanks to James Taylor Dunn, who opened his personal files to me for research. Mr. Dunn also carefully perused the manuscript, editing and making sure it was historically accurate, a Herculean task for which I am most grateful.

Cover Art: "View on Mississippi River," by Ferdinand Reichardt. Courtesy of the Minnesota Historical Society.

Design: Corinne A. Dwyer

Library of Congress Cataloging-in-Publication Data

Buck, Anita.
    Steamboats on the St. Croix / Anita Albrecht Buck.
    176 p. 28 cm.
    Includes bibliographical references (p. 163) and indexes.
    ISBN 0-87839-060-X : $19.95
    1. Steamboats—Saint Croix River (Wis. and Minn.)—History.
2. Steamboat lines—Saint Croix River (Wis. and Minn.)—History.
3. Inland water transportation—Saint Croix River (Wis. and Minn.)—
—History. 4. Inland navigation—Saint Croix River (Wis. and Minn.)
—History. I. Steamboats on the Saint Croix II. Title.
HE566.P3B83   1990   90-7915
386'.22436'097751—dc20   CIP

Copyright © 1990 Anita Albrecht Buck
ISBN: 0-87839-060-X

All rights reserved. No part of this book may be reproduced in any form without prior written permission from the publisher.

Printed and bound in the United States of America by Sentinel Printing Company, Sauk Rapids, Minnesota.

Published by North Star Press of St. Cloud, Inc., P.O. Box 451, St. Cloud, Minnesota 56302.

Table of Contents

Introduction		v
1	Steamboat's a'Comin'	1
2	Back Paddling, a General History	3
3	Portrait of a Packet	9
4	Full Steam Ahead	19
5	Fuel Up	23
6	Boats that Plied the St. Croix	29
7	Boats Built on the St. Croix	43
8	Muller Boat Works	55
9	Osceola Boat Builders	61
10	Friendly Rivals	69
11	Captain Stephen B. Hanks	79
12	Captain David M. Swain	85
13	All Aboard, Meet the Crew	91
14	Laws, Lights, Whistles, and Mail	97
15	Winter Tales	105
16	High Water, Low Water	111
17	Good Times While the Boats Ran	117
18	Bad Times	125
19	End of an Era	133
20	The Steamboats Return	145
21	Steamboat Men	153
Vignettes		
	Battle of the Piles	48
	A Capitol Excursion	142
	Red Wing-Stillwater Boat Race	78
	St. Croix Boom	26
	St. Croix Ferries	34
	Steamboat Round the Bend	143
Bibliography		163
Index		
	Index of Steamboats	165
	General Index	167

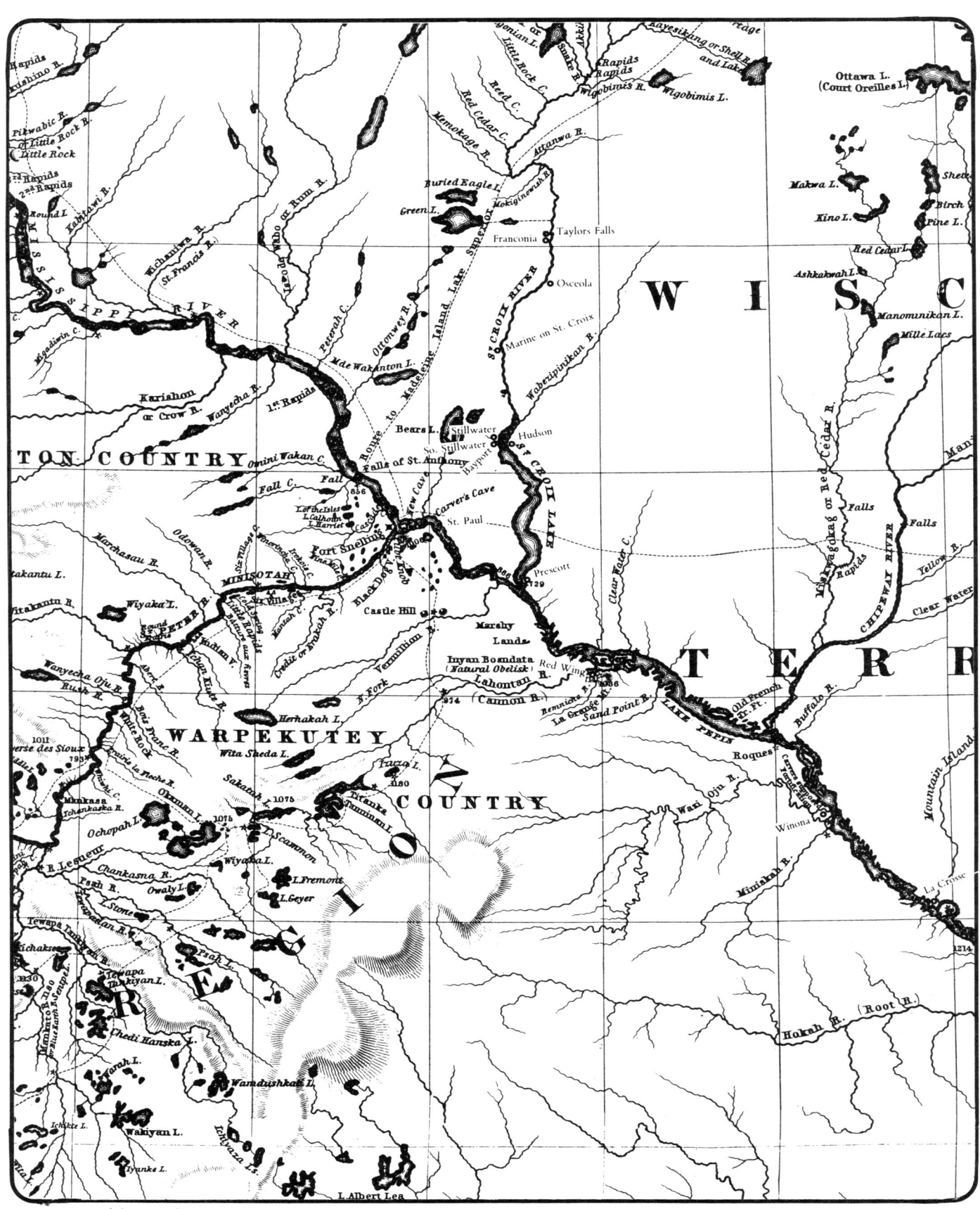

Reprinted from *The Hydrographical Basin of the Mississippi River, 1843*, a map by Joseph N. Nicollet. Town names along the St. Croix and Mississippi rivers added. (Courtesy of the Minnesota Historical Society)

Introduction

If rocks have memories, the bluffs and cliffs along the St. Croix, border river between Minnesota and Wisconsin, still echo to the whistle of steamboats, the chunking of paddle wheels, and the shushing of water tumbling off the paddle blades.

For three-quarters of a century, steamboats throbbed the pulse of the St. Croix Valley as the principal means of communication, travel, and shipping. They carried good news and bad, rascals and dignitaries, cargoes of dry goods and live goods, entertainment both lofty and base.

During the summer of 1975, I was on the excursion boat *Jubilee I*, owned by Capt. A. Carr Griffith of Stillwater, Minnesota. The boat headed north from the city's levee. I wandered to the back rail of the upper deck to watch water cascade off the rotating wheel. Mesmerized by the rhythmic beat of the paddles, I had a vision of a parade of boats, spanning scores of years, steaming between the tree-covered cliffs. I wondered how many paddles had churned through the tamarack-tinted waters of the St. Croix River, how many boats had passed the same islands and bluffs and sand bars we passed, how many lives were woven together or torn apart by steamboats on the St. Croix.

In the late afternoon, the *Jubilee I* returned to the dock. People were waiting on the levee to greet excursionists. I thought of the hundreds, even thousands, of times this scene had been enacted during the 19th century, with passengers arriving at the waterfront from both up river and down.

My first idea was to write an article about steamboats. I dredged up sparse references to the St. Croix steamboats, and worried about enough material to write any kind of comprehensive report. As I continued my research, I found a sentence in one book, a paragraph in another, an article in a newspaper, a reference in a history, a comment in a diary.

Surprised at the amount of material which began to surface, I decided to write a book. *Steamboats on the St. Croix* is the result. Even as the book goes to press, additional material surfaces. I know there are more steamboats and steamboat people and steamboat lore waiting to be discovered. Still, I hope in this volume to recapture the aura of the era of "Steamboats on the St. Croix."

Anita Albrecht Buck
Stillwater, Minnesota
August 1990

The *General Allen*, one of several paddle boats owned and operated by the United States War Department. The General Allen was built in 1916 and was used as an inspection boat on the St. Croix and other rivers of the Mississippi watershed. The hull is now used as a restaurant boat in St. Louis, Missouri. (Courtesy of A. Carr. Griffith)

Chapter 1

Steamboat's A-Comin'!

"Steamboat's a-comin'!"

The urchin on the levee was the first to shout the news. As he dangled bare feet and tangled fishing line into the swirling waters of the St. Croix, an inborn sensor made him look to the distant bend of the river. There, a plume of smoke waved above the trees. Soon, fluted black stacks appeared over the foliage. At length, a white palace glided into view around the point. Blunt bow shoving against the current, the steamer trailed a wake which joined with the water spilling from the paddle wheel.

"Steamboat's a-comin'!" he cried again.

The boat belched a puff of steam, and, a moment later, the sound of the whistle reached the boy.

"It's the old *Nellie Kent*." He quickly identified the boat by its whistle. Child of the river, he could distinguish dozens of boats by their whistles alone, and many more by their superstructures, even from a distance.

"Steamboat's a-comin'," he hollered once more.

The quiet town came to life. Clerks in warehouses and shops roused from routine, impatient to be at the levee. The town drunk stirred in his hole at the side of the mill, knowing the docking would mean excitement and a chance to panhandle the price of a drink. Sometimes, of course, he would be required to tote a valise to earn his handout. Frequently, though, the gift was freely bestowed.

Drivers of town drays and hacks hitched their teams and headed for the levee. The clatter of hooves resounded as every store and business readied its contribution of cargo. Each hotel sent a representative to meet expected guests, and to entice the unexpected to lodging.

"Steamboat's a-comin'."

Townspeople quickly finished chores and headed for the waterfront, casually hiding their excitement. Children imprisoned in school

Steamboat on the St. Croix, September 1, 1912. For three-quarters of a century, steamboats throbbed the pulse of the St. Croix valley. (Photo by John W. G. Dunn, courtesy of James Taylor Dunn)

When the steamboat arrived at the dock, there was usually a lot of activity. (Photo courtesy of Dick Anderson)

heard the deep-throated boat horn, and wiggled in their seats until dismissed to join the crowd at the waterfront.

Smoke trailing, flag flying, paddle wheel slapping, the steamboat neared the town.

The captain signaled the boiler room. The paddle wheels slowed, reversed, churned the river to foam. As the packet swung close to the levee, shaggy deckhands leaped ashore. With deft twists of rope, they moored the boat. The gangplank touched land.

Passengers jammed the upper decks, watching the shore, seeking a familiar face, assessing the unknown population. On board were adventurers who hoped to strike it rich in the West, lumbermen following the timber harvest across the nation, preachers wanting to pass the word of God to heathen Indians, gamblers and politicians confident they could make a fast dollar or a quick deal in new territory, merchants returning with new goods for frontier stores, mothers and children joining husbands and fathers who left them six months or a year earlier to forge a new life in a new land.

Waiting to board for a return trip were the same groups: adventurers who recognized that the lack of wealth was not something wrong with the country but with themselves; lumberjacks tired of the grueling winters, low pay, and monotonous meals; preachers who learned that their diluted brand of Christianity could not compete with the Indian's reverence for eternal nature; gamblers and politicians who discovered their tricks were already known to settlers; merchants whose supplies of watered-down gin and cheap goods rotted on the shelves during starving times on the frontier; families returning to the comforts of the East, leaving behind graves of children who could not fight the dual enemies of starvation and disease.

"Steamboat's a-comin'." The cry was an incantation that quickened the pulse of settlers in Taylors Falls, Franconia, Osceola, Marine Mills, Arcola, Stillwater, Hudson, and Prescott from the late 1830s until time turned the page to a new century and closed the chapter on steamboating.

Chapter 2

Back Paddling

There was little relationship between the hulking steamboats which braved the long trips on a storm-tossed ocean, and the shallow-draft paddleboats which plied the rivers of mid-America. Although both moved by means of paddle wheels pushing against water, the ocean steamships carried their machinery in deep holds, giving them stability. The side-wheelers and stern-wheelers of inland waterways had their boilers and engines on the deck; consequently they drew little water as they scuttled across the spiderweb of the Mississippi and its tributaries.

Robert Fulton is credited with the invention of the steamboat. His vessel had a deep, rounded hull and heavy keel, not at all suited to river travel. Flatboat and keelboat men who knew the nature of the nation's streams created the river packet. They fashioned craft that would be able to contend with sandbars, shallows, shifting channels, fluctuating water levels, and sunken snags that would hazard their trips. Using a wide-beamed keelboat for a model, they decked it over, and put machinery on the deck. This gave them a boat that drew mere inches of water. Instead of the single rudder of an ocean craft, two or three, sometimes more rudders steered the river boats.

The first steamboat to traverse the western rivers was the *New Orleans*, built at Pittsburgh, Pennsylvania, by Livingston and Fulton in 1811. In September of that year, the boat was given an experimental try on the Monongahela River. The boat then headed west from Pittsburgh to New Orleans. At the falls of the Ohio, the water was so shallow that the captain had to wait until rain in the upper drainage basin raised the river level.

Traveling at speeds of eight to ten miles an hour, the *New Orleans* arrived at the city of its name on January 12, 1812, proving that steamboats were practical for inland waterways.

The first steam vessel to travel up the Mississippi River was the

The *Ben Campbell* was a typical side-wheeler. It was one of many boats constructed at Osceola, Wisconsin, in the 1860s. The *Ben Campbell* was sold to the Galena-Minnesota Mail line. (Courtesy of Dick Anderson)

The *B. Hershey* was an example of a stern-wheeler. It carried freight and passengers on the St. Croix. (Courtesy of Dick Anderson)

Enterprise, which limped into port at Louisville on May 30, 1815. Henry Shreve had brought her up.

Shreve is credited with building the first real steamboat, the *George Washington*, which was constructed at Wheeling, West Virginia. Designed with a new oscillating engine, the *Washington* was 136 feet long, with a 28-foot beam. She looked like an overgrown keel boat. Small wonder. She was built with the shallow hull of a keel boat, then decked over. Shreve had the engines installed on the deck. The four boilers and two cylinders were put in a horizontal position instead of upright. The boilers and engines weighed 1/20 of the machinery used by Fulton, and consumed 3/5 of the amount of fuel. In addition, by having unconnected engines, the *Washington* could turn around in her own length by running one forward and the other in reverse. This was a very necessary advantage when boats began navigating the extremely narrow, frequently very crooked tributaries of the Mississippi. The keel for the *Washington* was laid on September 10, 1816. The boat was finished in June of the following year.

Reporting the trip of the *Washington*, the Niles *Register* wrote in 1816, "On Monday Evening last, the steamboat *Washington* sailed from Wheeling, Virginia, for New Orleans under the command of Captain Henry M. Shreve. In 45 minutes the boat had made about nine miles. She has no balance wheel, and her whole engine possessing the power of one hundred horses weighs only 9,000 pounds."

In March of 1817, the *Washington* swung away from the levee at New Orleans and headed north. Four days later, she arrived at Natchez, Mississippi. Whereas the Fulton ships had dug deep keels into the mud shoals and sand bars of the mighty Mississippi, the shallow flat-bottomed *Washington* skipped over the water's surface.

Early boats were not picturesque, however. They were designed merely to take people and freight from point A to point B and back again. Little was expended toward comfort or ornamentation. As for speed, 12 miles per hour downstream and 6 to 7 miles per hour upstream was the average.

Riverboats varied in design in different parts of the country. In the East, they were primarily passenger boats. Those steamers did offer comfort and speed, and carried little freight. They operated with low-pressure engines.

Western boats were designed chiefly for hauling freight. They were flimsy, jerry-built craft with high-pressure engines. They wasted fuel and wore out quickly.

By 1838, there were some 400 steamboats operating on the western and southern rivers alone. Most of them were built on the Ohio River. Steamboats ranging from 100 to 700 tons were built in great numbers at Pittsburgh and at Cincinnati. A few were manufactured at St. Louis. Those destined for the lower Mississippi trade had draws of 6 to 8 feet of water.

As travel and commerce expanded to the upper Mississippi, St. Croix, Missouri, and Minnesota rivers, the boats were modified. Steamboats were designed with shallow drafts to traverse the low waters of the northwest. Some boats needed as little as 18 inches of water. Average life of a river boat was five years, although some lasted as long as fifteen and sixteen years.

By 1859, there were railroads at six points along the upper Mississippi River from St. Louis to St. Paul. Steamboats flocked to these depots to make the most of the boom caused by freight shipments.

In their early years, railroads offered little competition to the steamboats. Trains were much more dangerous. They were noisy, dirty, and crowded. The boats, by contrast, had become floating palaces, with the ultimate in luxury designed to please the most elegant passenger.

During the Civil War, the luxury steamers were replaced by iron-clad craft which patrolled the waterways. After the close of the conflict, new luxury packets replaced war boats on the Mississippi. Railroads by then were posing a real threat to the river for transpor-

Steamboat and barge from Moline, Illinois, at the Stillwater levee July 8, 1923. (Photo by John W. G. Dunn, courtesy of James Taylor Dunn)

tation and freight. Ship builders were spurred to offer greater elegance and comfort in order to keep their passengers. Railroads made their own improvements, and added "palace coaches" to lure passengers from the steamboats.

By the 1870s, the only advantage river boats had over railroads was lower rates. Railroads could move freight and passengers faster. The routes they followed were straight, not the meandering paths of the rivers. Weather favored the iron horse, too, for shipments were never delayed because of freeze-ups, storms, or low water.

A song of the roustabouts who stoked the furnaces on the packets flaunted a brave theme:

> "O, shovel up the furnace
> Til smoke put out de stars.
> We's gwine along de river
> Like we's bound to beat de cars."

In spite of this bravado, it was clear the railroads were winning the battle. New steamboats showed restraint in their furnishings and fittings. By 1876, steamboat passengers were diverted to railroads for travel along the Mississippi routes, and steamers were mainly freight carriers. Mark Twain said that in 1882 there were locomotives in sight from the deck of a steamboat almost the whole way from St. Louis to St. Paul.

There were a few years after that in which river travel by steamboat was still a way of life, but no new river queens were built to accommodate passengers. Instead, the boats finished out their days pushing rafts of logs from lumber booms to mills along the St. Croix and Mississippi.

By 1900, the boats had outlasted the lumber industry and turned to hauling grain to justify their existence. Many of them were rebuilt as excursion boats.

From 1870 to 1910, the number of steamboats on the Mississippi network declined from 113 to 53. Tonnage delivered annually was down from 41,600 to 8,157. During the same period, the number of towboats went from 77 to 57, and tonnage moved by them was reduced by half.

World War I jammed the railroads with war materials. The nation turned again to her waterways. Old steamboats and barges were reconditioned for another hitch on the rivers. Retired pilots were rehired. New fleets were built to meet the demands of the years 1918 to 1920.

The revival was short-lived. As war use fell off, the railroads again took over the freight business. Towboats remained, along with a few excursion boats and commercial barges, but the romance of the river had faded.

The coup de grâce had been given to the high pressure steam engine in 1909 with the invention of the internal combustion engine. The few boats that remained in the 1920s and 1930s were relics. New boats were driven by deep-throated diesels.

The 1930s saw a feeble attempt to revive the rivers for passenger transport, but it was a success only as a novelty. Week-long cruises were enjoyed once, then forgotten. Daily excursion boats offered diversion, popular bands, and an escape during the depression. Another war, and even this brief revival was doomed.

In the past decades, a few steamboats have reappeared on the Mississippi and St. Croix. Some are anchored as showboats, restaurants, and museums. Several offer excursions of varying lengths.

These modern boats are token tribute to the vast fleets of steamboats which once plied the inland waterways of America.

The steamer *Columbia* with an excursion barge in 1900. The *Columbia* was built by Muller Boat Works to compete against the *Gracie Kent* in passenger service on the St. Croix. (Courtesy of the Washington County Historical Society)

Steamer *JS*, an excursion boat on the St. Croix River, seen here at the Stillwater levee. (Courtesy of the Washington County Historical Society)

Chapter 3

Portrait of a Packet

Early steamboats on the St. Croix were crude and ugly craft, put together with more eye for function than for beauty. Most of them measured less than 150 tons, with the average being about 100 tons capacity.

Although over the years, steamboats were usually referred to as "she," the early ones—and occasionally boats in later years—were so ugly they were referred to as "it."

Boats were of light draft, for the river was treacherous. Sandbars, snags, and deadheads waited to catch any boat whose hull penetrated too deeply into the water. If a craft drew more than 18 inches unloaded, it was headed for trouble. Many of them had only a 14-inch draw.

For years, boats were built without any plans or specifications. It wasn't until the 1880s that a formal design was followed. Early boats were constructed from experience. When an order came into the shop, the boss gathered his men around him, and told them what was wanted. Possibly he made a rough pencil sketch of the proposed steamboat. There was no scientific figuring of stresses and strains. Since the workmen had no technical schooling, they couldn't have followed a blueprint if they had had one.

The first steamboats evolved in the hands of men who were carpenters, flatboat builders, blacksmiths, and tinsmiths. They worked by the "cut and try" method, aided by the rule of thumb. Once they understood the general pattern, they went ahead and built it. After constructing two or three boats, they made few errors in "by guess and by gosh" plans.

Boats were of lightweight construction. To save weight, decks, floor timbers, bulkheads, and upper works were made of pine or poplar rather than sturdier and heavier oak. While light construction allowed steamboats to surmount sand bars and low water, it left them at the mercy of rocks, reefs, snags, high winds, and ice.

Interior of the *Redwing,* an elegant 1862 steamer, showing the elaborate chandeliers, elegant trapping and long dining hall in the salon. (Courtesy of Jim Johnson)

The pilot house of the *Isaac Staples,* a rafter used on the St. Croix and Mississippi rivers. Photographed in 1903. (Courtesy of the Washington County Historical Society)

A typical St. Croix River boat sat squarely on an even keel, with main deck, boiler deck, hurricane roof, and Texas deck all following the same general curve. Bow and stern were high, with the center of the cabin low. In post-Civil War days, steamboats were built with such a defined sheer that old men said you couldn't see from one end of the main cabin to the other. It was also said that as you walked through the cabin, you walked down hill and up again.

Machinery of a paddle-wheeler was located on the first deck, with the engine near the middle. Boilers were located toward the front of the boat, under two lofty smokestacks. Fire doors of the boilers opened forward, so as to produce a strong draft, and a resultant good flame.

The hurricane deck was at least 30 feet above the water, with the wheel house located to the front. The Texas deck appeared on boats in the late 1840s. This was situated atop the hurricane roof which housed the officers of the boat. The Texas deck was so named because it held the largest—hence "Texas"—stateroom.

Henry Shreve is credited with the idea of staterooms on steamboats. The earliest rivercraft had space partitioned off in the main cabin, with a large area for the men, and a smaller one for women, since fewer women traveled in early days. Shreve cut up these cabins into individual rooms. Because each of the rooms was designated by the name of a state, they obviously became "staterooms."

Travelers moving from the East to the waters of mid-America demanded the same luxuries and comforts which were offered on eastern boats. Steamboaters in the Midwest began to ornament hulls and cabins, as well as to install more dependable engines. The old distrust of steamboats and boatmen melted away. Demands for luxury resulted in the image of the "floating wedding cake." In the grand salon of a boat, first-class passengers were treated to every luxury possible. Elaborate chandeliers lighted the room. A grand piano was available for entertainment. Ornate carpeting padded the floor. Woodwork cut in intricate scrolls adorned cornices, window frames, and doors.

Staterooms surrounded the grand salon. Porcelain doorknobs, soft carpets, looking glasses, porcelain washbowl and pitcher were standard fittings. An oil painting usually graced the door.

Throughout the boat, gold leaf, gilt acorns, carved blossoms, and fancy wooden scrollwork filled every conceivable spot where a doodad could be located. Fine paintings were diplayed on cabin panels. Gaudy pictures decorated the very boxes of the paddlewheels, which also carried the name of the boat. The *Minnesota Belle's* paddle boxes, for example, were decorated with pictures of a beautiful girl, modestly clothed, carrying a bundle of wheat and a reaping hook. The steamer *Minnesota* was decorated with the seal of the state. Adding a festive air were the flags which streamed from the jack staff.

The glassed-in pilot house, perched on the Texas deck behind the chimneys, was ornamented with more gingerbread. Its lofty position gave the pilot a full view of the river in all directions. Hurricane deck, boiler deck, and Texas deck were all fenced in.

Tops of the heaven-kissing smokestacks had delicate filigree crowns. Each boat had a specific pattern. Sometimes a gilt ornament swung between the smokestacks. Many of the packet companies had trademarks identifying their boats. The Diamond Jo line placard displayed a diamond. The "Eagle" boats—*War Eagle*, *Gray Eagle*, and others, all sported a carved and gilded likeness of that bird suspended on lines between the stacks.

By 1850, packets which found their way up the St. Croix were built in the image of the classic Mississippi River steamboat. Waterborne palaces, they provided more luxury afloat than could be found ashore—for those who had the money to pay. Rates of passage were a cent a mile for first-class passengers, and a fraction of that for deck passengers. Fare for quarters toward the bow were lower than rates for cabins farther back. Reason—when (not if) the boat blew up, passengers near the boilers were in greater danger.

Although the term "steamboat" is applied to all the craft that plied the St. Croix, there were differences between packets, freight boats, and towboats. The towboats which pushed rafts of logs from the St. Croix Boom above Stillwater to mills as far south as Dubuque, Iowa, were fitted with powerful engines. They needed utmost control to maneuver their tows through the bends and currents of the river. Freight boats were the sluggards of the fleet. They didn't require the quality boilers and engines needed by the passenger packets, in which speed was a prime factor in luring customers.

Stern-wheelers were the most popular craft on the St. Croix. They could handle low waters and narrow river better than the less effective side-wheelers, dubbed "coffee mills." In later years, side-wheelers proved to be much less capable of controlling log rafts in adverse wind or current. Stern-wheelers could be reversed in shallow

A close-up of the government boat, *Minnesota*, at Stillwater, Minnesota. The *Minnesota* was built in Stillwater and was of all-steel construction. (Courtesy of the Washington County Historical Society)

areas to raise the level of the water under the hull to "grasshopper" over a sand bar. The paddle wheel was eased down from 24 to 14 revolutions per minute when the boat entered shallow water. The slow speed allowed the wheel to pull water through the narrow gap between boat hull and river bottom to move the craft ahead.

Despite their disadvantages, side-wheels were retained on some boats. Packets of the Diamond Jo Line had their side wheels so far back they almost looked like stern-wheelers.

Blades of the wheels were known as "buckets." Wheels were located so as to make the buckets bite into the curving swells from the boat's stem at just the right place to give it the most purchase on the water.

Water was taken into the boat's boilers by throwing the paddle wheels out of gear, and using their power for pumping.

The cry of "Steamboat's a-comin'" was frequently changed to "Steamboat's a-sinkin'." Early St. Croix boats were dangerous. The western craft used high pressure engines rather than the low pressure boilers popular on eastern rivers. Cheaper than low pressure boilers, the high pressure units took less deck space. They carried from 60 to 100 pounds of pressure. Unfortunately, there was no accurate way to gauge the buildup of steam. Frequently boilers exploded, driving hot metal through the top and bottom of the boat, jetting hot steam onto passengers and crew alike.

To prepare a boat and get up steam from a cold start usually took two days. Captains of boats making regular runs on the St. Croix simply kept the machinery running when they stopped at levees along the river.

Steamboats burned resin and pitch for an hour before leaving shore. Pent-up steam screamed through the gauge locks before the signal was finally given to draw the boat out into the current. Stillwater, Marine, Osceola, and Taylors Falls all had upper and lower levees. Usually at each town, the boats docked, let the steam down, unloaded, then built up steam again, moved to the second landing and repeated the performance.

In the mid-1850s, lights on a steamboat were pitch-dripping torch baskets, used mainly for landing. For night running, a pilot needed complete darkness, except for the red and green sidelights on the chimneys. Canvas shrouds, or "mufflers" were fitted in front of the furnaces on the main deck to block out the light from the fires. Others were placed on the boiler deck, and on the hurricane deck to block out the skylights. No one was even permitted to smoke a pipe or cigar in the pilot house because the glow interfered with the pilot's ability to see in the dark. He had to search for landmarks a mile away, and distinguish between the solidified darkness of the land, and the liquid darkness of the river.

When electricity became practical, shrouds became obsolete. Rivermen nicknamed the new searchlights "daylight in a box." With them, pilots could run at night or in fog with confidence. The many lights aboard the steamboats, and the corresponding lights from towns and villages glanced hundreds of twinkling sparks on the night surface of the water.

Passengers standing between the smokestacks on the *Julia B,* about 1890. (Courtesy of the Washington County Historical Society)

The engine room on the *Isaac Staples.* (Courtesy of the Washington County Historical Society)

The steamer *Ben Hur* at Stillwater after an excursion to Red Wing, Minnesota. Note the decoration between the smokestacks, an identifying embellishment for many steamboats. (Courtesy of the Washington County Historical Society)

When a steamboat prepared to leave the levee, freight was carried aboard in a procession of boxes and barrels. Belated passengers dodged roustabouts carrying cargo. Boats were loaded to effect the best draw. The mate in charge aimed for a slightly deeper draw forward than in the stern of the boat. He had to be an artist in his line to store cargo compactly, and at the same time preserve the trim of the boat. When it came to loading a few hundred tons of freight, balance was very likely to be shaken unless the mate knew his business.

That careful loading could be destroyed in an instant. At the sight of something interesting on shore, all the passengers rushed to one side of the deck, tilting the packet to starboard or larboard.

Cargo carried to St. Croix River settlements consisted of barrels of mackerel and codfish, beans, whiskey and flour, barrels of apples, and boxes of tobacco. Horses, cows, and poultry consigned to farmers in the area frequently shared deck space. Such exotic items as window glass and china dishes were loaded alongside cases of garden seeds and furniture of all kinds. The bells for the Chisago City Seminary and for the Presbyterian Church in Taylors Falls arrived in the valley aboard steamboats, as did the impressive safe for the Marine Mills company store.

Return cargoes consisted of bundles of wool, hides, skins, eggs, maple sugar, baskets of wild berries and barrels of cranberries, ginseng

The passenger boat, Verne Swain, showing the two levels with freight space on the lowest deck (Courtesy of the Washington County Historical Society)

roots, firkins of butter—and, of course, lumber.

Horace Greeley, famous editor of his day, visited the area, and said of Hudson and Prescott, "The cry is Wheat! Wheat." He also said that every steamboat goes down the river "with all the wheat on board she will take, and a couple of wheat-laden barges tied fast to her side." Wheat from Star Prairie and Somerset was delivered to boats via Harriman's Landing on the St. Croix. Grain was sent by chute from the top of the bluff to barges waiting on the river.

In 1857, downstream rates for freight were reasonable enough: items shipped 30 miles were charged at 5 cents per hundred pounds. From 30 to 50 miles, 4 cents a hundredweight. Over 60 miles, the rate was 3 cents a hundred pounds. Shipments made from Galena, Illinois, to St. Paul were charged at $1.50 per 100 pounds.

Steamboating was profitable in another way. A typical packet boat could carry 200 cabin passengers and 100 second-class passengers. Charge from St. Paul to Hastings, a distance of 32 miles, was $1.50 for cabin passengers, $1 for deck passengers. The longer the trip, the cheaper the rate. In 1875, a passenger traveling from St. Paul to St. Louis could make the trip for $18.50, which included meals and stateroom. St. Paul to Galena rates were $8 for cabin, $4 for deck passengers. Net receipts for a typical packet boat averaged over $56,000 a year.

While cabin passengers enjoyed a promenade on the second level, deck passengers on the bottom level were close to the hiss of the boilers, the bang of furnace doors which continued all day and all night long. They were the first victims of boiler explosions, or collisions.

Immigrants to towns and villages along the St. Croix surrendered as few of their precious coins as possible for boat passage. They squatted in whatever space they could find amid bags and bales of cargo. Men, women, and children shared the deck with cattle, horses, and poultry, part of their own worldly goods. They slept where they could—on bales of merchandise, in wagon beds, on the bare deck, or leaning against a woodpile.

One writer noted that every one of the immigrants seemed to have a baby in arms, and every baby was wailing. When disease struck the crowded steerage passengers, it spread rapidly. However, steamboats were the only means of transportation, so people had no other choice.

In trying to attract business, steamboats spared no expense in the culinary department. An average cook received the same pay as a first-class officer. And a first-class cook received the same pay as the captain. Competition was keen among boats to secure the services of a top-rated cook. He earned every cent of his pay. He had the responsibility of providing meals at stated times, offering good variety.

Many packets carried live passengers of two kinds—people and livestock. Sheep were part of the cargo off-loaded at this waterfront. (Courtesy of Dick Anderson)

Although some boats on the St. Croix were dry, whiskey was regarded as almost a necessity on the river. Men who owned the bar on a popular packet boat felt it was a better investment than owning a gold mine.

While cabin passengers enjoyed the finest of cuisine prepared by master cooks, deck passengers provided their own food. Many cooked their meal and porridge on a long sheet iron stove. Others doled out sausage, dried herring, water crackers, and cheese during their journey.

Immigrants crowded the guard in fair weather, huddled by the boilers when fog or rain blew in. The shaking of the engines, the jolting impact when the boat hit a log in the channel, offered a hazardous promenade indeed. Steamboat captains rarely stopped to rescue deck passengers who had the misfortune to topple overboard.

In spite of the differences between first-class and deck passengers, Mississippi and St. Croix steamers were considered more democratic than those in the effete east. Passengers and crew alike drank straight from the river. All were victims of mosquitos.

Price of passage could be reduced if a traveler was willing to haul wood when needed. When the mate called "Woodpile, woodpile, let's see the wood," the fuelers got up and scrambled ashore by means of a plank thrown out to the riverbank. Then with four, five, even six logs piled on their shoulders, the woodmen staggered back across the swaying plank and threw their load into the furnace room. An hour's labor and the bunkers were filled. The paddle wheel started turning again. Woodmen sank back to the bare deck for whatever rest they could manage.

During the day, cabin passengers went ashore to stretch their legs while the boat was refueled. If they strayed too far, they were called back to the boat with a gunshot or a blast from the steamboat whistle.

Sometimes, steamboats "wooded up" while continuing their progress on the river in an operation not unlike the mid-air refueling

The *Gracie Kent* at Taylors Falls. For many of the steamboats, "wooding up" meant stopping at the shore and cutting what was needed. (Courtesy of Durand Blanding)

of airplanes today. A large flatboat loaded with cord wood was lashed alongside. Logs were thrown aboard the steamer as it continued to push upstream.

Wood was no problem along the St. Croix. Maple, oak, beech, ash, and chestnut were favored, with sycamore and willow being accepted if necessary. On the rare occasions when a steamboat ran out of fuel, the crew cut up barrels, spars, and deck planks to stoke the boilers until the next stop. A boat used from 20 to 40 cords of wood a day, and fueled up twice a day.

At first, boat crew and passengers cut what wood was needed. As steamboat trade expanded, wood yard businesses developed. Squatters living on the islands and river banks provided fuel for a price. Farmers along the river had a steady income from wood. Levi W. Stratton, who arrived in the St. Croix valley in 1838 aboard the *Palmyra*, first steamboat to navigate the St. Croix, put up 25 cords of wood during the winter for use by steamboats. That was the first wood cut specifically for that purpose north of Prairie du Chien.

After the Civil War, coal became the river fuel on the Mississippi. St. Croix boats, though, burned wood as long as it remained so readily available.

Another ploy used to attract patrons was music. The steamboat *Excelsior* introduced a steam calliope about 1860, and other boats soon followed suit. Some tried brass bands in lieu of the shrill calliope, but the bands were expensive. Cheapest and most popular music was afforded by a cabin orchestra. This was a group of six or eight blacks who could play violin, banjo, and guitar. They were paid for services as waiters, barbers, or baggage men. But their main function was to play during meals, for dances in the cabin, and to attract passengers at landings.

For half a century, bells and whistles of steamboats were the voices of the St. Croix River. Bells grew larger over the years with some weighing 500, 800, even up to 1,500 pounds. Many of them had quarts of silver dollars melted into the metal to give the proper tone. The bell sounded when the steamboat landed, waking the roustabouts into action. It sounded the boat's departure, and faded in the rush and tumble of water shushing off the paddle wheels as the boat moved into the stream.

Whistles did not come into general use until the 1850s. Before then, signaling was done with bells alone, sometimes with vented steam. When first introduced, whistles were utilitarian, strictly for giving signals from one deck to another, from one boat to another. They, too, grew larger and more melodious. Captains took as much pride in the sound of the whistles of their boats as they did in their own skill on the river.

Each whistle was unique, having its own pitch and resonance.

There were three, four, or five tones to each whistle. They were grouped into a single musical chord. Anyone who spent much time along the river soon learned to identify packets by the mellow and individual trumpeting of their whistles. A pull of a brass ring above the pilot wheel, and the whistle blasted to signal the crew, a passing vessel, people on shore or levee.

A pleasant sound at any time, steamboat whistles took on a haunting tone at night. James Taylor Dunn wrote that from the time a boat was first heard down the river until it went by and was no longer heard in the distance was a lapse of nearly half the night.

Will Percey wrote, "There is no sound in the world so filled with mystery and longing and unease as the sound at night of a river boat blowing for the landing—one long, two shorts, one long, two shorts. The sound of a river boat hangs in your heart like a star."

The *Twin Cities*, an excursion barge, was pushed by the *Lora*, traveling from St. Paul to the St. Croix. Shown here in 1903, the barge was later pushed by the *Purchase*. (Courtesy of Durand Blanding)

Chapter 4

Full Steam Ahead

Following exploration by Daniel Greysolon, Sieur du Luth, in 1680, the St. Croix River became a channel for commerce. Indians, trappers, and voyageurs transported goods along the waterway between Lake Superior and the Mississippi. However, commercial enterprises on the river did not really begin until 1836.

In November of that year, a Mr. Pitt with a boat load of men went to the falls of the St. Croix to cut pine timber. He had the consent of the Chippewa Indians, but not of the United States authorities. No treaties had yet been signed with the Indians. This didn't bother Pitt. He continued his plans to become a lumber king.

At the same time, the first steamboat to navigate the St. Croix, most probably the *Palmyra*, was churning up the river. According to W. H. C. Folsom, it was under the command of Captain Holland, but W. E. Easton and William J. Peterson list Captain W. Middleton as commander of the boat. A single-engine side-wheeler, the 101-ton *Palmyra* was built in 1835 or 1836. It left St. Louis, Missouri, on July 5, 1838, with 50 men aboard. Calvin A. Tuttle, millwright, and Levi W. Stratton headed a crew of millwrights, carpenters, masons, lumbermen, teamsters, and laborers. On the *Palmyra* were provisions for four months, and the tools and machinery to build a sawmill and shops. This was the beginning of Franklin Steele's Northwest Lumber Company.

The boat reached Fort Snelling on July 15, bringing official notice of the Sioux treaty, which opened the St. Croix Valley to settlers. The boat then proceeded up the St. Croix. It reached the falls of the river on July 17.

The arrival of the boat astounded the Chippewa. The *Palmyra*'s shrill whistle and puffing engine earned it the name "ishkote' nabikwan" or fire vessel. Frightened by the mechanical monster, the red men rolled rocks from the high crags and bluffs down onto the steamer as it lay at anchor in the eddies of the river. Captain Holland responded to this action. The boat's bell clanged. The whistle shrieked. The stack belched billowing smoke. Terrified, the Indians vanished.

While the *Palmyra* had been churning up the river, the party of illegal lumbermen was making a hasty retreat. In anticipation of a treaty with the Indians, the lumberjacks had opened a camp at the mouth of the Snake River on the upper St. Croix and had begun cutting logs. The Chippewa, now feeling their rights had been invaded, chased the lumbermen off the claim. The whites took to their canoe and fled down the river. Indians pursued on the bank.

The red men expected the escaping lumber party to land above the falls, at which time they would have their revenge. The lumberjacks, aware of the fate that awaited them, elected to go over the falls in their frail craft. The canoe was lost, as were most of their effects, but all the men reached the shore in safety.

A short distance below the falls, they met the *Palmyra*. The boat brought the welcome news that the treaty with the Chippewa had been ratified. The lumbermen returned to the Snake River and took legal possession of their logs. The lumbering era was opened on the St. Croix.

The following year, the Chippewa along the St. Croix were scheduled to receive commodities which had been promised them when the treaties were signed in 1837. At the time, the Indians were near starvation. The *Palmyra* made the trip up the river, but carried no goods. It was not until late autumn that the promised supplies arrived.

The next craft up the river was the steamboat *Ariel*, which made its first trip on the St. Croix in August of 1838, then returned downstream. On September 10, 1838, David Hone and Lewis S. Judd left Marine Settlement in Madison County, Illinois. Possibly at the Mississippi port of Alton, Illinois, they boarded the steamer *Ariel*, owned by Captain Joseph Throckmorton. The two planned to make an exploratory trip up the St. Croix River to choose the best site for a sawmill.

On the 29th day of September, the two men left the steamer at the head of Lake St. Croix (near present-day Stillwater). From there, they poled a flatboat upriver to the falls, where they found Franklin Steele's mill. Hone and Judd explored further north, but returned to the lower St. Croix and staked a claim. The site later became the village of Marine.

The steamer *Gypsy* arrived at Fort Snelling October 21, 1838, with the load of goods destined for distribution to the Chippewa under the terms of the recently-signed treaties. The *Gypsy* was chartered for $450 to carry goods to St. Croix Falls. In passing through Lake St. Croix, the steamer grounded near the site of the projected town of "Stambough." Eventually, the boat was hauled off the sand bar and continued its journey. Goods from the *Gypsy* were landed at St. Croix Falls on October 26. Some 1,000 Indians arrived in canoes. Then the St. Croix River froze up, and deep snow fell. All goods were sacrificed except what the Indians could carry away on their backs. The Chippewa destroyed their canoes so the Sioux would not get them.

The following year, 1839, the side-wheeler *Fayette*, loaded with the complete machinery for a mill, left St. Louis in April and headed north. She carried eight partners of the Marine Lumber Company. On board, too, were farming tools, household goods, several cows, and three yoke of oxen.

Passengers included a millwright, a blacksmith, and Mrs. David Hone, who was to be cook for the company. The *Fayette* reached Fort Snelling in mid-May, and landed settlers' stores for the fort. The following night, the captain reversed his course and headed back downstream to the mouth of the St. Croix, where the boat turned north again. A heavy rain on May 12 had raised the level of the St. Croix, so the *Fayette* had no trouble reaching the Marine mill site the following day.

J.M. Mullen, a steamboat captain, described the early years on the St. Croix River in a letter written in 1877. While interesting, the letter was more fiction than fact. Mullen wrote,

> It was April, 1841, that the old steamer *Tennessee* could have been seen lying at the landing in St. Louis, with steam escaping from her steam pipes, and the black smoke rolling from her chimneys. The crew was busy engaged in taking on board a large supply of stores, mill machinery, and general merchandise. About eighty passengers were on board, the boat having been chartered by the St. Croix Lumber Company for a trip to the falls of the St. Croix, then the new "Eldorado," the pine region of the then territory of Wisconsin. Everything being aboard, the lines were let go, the last tap of the bell was heard, the steamer slowly moved from her moorings into the stream and headed on her course. The city was soon passed and lost sight of by the bends in the river; almost every nook and corner was covered with freight. The cooks were busy preparing meals for passengers and crew, while the clerk had registered on his books the names of W. S. Holcombe, Dr. Fitch, W. S. Hungerford, J. L. Taylor, W. S. Libby, J. W. Furber, Daniel McLean, and W. C. Mahoney, names that have since become historic in the St. Croix valley. But few small towns were seen along the lone banks of the Mississippi, and after passing the little town of Dubuque, the evidences that they were beyond the bounds of civilization and near the haunts of the red man, were plainly visible. Frequently would be met a lot of natives in their birch-bark canoes, hideous in their war paint, and as the steamer passed they would make the woods ring with a savage war whoop.
>
> After a voyage of fourteen days, the boat entered Lake St. Croix, an event that pleased all on board, glad that the journey was so nearly ended. The steamer glided swiftly over the lake's smooth surface, and soon reached its head, at which place was a trading post kept by Joe Brown. About twelve miles up the river could be seen a lone cabin. As the steamer approached the landing, the entire population was on hand to greet the boat, among them Orange Walker, Hiram Berkey, Asa Parker, David Hone, William Dibble, Samuel Burkleo, and others. Mrs. David Hone, the only white lady in the place, was standing in her cabin door. They were at work on getting the frame ready for a new saw mill; a portion of the machinery had arrived some time before. After passing Marine Mills, not a habitation of any kind was seen along the river. It was evening when the *Tennessee* reached the Dalles, and her passengers gazed with wonder on the high, perpendicular rocks

which rose majestically on either side. As the escape of steam from the pipes of the boat could be heard for miles, the entire population was on hand and looked with amazement at the steamer. It was indeed a mixed crowd, white, Indians, and half-breeds. Soon all hands had climbed the high cliffs, and took the trail that led to the village of St. Croix Falls.

The arrival of the *Tennessee* was the opening up of civilization, and the lumber business on the St. Croix.

According to historian James Taylor Dunn, the above letter was written by Mullen to the Taylors Falls *Journal,* and published in the February 2, 1877, issue. Five days later, the Stillwater *Gazette* clipped the item and reported it. When George E. Warner and Charles M. Foote, editors, published their "History of Washington County and the St. Croix Valley" in 1881, they reprinted the story.

Until 1918, the story of the *Tennessee* was accepted as fact. At that time, according to Dunn, the *Saturday Evening Post,* a newspaper published in Davenport, Iowa, came to grips with the truth. In the November 23, 1918 issue, the *Post* stated that the story of the *Tennessee* had "a foundation of fact with a good deal of misinformation."

First of all, it was the *Fayette,* not the *Tennessee,* which in April 1839, not 1841, brought the pioneers to Marine Mills. Capt. Mullen stated in his letter to the Taylors Falls newspaper that "the entire population was on hand to greet the boat"—Orange Walker, Hiram Berkey, Asa Parker, David Hone, William Dibble, and others. Mullen further stated that Mrs. Hone, "the only white lady in the place, was standing in her cabin door."

The truth is, said Dunn, that the population of Marine did not consist of those men named by Mullen. They were all on the boat—the *Fayette.* Furthermore, Mrs. Hone could not have stood at her cabin door—she was on the boat, too.

Other passengers on the *Fayette* for that trip were William Holcombe, who got off at Stillwater; WIlliam S. Hungerford and Joshua L. Taylor, who continued to Taylors Falls.

As a matter of fact, wrote Dunn, the *Tennessee* never traveled on either the Mississippi or the St. Croix. A paddleboat named *Tennessee* never existed!

Chapter 5

Fuel Up

While Marine was growing into a mill town, Prescott's Landing on the east shore at the mouth of the St. Croix was still an Indian trading post in the 1840s. The best general store in the area was across the river at Point Douglas, the regular stopping place for steamboats. There, and later at Prescott, large St. Louis-to-St. Paul boats landed daily. Passengers and freight were transferred to St. Croix steamers for the trip up the river. Two packets left each day for the St. Croix. The big boats refueled at Point Douglas before continuing their journey to St. Paul and Fort Snelling.

One of the first steamboats to attempt a landing at the site of the future city of Stillwater was the *Otter* under Captain Smith Harris, who came in the fall of 1843. The next spring, a regular line was established on the St. Croix. By 1849, Stillwater had a good steamboat landing on its waterfront.

During the season, boats came every two weeks, running from Stillwater to Galena, Illinois. First boat of the new passenger line was the *Lynx* under Capt. Hooper.

Two St. Croix valley pioneers and historians came to the area aboard paddle-wheelers. Anson Northup brought his family to St. Croix Falls aboard the *Indian Queen* in 1841. They boarded the boat at St. Louis.

W. H. C. Folsom and his family arrived at Stillwater on November 30, 1844, aboard the steamer *Cecelia* under Capt. Joseph Throckmorton. Earlier, Folsom had traveled from Prairie du Chien to Stillwater on the *Highland Mary*, with Capt. John Atchison. Deciding there was a future in the area, Folsom settled his family high on the cliffs at Taylors Falls.

During the early years, the only mode of travel, of communication, of cargo and freight shipment along the St. Croix River was the steamboat. Settlements relied on packets for their supplies. Gener-

A scene in the picturesque Dalles of the St. Croix River near Taylors Falls. This spot is one of the most scenic places on the St. Croix. The boat shown is the *Olive S.*, owned by James Teare of Stillwater. This boat made regular round trips daily between Stillwater and Taylors Falls. Visible on the opposite bank to the right of the *Olive S.* is a natural formation of rock known as The Holy Cross, one of many unusual rock formations in the Dalles. (Courtesy of the Washington County Historical Society)

ally there were two main shipments of goods each year, one in spring, one in fall. It required good husbandry on the part of settlers to make their provisions last from the arrival of one supply boat to the next.

Sometimes the final supply boat of the season would miss its run because of an early freeze up. If the water was low and the season late, steamboat captains did not want to risk being caught by ice, so adequate stores for the winter simply were not delivered. That happened more than once. Then, not a pound of pork or flour could be purchased above Prairie du Chien.

The winter of 1844 was such a "starving time." There were no provisions for two months. A few hardy men managed to cut a road through to Fort Snelling, 50 miles away. There they traded shingles for some condemned Army pork. This helped the settlers survive until the first supplies arrived by steamer in the spring.

By 1845, every boat that ascended the Mississippi also ascended the St. Croix. Between 1840 and 1848, 34 steamers traversed the river.

In later years, as larger boats were introduced, navigation on the St. Croix was restricted to smaller craft. Eventually, trade was carried on in boats built specifically for the border river.

Hudson was the principal port of debarkation along the St. Croix River on the Wisconsin side. The first steamboat to dock at Hudson's lakefront wharf arrived at the foot of Buckeye Street on April 15, 1847. That date has a double significance, for on that date, too, the first white child was born in Hudson. She was Abigale Page, daughter of Captain John Page. A pioneer lumberman in the St. Croix Valley, Page was the first lumberman in the Hudson area, working on the Willow River. Earlier, he had followed that trade in Maine, and had been a sea captain prior to that. Captain Page arrived in Wisconsin from the Mormon colony at Nauvoo, Illinois. He was instrumental in river improvement, opening up and dredging the channel from Lakeland to the Hudson drawbridge.

The village of Taylors Falls was formally platted in 1851. Since there were no roads to the village until the government road opened in 1856, the community depended on the river. Mail and passengers could reach the Falls only by steamboat—or by bateaux or birch bark canoe if the water was low. In time of high water large boats wended their way through the Dalles of the St. Croix. The 182-foot side-wheeler *Excelsior* made the trip in 1851. One of the largest boats to reach the Falls, it had a capacity of 272 tons. In 1857, an even bigger boat, the 313-ton *Metropolitan* of St. Louis, got as far as Marine Mills. The *Minnesota Belle*, a veritable floating palace, also tied up in Marine Mills. In April 1859, the 225-ton side-wheeler brought freight to Marine Mills for Judd, Walker and Company, and Ballard, Draper and Company.

The *New St. Croix*, a boat out of Oquawha, Illinois, came into the St. Croix trade in 1854. According to the *Saturday Evening Post* of July 3, 1915, the boat was a new hull, using the old machinery from the *Enterprise*. Sunk by ice on April 30, 1857 in Lake Pepin, she was raised, repaired, and again put into service.

The growing lumber industry had a double effect on steamboat trade on the St. Croix. First, traffic increased as it was found to be practical to move the large rafts of logs by steamboat. Stern-wheelers proved to be exceptionally capable of guiding the unwieldly rafts. Side-wheel boats were abandoned for that purpose because they lacked the control of the staunch stern-wheelers.

At the same time, the lumber business brought about the establishment of the St. Croix Boom Company, where logs were caught to form the rafts. First operated near Osceola, the company was later moved to a location about a mile upstream from Stillwater. Navigation was continually interrupted, because boats were unable to pass around the boom. They had to bump their way through floating timber.

Logs often piled up between the narrow cliffs of the Dalles at Taylors Falls. It required weeks of exhausting and dangerous work to break the jams. Frequently, whichever steamboats were handy were pressed into service to haul off the key logs.

During the seven-month long season of 1869, 230 steamers reached the levee at Taylors Falls to unload passengers and freight.

Logs passing through the Gap of the St. Croix Boom. A small army of men was engaged in bringing logs to the Gap, the narrow space that allowed only a few logs at a time. Once through, experienced men gathered the logs into brills, then rafts and floated down to the mills. The earliest statistics of log production on the St. Croix was the winter of 1837-38. By 1849 75,000,000 feet of lumber were cut. In 1893 this figure had climbed to 450,000,000 feet. (Courtesy of the Washington County Historical Society)

Steamer *Vernie Mac* with excursion at Red Wing, Minnesota, in 1898. Owned and operated at this time by the Interstate Navigation Company on the St. Croix River, it was purchased to replace the *Gracie Kent*, which was too light for the Stillwater-to-Taylors Falls passenger run due to rafts of logs on the river. Many lawsuits occurred because of logs blocking the river. One Sunday morning, the *Vernie Mac* and the *Columbia*, a competing boat owned by the Boom Company, left Stillwater together for Taylors Falls. The *Vernie Mac* reached there first, though both left at the same time. After a fast run, it also beat the *Columbia* back to Stillwater. (Courtesy of the Washington County Historical Society)

The St. Croix Boom

The biggest impediment to steamboat service on the St. Croix was the log boom just north of Stillwater. Every year millions of feet of lumber were floated down from the pineries on the upper reaches of the river. At the head of Lake St. Croix, the Boom Company caught the floaters by means of log chains anchored to the cliffs. Logs were sorted according to the timber marks of the owners, then rafted, and towed by steamboat to various lumber mills along the St. Croix and to markets on the Mississippi.

A large influx of logs often blockaded the river channel and boats were unable to get through. In August 1864, when Capt. Oscar Knapp commanded the *Enterprise*, he gave praise to a five-foot sturgeon speared by one of the boat hands. With typical Knapp humor, he observed, "This must have been the fellow that broke the St. Croix boom and ran the log blockade a a few days ago."

The following May and June, there was despair among steamboat people because of a blockade of logs. "With this kind of interruption, we may as well give up trying to improve and settle this part of the country," was a comment heard along the river. Another blockade in June and July 1867 caused the Polk County *Press* to sound a "call to action on the invasion of the rights of the people of the Upper St. Croix Valley by the upstart mushroom aristocrats who own and control the St. Croix Boom Company." Particular attention was paid to a "certain clique in Stillwater" that wanted to make that city the head of navigation, and the greatest log market of the West.

In February 1868, citizens of the upper valley formed an association whose purpose was to keep the river free and open for navigation. Delegates from Osceola, Marine, Franconia, Taylors Falls, and St. Croix Falls met at the Dalles House in Taylors Falls to discuss the matter. The group, known as the Upper River Convention, met for the next twelve years. During that time, only one blockade of any serious consequence occurred. That was in 1878, when river traffic was halted for 33 days.

Two steamboats managed to break through the blockade. In 1878, the *Ada B*, a small wannigan-shaped boat, abandoned most of her freight for upper river ports. Taking just a few passengers and a few barrels of beer, she left Stillwater, traveled up Page's Slough to Arcola, ramming the bank several times en route. At Arcola, the passengers and freight crossed the island and boarded the *G. B. Knapp* to continue their journey up the river, thus circumventing the blockade.

Starting in 1878, and for ten years, the United States Congress made appropriations for work on the St. Croix. The U.S. Army Corps of Engineers removed snags, stumps, sunken logs, overhanging trees, sandbars, and boulders. Side channels were closed. Revetments, dikes, spur dams, and wing dams were constructed to improve navigation.

In 1879, logs backed up for about seven miles above Stillwater, covering the entire river. Occasionally a small passage was opened for steamers, but travel was greatly restricted.

The district engineer, Maj. Charles J. Allen, realized that the main obstructions to navigation were the floating logs and the log booms. He wrote to the Secretary of War in 1880 that if the engineers "are to remove all natural obstacles [in the St. Croix River] then something must be done to prevent the placing of artificial ones."

For the balance of the 1880s, the Boom Company kept an open channel near its operations, possibly because it did not want to tangle with the War Department. However, in 1882, traffic was stopped by a tremendous blockade at the boom. On June 27, the Boom Company chartered the boat *Aunt Betsy* to ferry freight and passengers up the river to Arcola. There teams and carriages waited to convey people and cargo to Marine. At that point, travelers boarded the *Jennie Hayes* to complete the trip to Taylors Falls. The problem —the greatest log jam then known on the St. Croix began forming. Eventually, it grew to nine miles in length, and seven feet high, stretching from Arcola to Marine. Boats were unable to get through that stretch of the river until the middle of July.

Freight was brought to Taylors Falls by the newly-completed railroad and transferred to the *Jennie Hayes* for delivery to Osceola and other ports as far south as Marine.

In 1888 and 1889, the boom again blockaded the river for three months. The Corps of Engineers was given no more funds for improving the river. Railroads provided alternate transportation to valley towns.

Although mammoth log jams occurred in the narrow channel of the river at the Dalles, blocking off the steamboat landings at Taylors Falls and St. Croix Falls, they did not interrupt commerce of the lower river as did the Boom Company blockades.

The entry of the locomotive into the St. Croix Valley in 1870 marked the beginning of the end for the river business. In 1870, the *Wyman X* carried 5,776 paying passengers between Stillwater and Taylors Falls. Nine years later, two boats, the *Mary Barnes* (originally the *Nellie Kent*) and the *G. B. Knapp* together carried only 2,000 passengers up, and 1,894 down.

Railroads brought many changes to the St. Croix Valley. Residents of Taylors Falls rejoiced that trains would reach their village in 1880.

> And when we want to travel,
> No more we'll have to crawl
> All the way to Minneapolis,
> Stillwater or Saint Paul.
>
> Three cheers for Washburn's railroad,
> Join voices one and all.
> Goodbye old lumbering steamboat,
> And Donnelly's ship canal.
>
> Rumbling through the ledges,
> Skimming o'er the vale,
> Won't it then be jolly—
> Riding on the rail.

It is ironic that the biggest of all St. Croix steamboat excursions was held for railroad conductors in June 1901. Some 2,000 of them, attending a convention in St. Paul, boarded 28 rail cars, and entrained for St. Croix Falls. After a tour of Interstate Park, they boarded the *Columbia* and the *Lora* for a river journey to Stillwater.

For the St. Croix, the heyday of steamboating was from 1860 to 1890. Although in 1892, the steamer *Atlanta* was busy towing lumber and wood between Marine, Franconia, and Taylors Falls, she was an anachronism. After that, civilization caused a marked change in the river. Cut and burned-over timberlands in the upper valley no longer held the soil. The river filled with silt and sand from eroding hillsides. When in July 1905, a group of 1,100 retail grocers boarded the steamer *Purchase* and its excursion barge the *Twin Cities*, they got only as far as Log House Landing, near present-day Otisville, before grounding because of low water. The *Purchase* made one more excursion on the St. Croix. She took about 800 sight-seers to Taylors Falls in July 1914.

When the lumbering industry faded and the last of the logs floated through the boom, steamboats turned to hauling grain. By 1916, only two paddle-wheelers were operating regularly between Stillwater and the Dalles. They were the gasoline-powered *Olive S*, and the *St. Croix*, last of the paddle-wheelers.

Chapter 6

Boats That Plied the St. Croix

Records of the many boats that plied the St. Croix are at best sketchy. They are not reliable as to which boat was which. Before getting into a listing of them, it is necessary to note that frequently the same name was used time after time. There were at least three St. Pauls, and three War Eagles. There were undoubtedly seven boats with the name Dr. Franklin, for one of them was registered as "Dr. Franklin 7." A boat had hardly sunk into the mud when the order was placed for a replacement. Invariably, the second one carried the name of the first.

Sometimes, a wrecked steamboat was cannibalized, with boilers going into a different boat. The hull may have been used again, but the new boat carried a new name.

A SUMMER TREAT

THE "OLIVE S," one of the niftiest little steamers to be found anywhere, makes daily trips up and down the drowsy waters of the Beautiful and Historic St. Croix River. You can't afford to miss this opportunity. . .

...SCHEDULE...
Leaves Stillwater at 9:15 a. m.
Arrives Taylors Falls at 1:45 p. m.
Leaves Taylors Falls at 4:15 p. m.
Arrives Stillwater at 7:15 p. m.

INTERESTING AND REFRESHING

NOTICE:—Capt. Teare will make special trips to Osceola and return for parties numbering 25 or more making a 30 minute stop at Osceola, round trip 50c each

The Standard-Press Print—St. Croix Falls

"A Summer Treat." Flyer for the steamer *Olive S*, printed by the Standard-Press Print of St. Croix Falls. (Courtesy of Jim Johnson)

The passenger boat, *Olive S*, on its way from Stillwater to Taylors Falls on the St. Croix River. The boat was built by George Muller of Stillwater and was owned by Jim Teare. It made daily passenger trips to the Falls. Photographed by H. E. Jackson in 1915. (Courtesy of the Washington County Historical Society)

Printed in the Friday, February 4, 1927, edition of the Stillwater *Evening Gazette* was "The Rhyme of Old Steamboats." The contributor was F. X. Ralphe of Hastings. Mr. Ralphe had found the ballad among some old papers, and didn't know who had composed the poem.

"Mr. Ralphe writes us that he worked on the Matt Clarke line of boats with John Goff, one of the trio of the Last Man's Banquet, when John was cooking," was the explanatory note published with the poem. "When the following was written, it was no uncommon sight to see at our levee or on the lake from half a dozen to possibly a dozen boats at one time."

Owned by Schulenburg and Boeckeler of St. Louis, the *Charlotte Boeckler* was used on the St. Croix to carry log and lumber rafts between Stillwater and St. Louis and was built in 1881. (Courtesy of the Washington County Historical Society)

RHYME OF OLD STEAMBOATS OF MANY YEARS AGO

The Fred Weyerhauser and the Frontenac,
The F. C. A. Denkman and the Belle Mac,
The Nominee and the Louisville,
The R. J. Wheeler and Jessie Bill,
The Robert Semple and the Golden Gate,
The C. J. Caffery and the Sucker State.

The Charlotte Boeckler and the Silver Wave,
The John H. Douglas and the J. K. Graves,
The Isaac Staples and the Helen Mar,
The Henrietta and the North Star,
The David Bronson and Netta Durant,
The Kit Carson and J. W. Van Sant.

The Chauncy Lamb and the Evansville,
The Blue Lodge and the Minnie Will,
The Saturn and the Satellite,
The LeClair Belle and the Silas Wright,
The Artemus Lamb and the Pauline,
The Douglas Boardman and the Kate Keen.

The *LeClaire Belle*, a famous rafter of the seventies (built in 1873) was owned by Capt. Samuel Van Sant and others. (Courtesy of the Washington County Historical Society)

The *Stillwater*, a miniature steamer that operated as the Deephaven-Wayzata Express on Lake Minnetonka. It offered service to Wayzata, Deephaven, Cottagewood, Linwood, and Breezy Point, among other ports of call. (Courtesy of the Washington County Historical Society)

The I. E. Staples and the Mark Bradley,
The J. G. Chapman and the Julia Hadley,
The Mollie Whitmore and the C. K. Peck,
The Robert Dodds and the Borealis Rex,
The Pete Kerns and the Wild Boy,
The Lily Turner and the St. Croix.

The Dan Hines and the City of Winona,
The Helen Schulenberg and the Natrona,
The Flying Eagle and the Moline,
The E. Ruthledge and Josephine,
The Taber and Irene D,
The D. A. McDonald and Jessie B.

The Gardie Eastman and the Vernie Swain,
The James Melbon and the L. W. Crane,
The Sam Atlee and William White,
The Lumberman and the Penn Wright,
The Stillwater and the Volunteer,
The James Fisk Jr., and the Reindeer.

The Thistle and the Mountain Bell,
The Little Eagle and the Gazelle,
The Mollie Mohler and the James Means,
The Silver Crescent and the Muscatine,
The Jim Watson and the Last Chance,
The Kate Waters and the Ed. Durant.

The *Muscatine*, a government boat, at Stillwater. (Courtesy of the Washington County Historical Society)

The Dan Thayer and the Flora Clark,
The Robert Ross and the J. G. Park,
The Eclipse and the J. W. Mills,
The J. S. Keaten and the J. J. Hill,
The Lady Grace and the Abner Gile,
The Johnnie Smoker and the Georgie Lysle,
The LaFayette Lamb and the Clyde,
The B. Hersey and the Time and Tide.

Quite a few more paddle-wheelers regularly thrashed the waters of the St. Croix to foam. With apologies to the poet who wrote the original "Rhyme of Old Steamboats," these are added to the list:

The Humboldt and the G. H. Gray,
The Aunt Betsy and the steamer Spray,
The Arkansas and the Ida Clark,
The Sidney and Gen. Hyde Clark,
The Baby and the Edwin C.
The Lorene and the Ada B.

The Mark Painter and the Olive S.
The Sterling and the George S.
The Tidal Wave and the Brother Jonathan,
The Wyman X and Bill Henderson,
The Fannie Thornton and the Juniata,
The G. B. Knapp and the Viola.

The steamer *Edwin C* in 1904. (Courtesy of the Washington County Historical Society)

The steamer *Ben Hur*, an excursion boat, leaving the levee at Stillwater with a load of excursionists on their way to Red Wing in 1912. (Courtesy of the Washington County Historical Society)

The Pearl and the Lydia Van Sant
The Dalles and the Nellie Kent,
The Enterprise and the Pioneer,
The Morning Star, and the Lake Superior,
The Maggie Reaney and Minnesota,
The Jennie Hayes and Osceola,
The Cleon and Nellie Sheldon,
The Bun Hersey and H. S. Allen.

The *War Eagle*, a 296-ton side-wheeler operated on the St. Croix and Mississippi rivers from the 1840s until she burned and sank on May 14, 1870, near La Crosse, Wisconsin. Notice the elaborate painting on the wheel box. (Courtesy of Durand Blanding)

The War Eagle

Doubtless, even with this addenda, there are steamers whose names have been omitted from the poem, yet some of them left their ripples on the St. Croix even after they disappeared from the river.

One of these was the steamer *War Eagle*, built in Fulton, Ohio. Under Captain Smith Harris, the boat was operated for W. H. C. Folsom of Taylors Falls. Prominent settler and historian, Folsom wrote *Fifty Years in the Northwest*, published in 1888 by the Pioneer Press Company.

James W. Mullen of Taylors Falls wrote of a trip he made in 1846 from St. Louis aboard the *War Eagle*, serving as cabin boy. The last tap of the bell, the lines were loosened, and "the wheels of the *War Eagle* revolved slowly at first, soon headed northward in a wake of black smoke of the steamers *Ocean Wave*, *Tobacco Plant*, and *Western Belle*. The packet *Luella Alton* followed closely, racing with us. At the mouth of the St. Croix, we passed Prescott Landing, where lives old pioneer Philander Prescott," wrote Mullen. The boat landed first at Fort Snelling, where Mullen visited the post. In the afternoon, the boat retraced its passage down the Mississippi. The following morning, the prow of the *War Eagle* rested against the landing at Stillwater. The boat's Captain Harris greeted friends and was warmly welcomed. Although he had visited St. Paul en route, Mullen wrote, "So far, Stillwater seemed the most active and enterprising village on the whole route." He further stated that Stillwater was the only business port in the territory now called Minnesota. "Men with red shirts could be

St. Croix Ferries

In accordance with the act creating St. Croix County, Wisconsin, in 1840, an election was held. Among the first acts of the board was to grant a license to Philander Prescott to establish a ferry across the St. Croix River, at or near its mouth. The ferry was initiated, leading to the beginning of the town of Prescott, Wisconsin.

William Dibble was among those who realized the necessity and profit of ferries. He came to the St. Croix Valley in 1839 and was one of the founders of Marine Mills. He, along with Joseph R. Brown, was granted $30 by the St. Croix County board to carry the election returns to Prairie du Chien in 1840. In 1844, Dibble moved to Point Douglas and engaged in farming. He also established ferry service across Lake St. Croix to Prescott, and across the Mississippi River to Hastings.

On the first Monday of January 1849, county commissioners of St. Croix County met at the home of Dr. Philip Aldrich in Hudson. They granted him a license to operate a ferry boat from Hudson to Lakeland. Fees were established for the service—25 cents for a footman, 75 cents for horse and rider, $1.00 for horse, driver and single buggy, $1.25 for one span of horses with wagon or buggy, $1.50 for wagon with four horses or wagon with four oxen. Horned cattle, mules or horses were charged at 25 cents each. Sheep and swine, 12½ cents each. The fee for transporting lumber was set at 37½ cents per 1,000 feet. Freight was carried at 8 cents per hundred pounds.

In June of the same year, a license was given to M. H. Moses to operate a ferry for three years across Lake St. Croix between Hudson and Baytown. The Monroe brothers were proprietors of the Lakeland-Hudson ferry, with Capt. Frank Maquire commanding. The Monroes started their service with a boat on a rope line. When steam was introduced, a little steamer, the *J. O. Henning*, was put into operation.

Running a ferry between Lakeland and Hudson from 1850 to 1869 was Capt. John Oliver. Born in England, he shipped as a

cabin boy at age nine. Ill-treated, he abandoned ship in Calcutta, India. In Bombay, he joined a ship to China. There he claimed to be an American and found a berth on an American ship. The vessel went to the Marquesas Islands for sandalwood. Oliver was one of those who stayed on the islands to collect the wood. In 1812, while the party was at work, war broke out between the United States and England. The men were stranded. Finally, Oliver reached the United States, and he became a pilot in Boston. He arrived in the St. Croix valley in 1849, and settled on a farm in Lakeland. There he built an impressive Greek revival home, and ran the ferry.

Before the interstate bridge was constructed at Stillwater, two ferries operated—one crossing the St. Croix at the Willow River site; one running between Mulberry Point and "St. Petersburgh," (now Houlton), operated by S. W. Masterson.

To continue "the ferriage business" at Prescott, the stern-wheeler *City of Prescott* was built during the winter of 1869-70. The 80-foot long ferry made five trips daily. Fare between Point Douglas and Hastings was 10 cents. Fare from either Prescott or Hastings to Point Douglas was 5 cents. The *City of Prescott* was still in service in 1918.

Ferry service was necessary to get from one side of the St. Croix to the other. Boats were operating at Franconia in the 1870s and 1880s, as well as at Osceola and at Taylors Falls.

For almost 100 years a ferry operated at Marine on St. Croix. On February 11, 1856, a bill was introduced in the Minnesota House of Representatives to grant Hiram Berkey "the right to establish a ferry across the St. Croix River at Marine Mills." For many years it was the only means of crossing the river between Taylors Falls and Stillwater. Until the 1920s, the craft was pulled by hand on a cable. After that, a motorized boat was used. Among those who operated the service were Mathias Heller, Henry F. Otis, Charles Westergren, Swen M. Magnuson, August Lund, and Gilbert Walker. On March 9, 1942, Walker sold the Marine ferry to George T. Mills of Star Prairie, Wisconsin. Mills once said that on a good day he could carry as many as 55 cars across the river in an hour. Ferry service was discontinued at Marine in 1954.

Construction of the Interstate Bridge at Stillwater in the mid-1870s put an end to the need for a ferry at that point. But when the bridge collapsed in 1904, river transport was needed. The steamer *Two Brothers* was brought from Hudson and provided free ferry service until the bridge was repaired.

Temporary ferry service was in operation in Stillwater in 1931 because the wooden bridge was again in disrepair, and the new Interstate Bridge was under construction. Operating from Mulberry Point to the beach directly across the St. Croix, a passenger boat carried 30 people at a time, with no charge. Many school children and workers from Houlton used the ferry daily to reach school and jobs. The boat ran from 5:00 a.m. until midnight, running every half hour, and more if necessary.

An automobile ferry built by the Minnesota Highway Department was capable of carrying heavy trucks as well as numerous automobiles. The ferries were in operation only until the new bridge was completed in 1932.

(Photos courtesy of the Washington County Historical Society)

seen along the banks handling logs with their poles, getting them together for gathering them into rafts. Towing in those days was unknown, and the rafts were gotten through the lakes by very slow progress. When the *War Eagle* arrived, there were a number of rafts ready at Stillwater, and the steamer was chartered at $50 an hour to tow the fleet through Lake St. Croix. By evening she was surrounded by 10 rafts of logs moving down the lake. Next morning, the steamer struck the Mississippi, where she left her fleet and steamed down the river to St. Louis."

Again in 1847-48, the *War Eagle* towed a fleet of ten acres of logs through Lakes St. Croix and Pepin for W. H. C. Folsom. She opened the navigation season in 1855, arriving in St. Paul on April 14 with 814 passengers. In 1861, author and naturalist Henry David Thoreau and his companion Horace Mann Jr., son of the famous educator, spent about a month in Minnesota. The *War Eagle* carried the two from Red Wing to Prairie du Chien on their return trip to the east. During the Civil war, the boat carried the Winona militia to the South.

The *War Eagle* continued to work on both the St. Croix and Mississippi rivers until 1870. In that year, tragedy struck.

About 6:00 p.m. on May 14, the 296-ton sidewheeler docked at the Milwaukee Road depot on the Black River wharf. It was waiting for the midnight train to arrive from Milwaukee with passengers heading for St. Paul. Around midnight, Captain Thomas Cushing noticed coal oil leaking from a barrel. He sent a watchman to find the ship's carpenter, William T. Bennett. Bennett started to tighten the metal hoops on the leaking barrel. Moments later, flames spread across the deck to the forty-six passenger staterooms.

Later, Bennett gave this account of the fire:

> I took my hammer and a piece of iron out of my ship kit, and commenced tightening the hoops. The watchman held the light for me until I was about through. Someone then called the watchman away, so he handed me the lantern which I held in one hand and my hammer in the other, when all of a sudden the lantern was ablaze inside and in a minute it burst and the kerosene on the floor caught fire. In an instant the entire deck was in flames and the cabin was on fire, and my pantaloons caught fire too. A mate standing nearby said "Jump in the river" and I did so.

Roused from their sleep, some passengers climbed into a yawl that was then lowered to the river. However, there was not room for everyone. Five passengers were drowned, including Mary Ulrich, eighteen, who was on her way to attend a wedding in Alma, Wisconsin, and the boat's black barber, Felix Spiller. The *War Eagle* went down in flames at the mouth of the Black River near La Crosse, Wisconsin. She came to rest in about thirty-five feet of water.

According to Ralph DuPae, an engineer in that city, the ruins of the craft remain beneath the water there. Supposedly it contains a large amount of cash, a great deal of passengers' jewelry, and possibly seven barrels of bourbon and rye whiskey, which would be mighty well-aged by now.

One of the smaller packets on the St. Croix, the *WW* operated between Hudson, Prescott and Taylors Falls (Courtesy of Jim Johnson)

More Boats on the River

Minnesota was not yet a territory, nor was there a settlement at Stillwater at the time Joseph Renshaw Brown platted the town of Dakotah. Located at the point where a small stream (now known as Brown's Creek) flows into the St. Croix, Dakotah consisted mainly of Brown's house, Brown's trading post, and Brown's dream. Still, the site was the stopping place for early steamboats.

In April 1840, the *Eldora*, chartered in St. Louis by eighty passengers, headed north. The purpose was to explore the upper Mississippi and the St. Croix to find the spot for a settlement. It is recorded that the boat landed at Brown's trading post on the north end of Lake St. Croix, but there is no record of what happened to the passengers aboard the *Eldora*.

Another boat on the St. Croix in the early years was the *New Brazil*. Under Capt. Orren Smith, the 160-foot boat with 20-foot beam was reported on the river in 1842.

The *Argo* was one of the earliest of regular upper river packets, with M. W. Lodwick as captain, Russell Blakeley as clerk. Captain Lodwick established a packet line in 1847. By that time, Stillwater had become a town. Packets ran from Galena, Illinois, to St. Peter, Fort Snelling, and Stillwater.

The *Argo* made the trip to St. Croix Falls in 1847 with 100 passengers. Edward White Durant recalled shipping corn on the boat. The *Argo* struck a snag just above Winona, near a small island, which consequently was named Argo Island. The boat sank where she struck in the fall of 1847. Capt. Lodwick replaced the *Argo* with the *Dr. Franklin*.

Captain Edward Grant commanded the *Dispatch* on the St. Croix in 1850-51. Later it was commanded by C. J. Bradley. Grant lived in Somerset. The boat was possibly owned by Gen. Sam Harriman of that city, and was used to haul flour from his mills to Stillwater.

The *Caleb Cape* was the first towboat engaged on Lakes St. Croix and Pepin to tow log rafts through. Large oars, some 45 feet long, one on each end of a string of logs or lumber, helped manage the rafts.

"A dry goods box with legs standing on a floating plank" was the description of the *Humboldt*, which first made its appearance on the St. Croix in 1852. The engine was reported to have "one teakettle power." The boat made tri-weekly trips between Stillwater and Taylors Falls.

The *Humboldt* gave passengers a longer ride than any other craft, so far as time was concerned, said John Philips Owen, editor of the *Weekly Minnesotan*. He wrote of taking passage on the *Humboldt* in June 1853. The boat stopped anywhere along the river to do any kind of business that was offered. It was a temperance boat, allowing no liquor aboard. There were no facilities for cooking or serving, so the *Humboldt* stopped at Marine Mills, both ascending and descending the river, to allow passengers to get a substantial dinner.

During the decade of the 1850s, some 25 steamboats navigated the waters above Stillwater either on regular schedules, or once or twice a week carrying freight or excursion parties. Boats ranged in size from the 226-ton *Minnesota Belle*, a classic floating palace, to the 20-ton *Queen of the Yellow Banks*, one of the smallest steamboats ever

Wrecked on its first trip on the St. Croix, the *J. C. Farrell* was repaired and put into service again. (Courtesy of Jim Johnson)

The steamer *Vernie Mac* at the boat landing at Taylors Falls in 1899. (Courtesy of the Washington County Historical Society)

seen on the river. The *Belle*, a side-wheel boat, was a regular visitor at the Stillwater levee. The craft sank at Liverpool Landing on the Illinois River in April 1862. It went down so rapidly that holes had to be cut through the ladies' cabin in order to extricate a number of deck hands whose escape had been cut off. No lives were lost. The

Belle paddled as far north as Marine carrying freight for Judd, Walker and Co.

The 40-foot *Queen*, with Captain Albert Eames, made tri-weekly trips from Stillwater to the Dalles at a cost of one dollar for a round trip. She was the first boat to offer even slightly regular service. The *Queen* burned a cord of wood every twelve hours, and according to historian James Taylor Dunn, looked like two lumberjack wanigans fastened together with a pilot's wheel stuck in between.

In the early 1850s, Prescott, Wisconsin was a typical frontier settlement. Some 200 white settlers were planted among 500 Chippewa Indians. The levee was fronted by a row of stores and warehouses. The town was the transfer point for freight consigned to Afton, Lakeland, Hudson, Stillwater, Osceola, and St. Croix Falls. Big boats, unless carrying large amounts of freight for Stillwater and Hudson, did not enter the St. Croix. Freight was put ashore at Prescott and reshipped on smaller boats. This necessitated large warehouses in which to store the goods. In summer, they were filled with goods in transit. In winter, they held wheat awaiting shipment to the East after the river opened in spring.

Rafts of logs and lumber from the St. Croix were pushed to Prescott by towboats from Stillwater. Stores of pork, beans, flour, molasses, and whiskey were laid in at Prescott by the crews of the towboats.

The little 105-ton steamer *Eolian* inaugurated the first regular tri-weekly trade between Prescott, Stillwater, and Taylors Falls in 1856. A passenger and freight boat, it also carried the United States mail. The captain was Stephen L. Cowan, with David Bronson as clerk.

On July 31, 1855, the *Falls City*, a boat over 155 feet long, brought an excursion from St. Anthony and St. Paul to the St. Croix. In September, the stern-wheeler *Montello* transported passengers and freight, including supplies and equipment for the mills and store of Judd, Walker & Co. at Marine.

The steamer *Equator* made its first trip the same month, with C. H. Maxwell as master, B. W. Brunson as clerk, and a Mrs. Jackson as chambermaid. Wages for the crew ranged from $20 to $75 per month. Several of the crew on the *Equator* were unable to write, so they signed their shipping papers with an "X." The *Equator* made six trips on the Minnesota River in 1855, and about thirty-five trips the following year, traveling between St. Paul and Stillwater.

Captains and crews vied for the honor of being the first boat up the river in spring. The navigation season usually opened in April and ran through November.

In 1856, the *Excelsior* was the first craft to make it up the St. Croix for the season. At Hudson, her whistle shrilled her arrival. Nearly everyone in the village ran to the landing to swing their hats and shout "Huzza," as much in welcome of the coming of spring as in welcome of the *Excelsior*. The side-wheeler was a 182-foot boat with a carrying capacity of 272 tons.

And what a day it was when the circus came to town aboard the two showboats, *Banjo* and *James Raymond*. These were the first floating theaters on the river. The *Banjo* had a "nigger show" when it first appeared on the St. Croix at Prescott in 1855. Captain William Fisher who served one season on the boat, said his job was the softest he ever had. The boat averaged less than 20 miles a day because of stopping at every landing that promised a crowd for a show.

It was a bright day in June 1858 when the two showboats brought Spaulding and Rogers' "Great Monkey Circus and Burlesque Dramatic Troupe" to Stillwater. Afternoon and evening performances were given in the "audience chamber," which seated 800. Acts featured monkeys and trained dogs, bearded ladies, giant and pigmy women, Swiss bird warblers, among others . . . a greater variety of amusements "than ever before exhibited in the upper Mississippi Valley," according to the Stillwater *Messenger*. The story is told of a banker in Hudson, where the troupe played after leaving Stillwater, who arranged admission for the entire town. He paid the bill with what was then acceptable currency—pine shingles.

Largest steamboat known to have traveled on the river above Stillwater was the side-wheel packet *Metropolitan*, under Capt. Thomas B. Rhodes. The 313-ton craft went north to Marine on May 15, 1857.

The *Grey Eagle* was built in 1856 for the Galena and Minnesota Packet Company. She was seen frequently on the St. Croix. In the fall of 1858 the *Grey Eagle* and the *Itasca* staged a legendary race. Both paddled with a full head of steam for Minneapolis. The *Grey Eagle* won, and had the singular honor of bearing word that the first Atlantic cable message had been successfully completed between the United States and England. In 1861, while surging downstream near Rock Island, the *Grey Eagle* hit a bridge pier, and sank. The boat could have been properly called the *Grey Hound*, for it was said to be a long, lean boat, as graceful as a greyhound. The packet carried the emblem of the company, a golden eagle, which was later hung in the new *Helen Blair*. (Another source said the emblem was a guilded rooster, ready to crow, which perched on a jack staff.)

The stern-wheeler *Altair* carried passengers and freight on the Mississippi and St. Croix rivers. It is shown here at Samuel Peters' boatyard at Wabasha, Minnesota. (Courtesy of the Washington County Historical Society)

Among the boats visiting the St. Croix during the late 1850s was the *Lottie Lyon*, owned by a Mr. Trumble, who served as captain, clerk, pilot, engineer, steward, and fireman. The excursion packet *Kate Cassel* was an essential part of life on the river.

One of the most popular boats ever seen on the St. Croix was the 41-ton stern-wheeler *H. S. Allen*. Built in 1857 for the Chippewa River trade, she was named after H. S. Allen, an area lumberman of Chippewa Falls, Wisconsin. After a short run there, the *Allen* was brought to the St. Croix. Captain E. B. Strong was in charge of the boat in the summer of 1858, but he ran her into debt. Law officers seized her. Strong seized her back, and tried to run away. Pursued, he attempted to elude the officers by running up the Kinnickinnick River below Hudson. G. M. Stickney, sheriff at that time, headed the pursuing party. Believing capture was imminent, Strong ran the boat ashore and escaped. The *Allen* was apparently pulled off, and refloated. Former hotel keeper Isaac Gray was captain of the boat for a time, traveling up to the Dalles of the St. Croix one day, and back to Stillwater the next. Gray boasted that even if the St. Croix should dry up entirely, he still would be able to get through with the *Allen* on a heavy dew.

The *Allen* was popular for charters, picnics, and excursions. On the Fourth of July, she steamed through the valley with decks and cabin gaily decorated with colored streamers and bunting. Bands, either brass or cotillian, played for dancing. The *Allen* was the first boat to reach Taylors Falls in the spring of 1860. Her arrival in mid-April was followed closely by the *Bangor*. That same year, the *W. A. Knapp* joined the packets on the St. Croix.

The *Allen* rescued passengers from its rival boat the *Equator* when things went wrong on a "Grand Excursion." In 1858, spring had come early. Captain Asa B. Green planned a March 29 excursion on the *Equator*. Two hundred guests accepted the captain's invitation for the outing. The high spirits of the crowd were somewhat dampened when a crew member fell overboard, and an hour's search proved fruitless. Later in the afternoon, just above Marine, the engine of the boat quit working. The *Equator* was stranded in midstream. Some of the passengers danced while others wondered if the food would hold out. All were concerned whether they would have to spend the night on board, or have to swim to shore and walk home. About this time, the rival *H. S. Allen*, on a return trip from St. Croix Falls, came downstream. The *Allen* rescued most of the passengers from the stranded boat, and took them back to Stillwater.

The *Allen* ran on the St. Croix for a few years, then was taken from the river, and never returned.

Entering St. Croix trade in 1861 as a rival to the *Allen* was the *Enterprise*. She was said to look like a wood barge with a dry goods box on top for a cabin. The boat was built in 1853 on the Fox River in Wisconsin. Some time in the late 1850s, she was remodeled with a new hull. Professor Elijah Edwards who arrived in Taylors Falls in late 1860 to teach in the Chisago Seminary and be pastor of the Methodist Church, said that the *Enterprise* was "a toy steamboat, adapted to the shallows and narrow turns of the St. Croix." A stern-

The *Andiamo Too* docked at the levee in Stillwater. (Courtesy of the St llwater *Gazette*)

wheeler, she was 60 feet long, 12 feet wide. The *Enterprise* under Capt. Oscar Knapp, operated on the St. Croix until 1866. She then was cannibalized to fit out the steamboat *Dalles*.

During the 1860s, George Byron Merrick shipped on the *H. S. Allen*, working under Captain S. E. Grey, on the Prescott-to-St. Croix Falls run. Merrick later wrote several books which are invaluable to the student of steamboating on the Upper Mississippi waterways.

When war broke out between the North and South, the *H. S. Allen* and the *Enterprise* both carried recruiters to St. Croix Falls and Taylors Falls to enlist soldiers for the Civil War. The boats returned with enlistees who joined the recruits in Stillwater and became part of the First Minnesota Regiment.

Recruits from outlying districts went to Hudson during the Civil War to embark for the south on barges towed by steamboats. Some of the men lodged in a barn while waiting passage. One day, Henry Densmore led the recruits from the barn to the boats to the tune of "The Girl I Left Behind Me," played on his flute.

With men leaving from communities all along the St. Croix to fight in the Civil War, an excursion party was organized at Taylors Falls. Friends and families boarded the *Enterprise* to go to Fort Snelling to say goodbye to the men when they left for the battlefields.

The *Enterprise* played an unusual role during the Civil War. Prof. Elijah Edwards had taken a pastorate at Hudson. When the editor of the newspaper at Taylors Falls, one David A. Caneday, decided to take off to prospect for copper, he enlisted Edwards as editor. The professor commuted from Hudson to Taylors Falls on the *Enterprise* to put out the paper. The steamboat made at least one trip down the Mississippi carrying soldiers to the battle area in Tennessee and Kentucky.

Captain David Hanks took lumber to Memphis during the Civil War. The men on the towboat and the rafts were targets for guerillas shooting from shore.

Several paddle-wheelers offered competition to the *Enterprise* during the summers of 1864 and 1865. The *Spray* made regular connections with stage coaches which came from St. Paul to Stillwater. Another, described as a "common barge with a little engine," was the *Staver* built on Swede Lake at Chisago City. A queer-looking flat-bottomed scow, it transported wood from Marine to Stillwater, and ran regularly from Arcola to the Falls.

The *G. H. Gray* was a real threat to the *Enterprise*. To secure patronage, her captain, Oscar F. Knapp, in 1865 offered to carry citizens of Prescott on an excursion from there to Taylors Falls and back for free.

The Diamond Jo Steamer Company was established in 1867. Its boats carried a diamond emblem on all four sides of the pilot house, with "JO" for company president Jo Reynolds, lettered between the chimney braces. The firm proved to be quite successful in river trade. It operated with an average of six steamers on the rivers each year. The line was active on both the upper Mississippi and the St. Croix for 15 years.

Chapter 7

Boats Built on the St. Croix

Steamboat building was an important industry in the St. Croix Valley for half a century. A large number of the best boats on the Upper Mississippi, as well as those that navigated the St. Croix, were built on the banks of the border river. One reason was that the best material for construction of steamboats was found in the timber regions along the St. Croix. Black oak was found in quantity. It was very tough, and adapted well to the construction of first-class boats.

In many of the villages and towns along the river, steamboat captains, furniture builders, and adventurers all tried their hand at boat building. St. Croix boats averaged 100 tons in size.

The first boat built in the valley was probably the side-wheel *Osceola I*, constructed in 1854 by Humes and Cummings in the city for which the boat was named. When the woodwork was complete, the *Osceola* was towed to Davenport, Iowa, where the machinery was installed. The side-wheeler made one trip on the St. Croix. Because the 100-foot boat drew too much water, it was taken to Rock Island, Illinois, and sold.

The *Osceola I* ran on the Mississippi between Rock Island and Muscatine, Illinois. Captain of the *Osceola I* was Capt. George Hermes of St. Croix Falls. The *Osceola I* sank in the Mississippi below Rock Island in 1857.

The *Osceola II* was built in 1872 at the Munch Brothers and Company boat yard at Lakeland. Operated by Capt. Charles Timmers of Henderson, Minnesota, it carried freight and passengers between St. Paul and St. Croix Falls. It met an early end, being wrecked on the Yellowstone River in a July storm in 1877.

The *Arcola*, first boat built at Arcola for the St. Croix trade, was constructed in the early 1850s, possibly by Martin Mower. She was wrecked in a windstorm on Lake Pepin near Stockholm, Wisconsin, on May 2, 1857. A second *Arcola*, a rafter, was built at Prescott in

1873. She was still operating as late as 1882, with Stillwater as her home port. A pile-driver named *Arcola* was put into service after the wooden pontoon bridge at Stillwater burned in 1904. The *Arcola* was sent to Hudson to pull some 40-foot pilings out of the ground and bring them to Stillwater to be used in repair of the bridge.

A stern-wheel packet, the *Delta*, was built in Stillwater in 1857. She was sold south for the Des Moines River trade in 1858.

During the 1860s two or three steamboats were built at Franconia, Minnesota, by E. White, a Mr. Thornton and John S. Irish. One of these was the 130-foot *Viola*, for the St. Croix and Mississippi Packet Company. The boat made its first trip on June 19, 1865. Described as "One of the neatest and most perfect little packets that ever kissed the blue water of our beautiful river," the *Viola* cost $15,000. It was named for Capt. Oscar F. Knapp's daughter Viola. The boat burned at Rock Island on November 14, 1882. Another, the *Pioneer*, was built on Green Lake near Franconia, 1861-62, by two proprietors

The steamer *Arcola*, a pile driver built in 1898-99 by George Muller at Stillwater, Minnesota, for the St. Croix Boom Company. The *Arcola* operated between Taylors Falls and Prescott and on one occasion did work as far south as Winona. She was used to drive piling, break up log jams and pull logs off sand bars during log drives. The hull of this sidewheeler was 100 feet long, with a beam of 20 feet and a draft of 18 inches and was equipped with 52-foot leads and a 3,500-pound hammer for driving piling. Its crew of about nine men lived aboard the boat. The last pilings driven by the *Arcola* were at the Stillwater Boat Dock in May 1916. The boat was dismantled at Stillwater shortly after this. Harvey Ferguson was the first pilot, Mike Collins the second, Dan Flynn the third, and Pat Connors the last. The engineers were: Frank Johnson, John Johnson, Danny Robinson, Gus Beyle, Mell Sparks. The firemen were: John Mackey, George Johnson, and John Connors. Ed Stack and Arthur Raymo were the cooks. Bill Sullivan, because of his ability to judge the length of piling needed, was chief axeman; he sharpened all piling used. (Courtesy of the Washington County Historical Society)

of the stave mill, to tow rafts. When completed, the *Pioneer* was hauled from the lake to the river. Eventually, the hull of the boat became a barge. A second *Pioneer* was built by Stover and Barnes in 1866, probably at Osceola. It used the boiler from a mill at Amador, Minnesota.

Yet another Franconia boat was the *Fanny Thornton*, built by Truman Foster and Otto Thornton in the winter of 1862-63. After a few runs, the boat was sold and "went below," meaning it was used on the lower Mississippi for rafting, towing, and in the cotton trade. The *Dexter* and the *Jennie Hayes* also came into being at Franconia. The firm also manufactured a number of barges. (A different source puts E. White, Thornton, and John S. Irish in Osceola, Wisconsin, from 1861 to 1865, building boats in that location. Boats constructed there were reportedly the *Jenny Thornton*, followed by the *Ben Campbell*, and the *Jennie Hayes*.) The *Jennie Hayes*, launched June 7, 1879, was taken to Stillwater for its machinery. Named for the wife of David Hayes, the boat cost about $3,000.

Capt. Isaac Gray had the *G. H. Gray*, a stern-wheeler with 82-ton capacity, built at Stillwater in 1863. Seven years later, he ordered the *St. Croix* built at Maiden Rock. She was 115 feet long, with a 20-foot beam and 4-foot hold with 98-ton capacity. The *St. Croix* worked from Hudson to Taylors Falls for two summers, then was sold as a tow boat. She worked for 13 seasons, then sank in 1893 at the Dubuque Bridge.

There is a story about Henry W. Crosby, one of the few people in Hudson to build a boat. Crosby was born in Albany, Albany County, New York, on October 19, 1819, and had a common school education in Buffalo, New York. In May 1840, he headed up the Mississippi River from St. Louis aboard the *Indian Queen*, along with 50 other people, bound for the falls of the St. Croix. The boat landed at the head of Lake St. Croix, because the boat captain could not find the channel of the river. The rest of the trip was completed on a flat boat. Due to sleet, rain, and snow, it took three days to travel to the falls. In spite of that introduction to Minnesota, Crosby settled at Lakeland. Crosby served in the Civil War, then returned to the St. Croix and settled in Hudson. He decided to construct a steamboat in a building (located either at Third and Locust, or on Second Street between Walnut and Commercial streets). Crosby built a good-sized river boat. But somewhere along the line, his calculations went wrong. When the steamer was completed, Crosby had to tear out a large section of the store front to get it to the river.

Another boat builder was Cyrus J. Bradley, born in Kasaskia, Illinois, in March 1825. He arrived at Osceola in 1848. In 1865, Bradley hired a steamboat to see whether or not it was practical to use a boat to run logs to market. When he found it could be done successfully, he ordered Josiah Batchelder to build a boat for him, the *Minnie Will*. Completed during the winter of 1867, it was the first boat built especially for towing logs. When launched, the *Minnie* made a successful trip towing a raft to Clinton, Iowa.

The *Dalles*, originally called the *Mayflower*, or *June Bug*, saw the light of day in 1866 in the Osceola boat yard. Built by Capt. Marshall Winch, the boat used the machinery from the old *Enter-

One of several packets that bore the name *St. Croix*. This one was operated by Master A. B. Northey and made trips between Stillwater and St. Croix Falls every Sunday, offering "Sixty-two miles of unsurpassed scenery." The fare was $1.00 for the round trip. (Courtesy of the Washington County Historical Society)

Letterhead of the firm Bronson and Folsom. (The steamboat appeared to the left of the names.) The lumber firm operated the steamers *Isaac Staples, Clyde, Juniata, George S, Gypsy, Edwin C,* and the *Baby.* (Courtesy of Jim Johnson)

A rare photo of the *Wyman X* (left, behind the *Tiger*) with the dock in front of it filled with cargo and barrels of freight. (Courtesy of Durand Blanding)

prise, a boat which Winch had purchased in the fall. After one season on the St. Croix, running between Prescott and Taylors Falls, the *Dalles* was sold to a company at Chester, Illinois.

The Honorable W. H. C. Folsom, a pioneer settler of the Northwest and owner of extensive lumber holdings on the St. Croix, could not resist the desire to enter the boat-building business. His Chisago Boat Yard adjoined his carriage factory and sawmill at the foot of the Dalles. John S. Irish moved to Taylors Falls from Osceola to become Folsom's master carpenter and builder. He built the *Wyman X* at Taylors Falls during the winter months of 1867 and most of 1868. One of the most powerful steamers on the St. Croix, the *Wyman* was said to be the first steamboat completely built and fitted in Minnesota. It was a first-class boat in every respect, and was made of the best materials by the most experienced workmen. The *Wyman X* was 120 feet long, with a 22-foot beam, 4-foot depth of hold, and 200-ton capacity. Loaded, she drew 18 inches of water. Twenty-eight staterooms held three people per cabin. The main cabin was finished in black walnut and fitted with upholstered furniture. The *Wyman X,* one of the largest paddle-wheelers ever built on the upper river, had two forty-horsepower engines locally constructed. The boat was towed to St. Anthony Falls where the engines were installed at W. H. Harrison's North Star Iron Works, Machine Shop, Iron and Brass Foundry. The craft was towed back to the St. Croix in November. Captain of the boat was the man for whom it was named, Wyman X. Folsom, elder son of W. H. C. The boat ran as a regular tri-weekly packet for the St. Paul and St. Croix trade during 1869, 1870 and 1871. In the spring of 1869, she was one of four boats on the river trying to beat each other out for patronage—the *Nellie Kent,* nicknamed "Old Reliable," and owned by Commodore William Davidson; *James Means,* owned by the Northern Lines; the *G. B. Knapp;* and the *Wyman X.* of Taylors Falls. "Sell tickets at any price" was the motto. A traveler could almost name his own fee for a trip. Twenty-five cents was considered top price from Prescott to the Dalles of the St. Croix. During 1870, the *Wyman X* alone carried 5,776 paying passengers between Stillwater and Taylors Falls.

For a short time during 1871, the *Wyman X* operated as a mail boat. That year, too, she was involved in the legendary "Battle of the Piles," (see pages 48 and 49.) The following year, she was towing logs out of Stillwater. Three years later, the *Wyman X* was on the Minnesota River. In 1877, when owned by lumberman Isaac Staples, the boat sank near Quincy, Illinois. She was then scrapped and the machinery used in a new Stillwater-built boat, the *David Bronson.*

W. H. C. Folsom commissioned the building of another boat, the *Frankie Folsom,* in 1886. The small stern-wheel packet was 83 feet long. After a short time on the St. Croix, she was sold to Parmlee Brothers of Stillwater, then to J. C. Losch on the Illinois River. In 1892, she was caught in a gale and sank, with the loss of nearly a score of lives.

E. H. Tilton, born in New York City, was a shipwright in Polk County. He arrived in the St. Croix Valley in 1869, and assisted in the construction of many boats.

Martin Mower of Arcola was involved in the St. Croix Boom

The stern-wheeler *Ada B* is shown here at the Taylors Falls landing in 1878. Built at Arcola during the winter of 1876-77, the *Ada B* was a 105-foot packet destined for St. Croix River trade. (Courtesy of Durand Blanding)

Company. As part of that business, Mower started building steamboats in the mid-1870s. Two pile drivers and two passenger steamers were launched from a shipyard at Arcola. Working with Mower was shipwright John Irish. During 1876 and 1877, they built the "very neat little steamer" *Ada B*, a 105-foot stern-wheel packet destined for St. Croix River trade. The *Eva*, built at Arcola in 1882, was used as a pile driver. Sold to Libby and Clark at Hastings, it was used as an excursion boat until 1893 when it was dismantled. Other boats constructed at Arcola were the *Gracie Mower*, and the *Plough Boy*, which ran between Prescott and Hastings. Mower also designed an ice boat, and that story is told in a later chapter.

Lakeland, Minnesota, was the site of the shipyard of Munch Brothers and Company. In 1871, a steamboat named *Osceola* (or *Osceolin*) was constructed there, as well as two or three barges. The business was short-lived, for it lasted just one year.

A wanigan had been built on the Namekagon River, a tributary of the St. Croix, during the spring of 1872. The boat was used to carry provisions and cooking utensils for the lumberjacks during log drives. Named the *City of Stillwater*, the boat was 100 feet long, and 25 feet wide. The cabin, 50 feet in length, could be taken down to enable the wanigan to pass under low bridges and other obstructions. The *City of Stillwater* was capable of carrying 200 tons of material and was constructed of white pine lumber. The woodwork was done by John Hejland and William Thompson, and the iron work made by blacksmith Peter Grant.

The *David Bronson*, a stern-wheel rafter, was built at Stillwater in the winter of 1878-79. Perhaps "rebuilt" would be a better word. The

The Battle of the Piles

The story of the "Battle of the Piles" that took place on Lake St. Croix in 1871, has been told and retold. It was more than a squabble between towns over the width of the draw through which steamboats could pass; it was almost a last-ditch stand in the bigger war between steamboats and railroads, a war that the steamboats could not possibly win.

For this book, the record as printed in "History of Washington County and the St. Croix Valley" edited by the Rev. Edward D. Neill, published in 1881, is quoted verbatim, as follows:

"The West Wisconsin Railway Company, in building their road, had secured the right to bridge the lake at Hudson, to make a western connection with the St. Paul, Stillwater and Taylors Falls railroad, and thereby securing an entrance into St. Paul as its western terminus. The building of the bridge caused hard feelings to rankle in the breasts of the lumbermen at Stillwater, because as they claimed, the passages were not wide enough. We clip the history of the 'Battle of the Piles': 'On the morning of the 7th of July, 1871, warlike preparations were noticeable at Stillwater. Six steamboats moved down the lake towards the nearly-completed bridge at Hudson, Wisconsin. They carried a force of two hundred active, able-bodied men. The work on the bridge had been progressing rapidly, much to the satisfaction of the people of Hudson. The "pile drivers" had placed a long line of piles, or supports, in position, and had left space for a draw of ninety-eight feet in the main channel of the river. The bridge was looked upon with displeasure by the people of Stillwater for various reasons, but they argued principally that the draw was too small. It may be that the rafts could have been diminished in size. But "may bes" don't count, and on Monday, July 3rd, an injunction was formally served upon the bridge builders. Their work was suspended temporarily and an agreement was made, the Stillwater folks thought, to stop further proceedings and take the matter from the "district" to the "circuit court." They found, however, that the bridge builders

The *Minnesota*, one of six boats to carry that name on the Mississippi and St. Croix rivers. (Courtesy of A. Carr Griffith)

continued the work. When the steamers, with their forces, arrived near the Hudson bridge at ten o'clock that Friday morning, it was discovered, by the aid of a glass, that more piles were being driven. So three of the steamers—the *Louisville, Whitmore,* and *Brother Jonathan* —were lashed together and ordered to the attack. They proceeded under a fire of invectives from the Hudsonites who had gathered at the bridge. Several of the attacking party were stunned by the force of the invectives, but they were carried to Dr. Morpheus, in whose care they soon recovered. At five minutes past ten a.m. the attack was commenced. A great hawser was uncoiled from the deck of one of the steamers. Several gallant, but slightly excited, men fastened it to one of the piles. The commander commanded, the bells rung, the engines moved, the wheels revolved, the hawser slipped off, and Hudson whooped with joy. The other three steamers moved toward the point of attack, hoping to be called upon. But the undaunted commander renewed the attack.

"'The hawser was again fastened, the command given, and this time the steamer was victorious. The pile was drawn, and from up river went a yell of delight that was repeated by the re-inforcements, and again and again repeated by both. Throughout the day eighty piles were drawn.

"'During the next day a steamer was left to guard the passage, and not till evening did she leave her post. Even then she finished the fight by capturing that great machine, the "pile driver," which she delivered into the custody of the good city of Stillwater. No record has been kept of the wounded feelings of the lost spirits. It is a matter of regret that they cannot enter into the "Battle of the Piles." A flag of truce was sent, a couple of conferences were held, and finally on Saturday, July the 16th, 1871, an agreement was entered into under which the building of the bridge went on, and the draw was made 140 feet clear above, and 136 feet clear at the water line for the passage of rafts. Thus was effected the bridge compromise; and soon Hudson celebrated the completion of the West Wisconsin railroad.'"

The Stillwater Gazette *reported afterward that the city council voted three to one in favor of repaying the steamboats for their part in the battle. The steamers* Louisville *and* Minnesota *received $100 each; the G. B. Knapp and the* Swallow *each received $50.*

The steamer *Louisville*, a famous Stillwater boat of the eighteen seventies, was owned by the pioneer rafting firm of Durant and Wheeler of Stillwater. Captain R. J. Wheeler was her master. This photo was taken in 1883. (Courtesy of the Washington County Historical Society)

The Bayport Boat Yard. In the background are the steamers *Ramora* and *Helen Schulenburg*. (Courtesy of Jim Johnson)

A large, powerful steamboat, the *Kit Carson* was built at Stillwater in 1880 for Capt. A. R. Young and the Burlington Lumber Company. (Courtesy of the Washington County Historical Society)

boat was formerly the *I. E. Staples*, which had been a rafter for Isaac Staples. Machinery for the *Bronson* was taken from the *Wyman X*. The name was changed when the 130-foot boat was purchased by the Matt Clark Transportation Company of Stillwater. (Clark was a son-in-law of Staples.) As the *Bronson*, the boat was commanded by Capt. James Newcomb. When Clark's business failed in 1886, the *Bronson* was sold to Durant and Wheeler, and the name changed again to *Henrietta*.

The Stillwater Dock Company, located in South Stillwater (the name was changed to Bayport in 1922) was organized in 1877. Capital stock was $10,000. Partners in the venture were Durant, Wheeler and Company; St. Croix Lumber Company; and Josiah Batchelder. R. G. Wheeler was president, Louis E. Torinus secretary and treasurer, and Batchelder was general manager.

The business looked promising. Steamers produced in the yard at Stillwater Dock were architecturally sound. Three steamers were built in 1880, the *Pauline*, the *R. G. Wheeler*, and the *Kit Carson*. This last boat was built for Capt. Augustus R. Young. Measuring 138 feet by 29 feet by 4 feet, it was a big boat, 237 tons. The *Carson*, a rafter, had two boilers, and was named for one of the daughters of Mr. Carson, of the Carson and Rand Lumber Company of Eau Claire, Wisconsin.

Others built by the firm were the *Netta Durant*, *Ed Durant Jr.*, *Gardie Eastman*, *Robert Dodds*, *Everett*, the United States government boat *Alert*, the *Louisville*, *St. Croix III*, *Ten Broeck*, and *Burdette*. Built in 1881, the *Burdette* was just 30.55 tons. It was used as a brail boat in Stillwater harbor, and finally dismantled at South Stillwater. The *Ten Broeck* was built in 1882. Master and pilot of the rafter was Capt.

The steamer *Ten Broeck* was built at Stillwater in 1882 for the rafting firm of Gillipsie and Harper of Stillwater. It was a large, powerful rafter with three boilers and was low and wide to reduce the effect of the wind. It could out-back and out-flank any boat on the river. This photo was taken four miles below Lynxville, Wisconsin. (Courtesy of the Washington County Historical Society)

Walter A. Blair. The boat was bought by Le Claire Navigation Company in 1886.

Also constructed at South Stillwater was the *Lora*. Launched in August, 1900, the *Lora* was equipped with boilers formerly on the *Abner Gile*. Its new engine was manufactured by David M. Swain. When the 140-foot boat was launched, a pennant at the bow carried the name of the steamer, and a new United States flag floated astern. Under the command of Capt. John A. Kent, the *Lora* made the round trip from Stillwater to Taylors Falls for fifty cents.

The *Dispatch II* was a 64-ton boat built in Stillwater for Durant, Wheeler and Company. It served as a brail boat and bow boat. On September 14, 1878, it was bumped and sunk by the packet *Red Wing* near Savanna, Illinois. Raised and refurbished, the *Dispatch II* was used as a raft boat until 1884. Portaged to White Bear Lake, it served as an excursion and pleasure boat for several years, then was dismantled.

The *Everett*, a stern-wheel rafter, was built by Josiah Batchelder for Capt. Charles H. Meeds. Machinery for the 110-foot boat was from the *William White*. The *Everett* was struck by a tornado April 19, 1889, near Burlington, Iowa. She was raised and sold to the Empire Coal Docks at Fulton, Illinois. The *Ed Durant, Jr.*, built in 1884, was fitted

The *City of Hudson*, under construction, or perhaps reconstruction, since the cabin, pilot house, and stacks are complete. (Courtesy of Jim Johnson)

The *Fury* was the last steamboat built at South Stillwater by Josiah Batchelder. The photograph was taken May 21, 1899. (Courtesy of Jim Johnson)

with machinery from the *A. T. Jenks* which had burned at Stillwater the previous year. In its turn, the *Ed Durant* was also destroyed by fire.

Two small propellor boats were built at Stillwater in 1887. The *Alice D.* was 60 feet long with a 12-foot beam, and 5.7-foot hold. Built by lumberman William Sauntry, it was used as a make-up boat for the Stillwater rafting works. The second was the *Ellen M.*, 50 feet long. It was built as a brail boat for the St. Croix Boom Company. Henry

Burkleo was master in 1893. Patsey Connors captained it in 1896. The following year, the boat was dismantled in South Stillwater.

Durant and Wheeler built a 122-foot rafter, the *Daisy*, in 1887. Charles White was master and pilot of the boat. She was sold down river in 1898. Another stern-wheel rafter, the 121-foot, 138-ton *Cyclone*, was built by the Durant and Wheeler firm in 1891. She ran on the St. Croix until 1898, when she was sold to Fountain City. The *Cyclone* burned in winter quarters in 1906 at Wabasha, Minnesota. Two boats of Durant and Wheeler made twelve to twenty trips each year and employed some thirty-five men. Stillwater Dock Company did repairs on boats as well as constructing craft.

One of the partners, the firm of Durant and Wheeler, operated twenty lumber camps. According to Warner and Foote, four were on the Snake River; one on the Kettle; two on the Yellow; two along the West Wisconsin Railroad; one on the Totogaticonce [sic] River; four on the Apple; six on the Totogatic; and one on the Namekagon. The corporation was formed in January 1881. In connection with their lumber business, Durant and Wheeler operated a towing business. It was natural that they would become involved in building steamboats.

D. M. Swain furnished the machinery for nearly all the boats built at Stillwater. In addition, he had several packets built, including the *Percy Swain*, *Verne Swain*, *Plough Boy*, and *Joseph Long*. The Swain story is told later in this book.

At the point where the St. Croix joins the Mississippi River, the Prescott Machine Shop was established by H. B. Fasiling. He did a large amount of repairing of river boats. He also manufactured row boats.

The *Annie Barnes*, a 20-ton boat was built in Prescott, Wisconsin, in 1880. She was named for the daughter of Charlie Barnes, steamboat agent there from 1857 to 1903. Charlie's job was to handle the great amount of transfer business for Lake St. Croix. He always wore a silk stove pipe hat, and met every boat. It was said that the pilots on the river "held on" Charlie's hat when they landed at Prescott. By lining up with the top hat, they brought the boat exactly to the warehouse.

Built at Prescott in 1884 by Hamilton West and Mr. Truax for John Dudley Lumber Company, the *Luella* was a 99.34-ton boat. She towed logs and lumber from Stillwater and St. Paul to the mill at Prescott. The *Luella* burned at Wabasha in 1898 or 1899. Another West boat was the *Mark Bradley*, built in 1872 for Capt. Cyrus Bradley of Osceola. After it ran many years in the rafting trade, it was dismantled at Stillwater in 1881.

The Muller Brothers were the most famous of the boat builders at Stillwater. Their story appears in a later chapter. There was another firm, Harper and Gillespie, which built the steamboat *Nina* during the winter of 1881.

It was in December of 1890 that word was out that a new pleasure steamer was being built at Baytown. Partners in the project were Capt. H. C. Doughty and Capt. John A. Kent. Unfortunately, no further information was available on that project.

One of the last boats built to ply the St. Croix was the *J. J. Hill*,

The *Baby* on the St. Croix River. The boat was so named because there were infants in both the Bronson and Folsom families, sponsors of the boat. (Courtesy of the Washington County Historical Society)

constructed at Hastings in 1902.

During the frenzy of boat building, there was competition among towns along the river for the honor of having a boat carry the town name. Frequently, though, names for boats came from the family of those who built the steamers. They usually were bequeathed with little formality. Generally some lady would crack a bottle of "Robert Slater's Elixer of Life" on the prow of the boat and dub it with the appropriate name.

The *Baby* was so named because there were infants of the same age in both the Bronson and Folsom families, sponsors of the boat. Rather than offend either family, a name was chosen which could refer to both.

Although boat launchings were frequent, particularly at Stillwater and Osceola, they were always occasions for celebration. Well-greased skids were laid between the boat and the water, and, when all was ready, the ropes holding the hull were loosened, the traditional flask of champagne was smashed on the bow, and the boat skidded into the St. Croix.

A tale was told along the river of a boat built for a man from Northern Wisconsin. He wanted the craft christened properly, but failed to supply the necessary bottle of liquid. He went off to find one, but neglected to return for several hours. The men on the dock got tired of waiting. They launched the boat with no ceremony. Eventually the owner arrived with the liquor. He found his boat floating in the middle of the stream. Rather than waste the bottle, he sat down on the levee and drank it.

Two shipping bills for freight being transported on the *Humbolt*, in the years 1853 (top) and 1854 (bottom). (Courtesy of the Washington County Historical Society)

Chapter 8

Muller Boat Works

The name "Muller" was associated with boat building, boating, and boat docks in the St. Croix Valley for more than a century. Five generations carried on the family tradition.

The Muller family arrived in Stillwater, Minnesota, from Pennsylvania in 1855. Philip Muller, a furniture and coffin maker, opened a shop at Sixth and Myrtle streets. His sons George and John learned the trade from him. Living near the St. Croix, the boys spent much of their free time on the river.

The two sons were in their early twenties when they got the idea of starting a boat works. They first made boats—skiffs and bateaux. In 1873, they opened a shop, 20 by 40 feet, on the riverfront at the south end of Stillwater, where they constructed the watercraft. Most of their work was done by hand. In addition to building boats, the two manufactured the peavies and cant hooks used by lumberjacks on log drives.

Muller Boats Works was closely aligned with the lumbering industry in the valley. Companies such as Hersey, Bronson, Doe and Folsom; McKusick, Anderson and Company; and Isaac Staples brought them the lumber for the construction of bateaux, sculls, and peavy stocks which were then fabricated by the Mullers. The items were then sold back to the lumber companies. A bill from Bronson and Folsom, dated 1874, shows that the company bought two bateaux from Mullers at $35 each.

The steamer *Arkansas* of the Diamond Jo line, and the *G. B. Knapp* of the St. Paul and St. Croix Packet Company were buying Muller products in 1875, according to records of that year. On July 19, 1876, Mullers paid the St. Paul Daily Railroad $1.15 to deliver a skiff to the steamer *Nellie Kent*. At that time, Mullers charged $35 for a 16-foot skiff.

The Muller brothers were reported to be at work on a miniature

Muller boat house above the Stillwater bridge on the St. Croix River, 1912. (Courtesy of the Washington County Historical Society)

Roy Muller in front of the Muller Boat Livery at Stillwater. Many of the boats used by tourists on the St. Croix were rented here. Photo taken in 1927. (Courtesy of the Washington County Historical Society)

steamboat in September 1875. It was launched late that month, and engaged in a cruise from Stillwater to Catfish Bar, near Afton. The purpose of the trip was to hunt geese. The Mullers bagged the first game of the season on September 26, according to a news report of that era. (The name probably was originally Müller with the German umlaut—two dots—over the "u," for the newspaper spelled the name "Miiller.")

That same year, George and John installed a four-horsepower engine and some other new machinery in their shop. They put a 50-foot addition onto their building. Three years later, because of a continuing increase in business, they expanded again, installing an 18-horsepower engine, two crosscut saws, two rip saws, and a number of lathes.

On November 10, 1880, eight years after the business originated, George purchased John's interest in the Muller Boat Works. George, operating with his two sons Roy and George A., who was always called "Mike," continued building boats for the river trade. Frequently, the boatworks leased a portion of land from the railroad for 90 days. They then proceeded to complete a steamboat in that

The steamer *LeRoy*, built by George Muller in 1885-86 and sold to Bronson and Folsom about 1889. The *LeRoy* was the first tugboat used to tow logs from the St. Croix Boom to the rafting grounds on the lake. (Courtesy of the Washington County Historical Society)

period of time. Often, though, only a month elapsed from the laying of the keel to the launching of the boat. Cost was as low as $3,000.

The tugboats *Alice D*, *St. Croix*, *L and M*, *Baby*, and the *LeRoy* were all built in the mid-1880s. Among the more than 60 steamboats built by Muller were the *Gracie Kent*, *Columbia*, *Isaac Staples*, *Flora Clark*, *Borealis Rex*, and the *Robert*, which operated out of Taylors Falls for many years as a sightseeing boat. The 82-ton stern-wheel *Columbia* was built by the Mullers at Baytown in 1900 to compete against the *Grace Kent* in passenger and excursion service to Taylors Falls. She left the St. Croix with the last load of logs in 1914. The *Grace Kent* was built by Muller for Capt. John Kent of Osceola in April 1887 for interstate navigation. The packet operated between Stillwater and the Falls for just one season. In autumn, she was sold in Louisiana after a trip south with several barges of Stillwater-grown potatoes.

Perhaps the most famous of the Muller-built passenger boats was the steamer *Ravenna*, built in 1889 for Anderson and O'Brien Lumber Company. Built as a raft boat, the *Ravenna* doubled as a packet or excursion boat, and carried passengers on many occasions. She was 122.6 by 22 feet, with a four-foot draft.

On June 12, 1902, while ascending the Mississippi River at a point known as Maguoketa Chute, about eight miles above Dubuque, Iowa, the *Ravenna* encountered a sudden, severe windstorm, and capsized. Out of the 26 people aboard—24 crew members and two passengers—four drowned: Capt. John Hoy, master; Bryon Trask, clerk; Louis Walker, fuel passer; and a deck hand whose name was unknown. Two

The steamer *Gracie Kent* at Taylors Falls in 1898. This boat was built at Stillwater in 1897-98 by George Muller for the Interstate Navigation Company operating between Stillwater and Taylors Falls. In the fall of 1898 the *Gracie Kent* made a final trip south with several barges of Stillwater-grown potatoes and was sold in Louisianna. (Courtesy of the Washington County Historical Society)

other people were slightly injured by escaping steam. The estimated value of the vessel was $8,000. The upper works were completely demolished, but the hull was raised and a new upper works constructed by Muller. In an investigation of the accident, no negligence was found, and the officers of the boat were exonerated.

The *Ravenna* was again damaged in May 1906. Going through the bridge at Hastings with the bow steamer *Bun Hersey*, the *Ravenna* was caught in a severe wind storm, and swept against the middle pier of the drawbridge. Guardrails on the larboard side of the steamer, on both the boiler deck and the cabin deck, were broken. The seams opened, which caused some leakage. The boat was returned to Stillwater for repairs.

When rafting ceased, the *Ravenna* was sold to Capt. H. C. Wilcox and Sons, who ran her for several years as a packet between La Crosse, Wisconsin, and Wabasha, Minnesota, changing her name in 1907 to the *LaCrosse*. She last was included in the Merchant Vessels listing in 1913. However, it is believed that the *Ravenna* was returned to the St. Croix, and operated until the 1920s when she burned.

In 1894, Muller Boat Works was hired to repair the pontoon bridge across the river at Stillwater. The company fashioned new pontoons on the levee, then placed them on the bridge. Pine for the repairs was imported from the state of Washington, even though millions of board feet of lumber were available from the forests along the St. Croix.

The most famous work boat constructed by the Muller firm was the *Edwin C*, built in 1897.

The steamer *Edwin C*, a very powerful boat for its size, on Lake St. Croix in 1904. It was built in 1897-98 by George Muller for Bronson & Folsom Company of Stillwater. James Sullivan was the captain, Raymond Fuller the engineer, Harry Jackson the fireman and Pat Fitzgerald the linesman. (Courtesy of the Washington County Historical Society)

A new hull for the pile driver *Arcola*, originally constructed by Martin Mower in 1882, was built in 1898 for the St. Croix Boom Company. The *Arcola* operated between Taylors Falls and Prescott, and once did some work at Winona. The boat was used to drive piling, break up log jams, and pull logs off sand bars. The hull of the sidewheeler was 100 feet long, the beam 20 feet. Her draft was just 18 inches. She had 52-foot leads, and a 3,500-pound hammer for pile driving. A crew of nine lived on board. Harvey Ferguson was first pilot of the *Arcola*. Following him were Mike Collins, Dan Flynn, and Pat Connors. Engineers of the boat were Frank Johnson, John Johnson, Danny Robinson, Gus Boule, and Mel Sparks. Bill Sullivan was the chief "axeman." His job was to sharpen all the piling used. He held the job because of his ability to judge the length of the piling needed. The last piling driven by the *Arcola* were at the Stillwater Boat Dock in May 1916. Shortly afterward, the boat was dismantled.

A popular passenger boat on the St. Croix was the *Olive S.*, built by George Muller. The boat, owned and operated by Capt. James Teare, made daily trips to the Falls of the St. Croix from Stillwater.

The passenger boat, *Olive S*, built by George Muller and owned and operated by Jim Teare, is shown here—aground—after hitting a snag in the St. Croix River during a race with the *St. Croix*. (Photo by H. E. Jackson in 1915. Courtesy of the Washington County Historical Society)

May 5, 1938, just before the move to Mulberry Point. (Courtesy of Dick Muller)

Muller boat houses during high water, May 5, 1938. From building steamboats and pleasure craft to operating a marina, the Muller family was a tradition on the St. Croix for 113 years. (Courtesy of Dick Muller)

Muller dynasty, October 1934. Left to right are Carl Muller, George Muller Sr., George (Mike) Muller, and LeRoy Muller. (Courtesy of Dick Muller)

High water, May 5, 1938, showing the Muller boat houses located at Mulberry Point in Stillwater, Minnesota. (Courtesy of Dick Muller)

The *Olive*, a trim little gasoline-powered packet, and the equally tiny *St. Croix*, a roomy little vessel, were the last paddle-wheelers to operate regularly between Stillwater and the Dalles of the St. Croix. Praise for the little *Olive S.* appeared in the Stillwater *Messenger* on June 17, 1916:

Who makes trips to Taylors Falls,
Every day, whether rain or shine?
Old Jim Teare with the *Olive S.*,
A craft that's fixed up fine . . .

In the early 1900s, George Muller raised a boat which had been built 40 years earlier. The *Abner Gile*, built at Le Claire, Iowa, in 1872, sank in 25 feet of water at South Stillwater on April 17, 1899. Muller raised the craft, and dismantled it.

When the last of the logs were harvested along the St. Croix in 1914, the river became unsuitable for steamboats. Muller and his sons Roy and George A. (Mike) turned to designing and building pleasure craft and small boats. (A third son, Carl, became involved with river boats, running excursions out of Taylors Falls.) The Mullers originated the first boat kits. Bateaux were cut and assembled temporarily, then dismantled and shipped to lumber companies on both coasts of the United States. A delivery skiff of pine, 17.5 feet in length, cost $30. Cedar skiffs were $5 higher.

Muller Boat Works manufactured raft skiffs at $1.99 per foot. They also turned out three- and four-stroke bateaux, pond skiffs, and hunting skiffs. Prices included two paddles and one pair of oars.

During the 1920s, the company designed and built racing boats. Mike Muller became well-known in racing circles, not only for the boats he designed, but also as a racer. George Muller retired from the firm in 1933 at the age of 80. His sons, Mike and Roy, who had grown up in the family tradition, continued to run the company.

Mike Muller and Chet Thomas added another dimension to water traffic in 1931. They took to the air. The pair invented what they called a "water glider." Made of airplane spruce wood, the 15-foot craft had a 37-foot wingspread. It was towed by a motor boat until it lifted off the water and soared aloft. It was first tested and proved successful by John Quinlan on March 3, 1931.

The third phase of the Muller Boat Works was operated by George's two sons, Dick Muller and Bill Murray, both of whom started in the family enterprise as young men. As their sons came of age, they, too, worked in the business. From the building of steamboats, then the building of pleasure craft, Muller Boats turned to marina services. Boats were docked, serviced, repaired, and stored at the facility. A canoe rental service operated from Muller Boat Works for many years, but was discontinued in 1968 when power boat traffic near Stillwater became too heavy for canoe safety. Muller Boat Works was sold in 1986 and became the Stillwater Yacht Club, ending a 113-year family tradition.

Chapter 9

Osceola Boat Builders

Osceola was home to two families of steamboat builders, the Knapps and the Kents, who dominated the boat-building business in that city. Between 1853 and 1887 the two families built ten steamboats at Osceola, and a few at Franconia. Members of the families also owned and captained boats on the St. Croix. The boats they constructed were particularly suited to the needs of the St. Croix trade and to the shallow waters of the St. Croix.

There were other boat-builders in the Wisconsin city. The first steamer finished at the Osceola boatyard was the *Osceola* in 1854, 100 by 18 feet in size, with a 65-ton capacity. Her cost was $10,000. But her owner-builders were neither the Knapps or the Kents; rather, they were Humes and Cummings, with construction by George Hermes, long-time resident of St. Croix Falls. After the wooden hull of the side-wheel boat was completed, the *Osceola* was towed to Davenport, Iowa, where the machinery was installed. Because she drew too much water, the boat was sent to the Mississippi after only one season on the St. Croix River. She ran between Burlington, Illinois, and Davenport, Iowa, and sank in 1857 below Rock Island.

A second steamboat named *Osceola* was built by the Munch Brothers at their boatyard in Lakeland in 1872. For three years, this boat plied the St. Croix and Minnesota rivers, but met an early end when it was wrecked on the Yellowstone River in a July storm in 1877.

In 1863 a new levee was built at Osceola. According to the Polk County *Press*, "When the new hill leading to it is repaired, and the new road built, Osceola will have the best landing on the St. Croix."

The hull of the light-draft *Viola* was built at Franconia by Capt. Oscar Knapp of Osceola in 1864. Knapp was one of the most experienced rivermen of the West. For construction of the steamer, a stock company was organized under a special act of the Wisconsin legislature. Businessmen all along the St. Croix became investors. The machinery was installed on the *Viola* at La Crosse. The boat, one of the fastest and best boats ever on the St. Croix River, was intended for trade between La Crosse and Taylors Falls. Knapp was the first captain of the *Viola*. However, because of difficulties among members of the company, he was replaced by Captain Bartlett of Hudson. According to the Stillwater *Republican* of April 6, 1869, the *Viola*, "born to bad luck, she will never in all probability win a fortune for anyone. . . ." The "company" ended in a great fizzle in 1867.

In the winter of 1865-66, the steamboat *Enterprise*, an old St. Croix packet, was overhauled at the Osceola boatyard. Brought from the Fox River in Wisconsin in 1861, she operated regularly on the river for five years. At the end of her first year, the *Enterprise* carried to the East a shipment of 800 bushels of cranberries for Judd, Walker, and Co. of Marine. Among her many passengers in the fall of 1865 were four or five Swedish families, about 50 people in all, who disembarked at Marine Mills.

The *Enterprise*, which ran tri-weekly between Stillwater and Taylors Falls, was owned by Robert C. Eden, who sold her to Capt. Oscar Knapp. He in turn sold the craft to Capt. Marshall Winch, who took out her machinery in Osceola, rebottomed her, and lengthened her by 15 feet. (A longer boat could travel more easily in shallow water.) The *Enterprise* was back in service in May 1866, but left the St. Croix at the end of that season.

Four new boats came into being at Osceola during the winter of 1865-66: The *G. B. Knapp*, the *Minnie Will*, the *Pioneer*, and the *Dalles*.

Capt. Oscar Knapp built the *G. B. Knapp*, which was on the St. Croix for more than twenty years. A stern-wheeler of 105 tons, 130 by 20 feet, she received her machinery at Stillwater. The engine was built by North Star Iron Works of Minneapolis. The *Knapp*, the most popular packet ever to ply the waters of the St. Croix, carried both freight and passengers, and was outfitted for towing logs from the Stillwater boomsite to distribution points on the Mississippi. She was frequently used for excursion parties to the Dalles, with stops at Marine Mills, and at Osceola to view Cascade Falls. In 1878, the boat was lengthened by 20 feet at Osceola. After twenty-two years of service in the St. Croix trade, the *Knapp* retired in 1889. She was floated to Stillwater in March. There, her machinery was put into a new boat. One source said the boat was used by rafting crews as a floating boarding house on the Lake St. Croix; another says the machinery was put into the steamboat *Ravenna*. (See Chapter 10, "Friendly Rivals.")

The *Minnie Will*, 90 by 16 feet, was built at Osceola in 1866. Machinery was taken from the dismantled side-wheeler *Active*. The *Minnie Will* was commanded by Capt. Cyrus Bradley, who designed her to tow large log rafts. Her first towing job was to take the *Knapp* to Stillwater to be fitted with machinery. The *Minnie Will*'s first trip as a rafter was in May 1866. Still under the command of Captain Bradley, her builder, in November 1877, she hit a rock in the Mississippi River near New Boston, Illinois. She sank in a few minutes. Crew members barely had time to save themselves. Machinery from the *Minnie* was salvaged, and her hull was sold for $20.

The *Pioneer*, 130 by 22 feet, was built by Capt. Augustus Storer. This boat was the victim of the only construction mishap on the Osceola levee in 1866. After the main deck of the *Pioneer* was laid and she was ready for her machinery, the breakup of the ice on the St. Croix knocked the blocking from under her bow. The weight of the unsupported bow caused the gunwale to break. Work on the craft was delayed for about a week. Her machinery was probably taken from the steamboat *Staver*, a small boat built in 1861-62 on Green Lake, and used for carrying staves. The boiler of the *Pioneer* came from a mill at Amador, Minnesota. She was launched in early May 1866. Later that month she was hauling wheat on the Minnesota River. In late summer, she was back on the St. Croix making regular trips. The *Pioneer* was in the St. Croix trade for the next two seasons. She then joined the *Minnie Will* towing logs to Clinton, Iowa.

In November 1872, the *Pioneer* was brought back to Osceola levee to be rebuilt. By January 1873, Capt. David Hayes decided that the project was too expensive. He had the machinery removed, sold, and taken to Breckenridge, Minnesota, where it was installed in a steamboat built to run on the Red River of the North. The hull of the

The steamer *G. B. Knapp* at Taylors Falls about 1880. It was built by Capt. Oscar Knapp in 1866-67 at Osceola, Wisconsin, and operated on the St. Croix between Stillwater and Taylors Falls as a packet. After the advent of the railroads, that business was no longer profitable, and the boat was engaged towing wood from the St. Croix River to St. Paul via Lake St. Croix and the Mississippi River. The boat was purchased by Anderson & O'Brien Lumber Company of Stillwater. In 1888-89 the *Knapp* was dismantled and the machinery placed in the new steamer, *Ravenna*, built that winter at Stillwater. The *G. B. Knapp* was named after George and Ben Knapp, sons of Oscar. (Courtesy of the Washington County Historical Society)

Pioneer lay on the levee for a year before it was made into a boat for hauling wood.

Fourth and last boat to be launched at Osceola in 1866 was the sternwheeler *Dalles*, built by Capt. Marshall Winch at the cost of $5,000. Machinery from the dismantled *Enterprise* was installed in the *Dalles*. Before her formal christening, the boat was dubbed the *Mayflower* (or *June Bug*). She ran for only one season on the St. Croix, then was taken to St. Louis and sold to a company from Chester, Illinois. She was wrecked in the 1868-69 season. Possibly the *Dalles* was repaired and operated again, or another boat was built to replace her, for there is a record that while she was in dock for repairs in 1875, the *Dalles* caught fire. The cabin was burned and then rebuilt. The boat worked for several more years. In 1910 another *Dalles* was built by George Muller at Stillwater.

In January 1867, Capt. William Kent began building the *Nellie Kent*. Captain Willie with four brothers constituted the founding family of Osceola. Brother Robert superintended construction of the *Nellie* at a cost of $12,000. A two-month blockade of the river by the St. Croix Boom Company prevented the *Nellie* from being towed to Stillwater for her machinery, so she could not be completed until 1868. She first appeared on the Osceola levee in June of that year. Soon the *Nellie* became known as the most reliable boat on the St. Croix. Originally 120 feet by 18 feet, she was lengthened by 25 feet in spring 1879 at La Crosse and renamed the *Mary Barnes*. Sold to the government in the early 1880s, the *Barnes* was taken to the upper Missouri River. In the winter of 1884-85, she sank to the bottom of the river and was frozen in. Only a part of her machinery was saved.

By the early 1870s, Capt. Oscar F. Knapp and Capt. William Kent were said to be the most popular steamboat men on the river. Knapp, whose career began in 1856 and spanned more than three decades, was regarded as "a kind, generous, and painstaking officer making comfortable all who rode on his boat." A boat builder and captain of boats, his career also included service in the employment of the United States War Department between 1878 and 1889; he worked to improve the main channel of the St. Croix for navigation. He was said to know the bottom of the river "as well as any man knows his own dooryard."

Genial, popular and affectionately known as "Uncle Bill," Captain Kent spent fifteen years on the river in command of the *Nellie Kent*. Once, after running a leaking boat ashore, pumping it out, and stopping the leak, he was praised by his passengers for his cool and gentlemanly conduct. The Prescott *Journal* in 1869 commended the lucky captain after he plowed the *Nellie* through fourteen inches of rotten spring ice for 10 miles to be the first boat of the season through Lake St. Croix.

In the 1870s and 80s, five other boats were built at Osceola.

Captain Kent and lumberman John Dudley of Prescott and Minneapolis engaged builders Wilson and West of Prescott to construct the *Helen Mar* in 1872. Although she was a stern-wheeler designed for towing logs, she was called the most beautiful boat on the St. Croix at that time. She was 120 feet by 24 feet, driven by two 12-foot cylinders, which had a 4-foot, 2-inch stroke. Steam was provided in two 6-foot boilers, each of which had six flues. She received her machinery at Stillwater. Captain Knapp made the first trip of the season on Saturday, April 12, 1872, in the *Helen Mar*. She started on a regular schedule of trips between Taylors Falls and Stillwater. The sailing was planned to meet with the St. Paul, Stillwater, and Taylors Falls train at the Stillwater end of the trip. Apparently, the boat then went into the Clinton, Iowa, log trade. In 1874 *Helen Mar* towed 14 strings of logs with 70,000 feet of timber in each string. She was sold in May 1879 to Knapp, Stout and Company of Menomonie, Wisconsin, and used on the Chippewa River. About 1904 the *Helen Mar* was dismantled.

Another Kent boat, the *Maggie Reaney*, built by Captain Kent and John Dudley, was begun in 1875 and completed in 1877. The largest boat constructed at Osceola, she was 130 by 24 feet, (128 by 25 feet according to another source). Captain Kent owned one-fourth of the boat, Capt. John H. Reaney of St. Paul three-fourths. In 1876, she was dubbed "the finest-looking hull that ever left the Osceola boatyard." The boat was "furnished with fine carpets, gorgeous furniture, beautiful chandeliers and the state rooms with furniture as minute as a hotel chamber, and costly silverware and dishes." She was probably the most luxurious boat on the border river. It was claimed she was also the fastest. Steward of the *Maggie* was Jim Mullen. His cuisine was said to compare favorably with "the palmy days of steamboating on the Mississippi."

On her first commercial appearance at the Osceola levee, the *Maggie Reaney* carried in her cargo "200 barrels of salt, 100 of flour and 500 sacks of wheat." She carried a Christmas excursion out of St. Paul in 1877 for the benefit of an orphanage. The *Maggie* ran for two seasons on the St. Croix, then was taken to La Crosse, Wisconsin, in late 1878. There, she was lengthened by 40 feet to lighten her draft. She never returned to the St. Croix.

In 1879, Captain Knapp in partnership with Capt. David Hayes built the *Jennie Hayes*. A small boat, 117 by 13½ feet, she drew 15 inches of water. She received her machinery and possibly her cabins at Stillwater. (Another source says she was built at Franconia, 117.4 by 14.5 feet.) The *Jennie* made regular runs on the river until August 1886 when she withdrew from the St. Croix trade and started towing logs.

The *Jennie Hayes* marked the emergence of Capt. Oscar Knapp's sons, Ben and George, in the steamboat business. Ben had had previous experience as captain of the *Aunt Betsy*. The *Betsy* was built in Allegan, Michigan, in 1867. A wooden boat, she was later lengthened by 24 feet, and changed from a sidewheel to a sternwheel boat. Captain Costaine ran her in 1878; Capt. Marcus Thompson commanded her in 1882. After the boat was rebuilt, it was rechristened *City of St. Paul*.

The Knapp brothers went into partnership with David Swain to buy out David Hayes' interest in the *Jennie*. By September 1885, after a contest with Swain over ownership, Ben and George Knapp took over the boat. In August 1886, the *Jennie* withdrew from the

St. Croix trade to tow logs on the Mississippi.

The *Germania*, a flat-bottomed boat just 65 feet long, was among the last of the paddle-wheelers built in the Osceola shipyards. In 1887, she was transported to Forest Lake on two flatcars of the Duluth Railroad, and used for the entertainment of guests at Michael Marsh's Hotel on the west shore of the lake. With a capacity of 100 people, the boat called for passengers at the railroad station, and made trips around the lake. By July 1891, the *Germania* was back in Stillwater. Purchased by George Torinus, the steamer was used on the St. Croix for towing and excursions.

In the spring of 1883, Captain Oscar started building his last boat, the *Cleon*, a stern-wheeler 129 feet by 21 feet, a 103-ton boat. She was modeled after the *G. B. Knapp* and, in fact, had the machinery which had been in the *Knapp*. The boat was named for Captain Knapp's daughter. The maiden voyage of the *Cleon* was in early September 1884. The Stillwater Cornet Band was engaged to play for the festive occasion. As reported in the Stillwater *Messenger* in November 1884, "The new steamer *Cleon* had her first explosion experience while lying in the wharf in Stillwater. Fortunately, no one was killed or seriously injured."

Ben and George Knapp, who then called themselves "Knapp Brothers and Company," successfully navigated the *Cleon* for three seasons. During that time, the *Cleon* towed steamboat wood from Franconia to St. Paul. She was used for excursions of Sunday schools, library associations, singing groups, and such. The *Cleon* took groups to entertainments at Chapin Hall House in Hudson, and to watch the breakup of log jams at Taylors Falls. In 1886, the Knapps donated the *Cleon* for an excursion to see the spectacular log jam of that year at the Dalles. The sum of $55.45 was raised by excursion sponsors for the benefit of Mt. Hope Cemetery Association of Osceola. Eventually, the machinery was taken out of the *Cleon* and put into the *Jennie Hayes*. (Was this replacement machinery? Was this a second *Jennie Hayes*? Did the two boats switch engines? Records are not clear on this point.) After Ben died late in 1887, the *Cleon* was sold to New Orleans. She burned April 2, 1900, at Rockdale, Louisiana.

The Knapp brothers finished the last boat built at Osceola, the *Lynn J*, in June 1887. Named for one of Captain Oscar's grandchildren, the *Lynn J* was 65 feet by 14 feet (or 70 feet by 13.3 feet). At 32.7 tons, the *Lynn J* was the smallest boat constructed at Osceola. Her novel feature was an electric light that could be seen clearly from a mile-and-a-half away, making night travel possible.

Mechanical problems plagued the *Lynn J* in her first season. Before it was even installed, the machinery for the boat had been damaged in a fire at the Staples foundry in Stillwater. She was laid up three times with boiler problems during her first six weeks of operation. Her boiler, designed by Captain Ben, apparently did not live up to expectations. Later it was explained that "the chain by which the wheel is navigated is liable to break without much warning." Capt. George B. Knapp took the *Lynn J* and the *Cleon* to New Orleans in the fall of 1889. The *Lynn* was sold to Capt. G. A. Muntz and Capt. William Leager. The boat burned August 17, 1900, ten miles above

Built by Capt. Oscar Knapp, the 103-ton *Cleon* was used as an excursion boat and a work boat. She hauled steamboat wood from Franconia to St. Paul. Here she is shown tied up to a rock boat. (Courtesy of Durand Blanding)

New Orleans.

St. Croix River traffic practically stopped after the Soo Line bridge was built in 1887. Early in 1889, Capt. Oscar Knapp said, "Steamboating is poor business this year." That year, three Osceola boats left the St. Croix trade. The *Cleon* and the *Lynn J* went south to work on the lower Mississippi and the Red River of the South. The *Lynn J* was sold, as noted above. For a season, the Knapps operated the *Cleon* on the Red, Ouachita, Black, and Mississippi rivers. On one eleven-day trip, the *Cleon* pulled six barges from New Orleans to Monroe, Louisiana. In spring of 1890, Captain Oscar sold the *Cleon*. After a thirty-year career of steamboating, he retired to enjoy his trout pond at Luck, Wisconsin.

Apparently, he did not stay retired, for a report in the Stillwater *Gazette* May 9, 1906, reads "Captain O. F. Knapp has plans for regular trips to and from Taylors Falls. The small steamer *Lorene* arrived yesterday from Dubuque, Iowa, where she was built for Capt. O. F. Knapp who proposes to use her in the pleasure excursion business on the upper St. Croix." The *Lorene* was designed for use in low water, with a draw of just two feet. Knapp had a barge built with a capacity of fifty passengers for use with the steamer.

His steamboating rival, Captain William Kent, had retired from the river in 1879 and started a mercantile store in Osceola.

The *G. B. Knapp* and the *Nellie Kent*. Friendly rivals, these were the two most popular packets in the St. Croix Valley for almost three decades. (Courtesy of Jim Johnson)

Chapter 10

Friendly Rivals

The two most popular packets in the St. Croix Valley during the 1860s, 1870s and early 1880s were the *G. B. Knapp* and the *Nellie Kent*. Both were launched in the mid-1860s, the *Knapp* in 1866, the *Nellie* in 1868. Both boats were constructed at Osceola. At 130 feet, the *Knapp* was about 10 feet longer than the *Nellie*. Both were sternwheelers and received their machinery at Stillwater. Each boat timed its trips to meet the trains which traveled to and from St. Paul and Stillwater. And both were determined to dominate the passenger and freight trade on the river.

Before the *Nellie* came along, the 139-ton *Knapp* enjoyed leisurely control of the St. Croix. She earned the name of "Gay Boat." After the Civil War, steamboat excursions were all the rage. The *Knapp* carried many excursion parties. One of them was a grand excursion from Osceola to Prescott and Hastings in 1866, with the Stillwater Cornet Band providing the music on board. Later at a hotel in Hastings, the excursionists danced most of the night away before making the return trip upriver.

In May 1867, the sternwheeler carried de Haven's Great Union Circus from Stillwater to Taylors Falls. As the menagerie passed Osceola, a delighted crowd boarded the *Pioneer* and followed the *Knapp* up the river to see the performance. In mid-July of the same year, a large party from the Falls and Osceola boarded the *Knapp* and went to St. Paul to see the scandalous leg show, "The Black Crook."

The following year, an excursion group bound for Log House Landing at Otisville stopped briefly at Marine. The Bohemian ferryman there, Diedrick van Hollen, was infuriated because the ferry cable was damaged as the steamer passed over it.

In spring of 1868, the *Nellie Kent*'s familiar whistle of two longs and three shorts signaled the beginning of a continuing rate war. The *Nellie* had been built for William F. Davidson, owner of the Davidson

Lines. Her competition was the *James Means*, owned by the Northern Lines, and local boats *Wyman X* of Taylors Falls and the *Knapp*.

"A little competition is what we want," wrote a reporter in the Taylors Falls newspaper. "Sell tickets at any price," was the order to the boatmen. Fares plummeted. Passengers found that it was cheaper to take a pleasure trip than it was to stay home. Steamboat clerks quoted twenty-five cents as the top price for travel between any two points from Prescott to Taylors Falls. Steamboat rivalry grew hotter. Both the *Nellie Kent* and the *G. B. Knapp* made daily trips, leaving Prescott early, and arriving at Stillwater between 8:00 and 9:00 a.m. They continued to the Falls, and returned to Stillwater again about 4:00 p.m.

The *Mollie Mohler* briefly took the place of the *Nellie Kent* while the latter boat was laid up for repairs in August 1868. The *Mollie* was built in Carver, Minnesota, by Capt. George Houghton, James Houghton, and William F. Davidson. She was dismantled in 1868, and her machinery was put into the *Nellie Kent*.

When the *G. B. Knapp* took Sabbath schoolers on a picnic and excursion in June 1869, the captain was rewarded handsomely. A committee of young ladies presented Capt. Oscar Knapp with an American flag for his boat.

Swedish immigrants came into the St. Croix Valley area beginning in 1850. By 1869-70, Sweden was in an extremely depressed state, and immigration increased. On July 3, 1869, "Count" Henning A. Taube of Stockholm, his wife, and son came to the Valley. With him were 100 Swedish immigrants who had paid in gold for land in Minnesota. When they reached St. Croix Falls, the would-be settlers learned they did not have title to the land. Count Taube announced that he would return to Sweden to raise more capital to build up the town. A crowd gathered at the levee in Taylors Falls to wish him Godspeed. The Count, the Countess, and their son left the Valley—never to return.

In spite of that chicanery, more settlers came. In August, the *Nellie* landed 30 families of Swedish immigrants at Marine.

One sport during the heyday of steamboating was shooting geese from the boiler deck of a packet. Frequently, passengers and crew of the *G. B. Knapp* and the *Nellie Kent* returned home with a good supply of birds. Paddle-wheelers were often chartered by hunters. In the autumn of 1870, ten Stillwater men chartered the *G. B. Knapp* to go hunting on Lake St. Croix. Each goose, counting rental of the boat, ammunition, food, and other incidentals, cost $2.50.

In May 1872, the *Nellie Kent* contracted with the railroad company to meet trains to and from St. Paul. The *Nellie* left Taylors Falls at 5:00 a.m. and arrived at Stillwater in time for her passengers to board the train to St. Paul. She then continued to Prescott, arriving there at 12:00 noon. The *Nellie* started her return trip at 2:00 p.m. and arrived in time to meet the evening train to take passengers home to the Falls.

The month of June found the *Nellie Kent* making a grand excursion from Osceola with passengers to attend the Great Eastern Menagerie and Circus at Stillwater. Two weeks later, on the Fourth of July, the *Nellie* took another Osceola group to St. Paul for the New York Circus. Some time later, the *Knapp* took Osceolans to a circus performance in Stillwater in late afternoon, and returned the next morning. The women slept in cabins on the boat, while the men toughed it out on the lower deck.

In August 1872, there was so little water in the channel of the St. Croix that the *Nellie* was forced to return to Taylors Falls rather than continuing downstream to Stillwater. There were only eighteen inches of water in the slough at the end of the Apple River, not enough to float the boat. The Boom Company management promised to open the boom within the next few days so there would be no difficulty in navigation for the rest of the season.

Once the keen competition between packets leveled off, new rates were established on the river. The *Nellie Kent* (which in 1872 was called the only reliable boat on the St. Croix) charged $1 fare from Stillwater to Taylors Falls; $2 from the Falls to St. Paul. Freight rates were ten cents per hundredweight from Stillwater to Marine, and fifteen cents to Taylor's Falls. The charge was twenty-five cents per hundredweight from Taylors Falls to St. Paul.

By November 11, 1872, winter was not far off. Steamer captains in the Valley were taking their boats off the river. The *Nellie Kent* was laid up at Taylors Falls to be repaired, and L. W. Mueller, a crewman of the *Nellie*, was on his way south for the winter. The towboat *Pioneer* was dry-docked at Osceola. The *Minnie Will* was laid up at Prescott, and the G. B. *Knapp* over-wintered at Osceola. In spring, workmen removed a portion of her cabin to make the boat easier to handle.

All the packets were ready for work when the ice went out in April 1873. In June of that year, the *Nellie* brought a safe to the firm of Walker, Judd and Veazie at Marine. (The safe may be seen today in Marine's village hall.) She also carried the body of a murder victim from Cottage Grove to Stillwater. The *Nellie* towed wheat barges to the Stillwater elevator from various landings along Lake St. Croix.

In 1875, the G. B. *Knapp* was designated as official mail boat. She appeared on the river "looking as gay as a girl in a calico dress with a white apron," with "U.S. Mail" painted in white letters on her bulkheads. She made daily runs upriver from Stillwater.

That year, too, Walker, Judd and Veazie of Marine purchased a half interest in the G. B. *Knapp*. They joined with other investors to provide regular passenger and freight service between Stillwater and Taylors Falls. A year later, Sam Judd, of Marine, and Smith Ellison, of Taylors Falls, became sole owners of the boat.

The people at Taylors Falls felt a particular ownership for the *Knapp* after Ellison became a partner in the boat. "When they want to go off, they just order the *Knapp* hitched up and off they go," wrote a Stillwater *Gazette* reporter. On a Saturday in June 1875, they felt like seeing a circus at Carli Field in Stillwater, so they took the steamer and off they went. After the circus closed at 11:00 p.m., they sailed home again.

An excursion to Osceola by 20 people on the *Nellie Kent* found slow going because of "logs running so thick that considerable delay

In 1880 an engraver from New York carved this scene of Marine on St. Croix on boxwood. On the reverse side was an engraving of the Grand Opera House seating arrangement. After the Opera House was destroyed by fire, the Stillwater *Gazette* janitor found the woodcut in the basement and gave it to Frank Giossi, *Gazette* printer.

The engraver was Peter Hugenine, who Dick Taylor of the Stillwater *Lumberman* brought from New York to work for the paper.

The cut was made in four sections. Over the years the wood blocks shrunk, so that when the picture was printed, white lines appeared. (This is evident in the reproduction.)

The boat shown in the *G. B. Knapp*. The long structure on the left is the Rose Flour Mill. Water drained from the top of the hill down a mill race, and provided power for the mill. An artificial island is shown in the lower part of the picture. (Stillwater *Gazette, July 7, 1938. Courtesy of the Washington County Historical Society)*

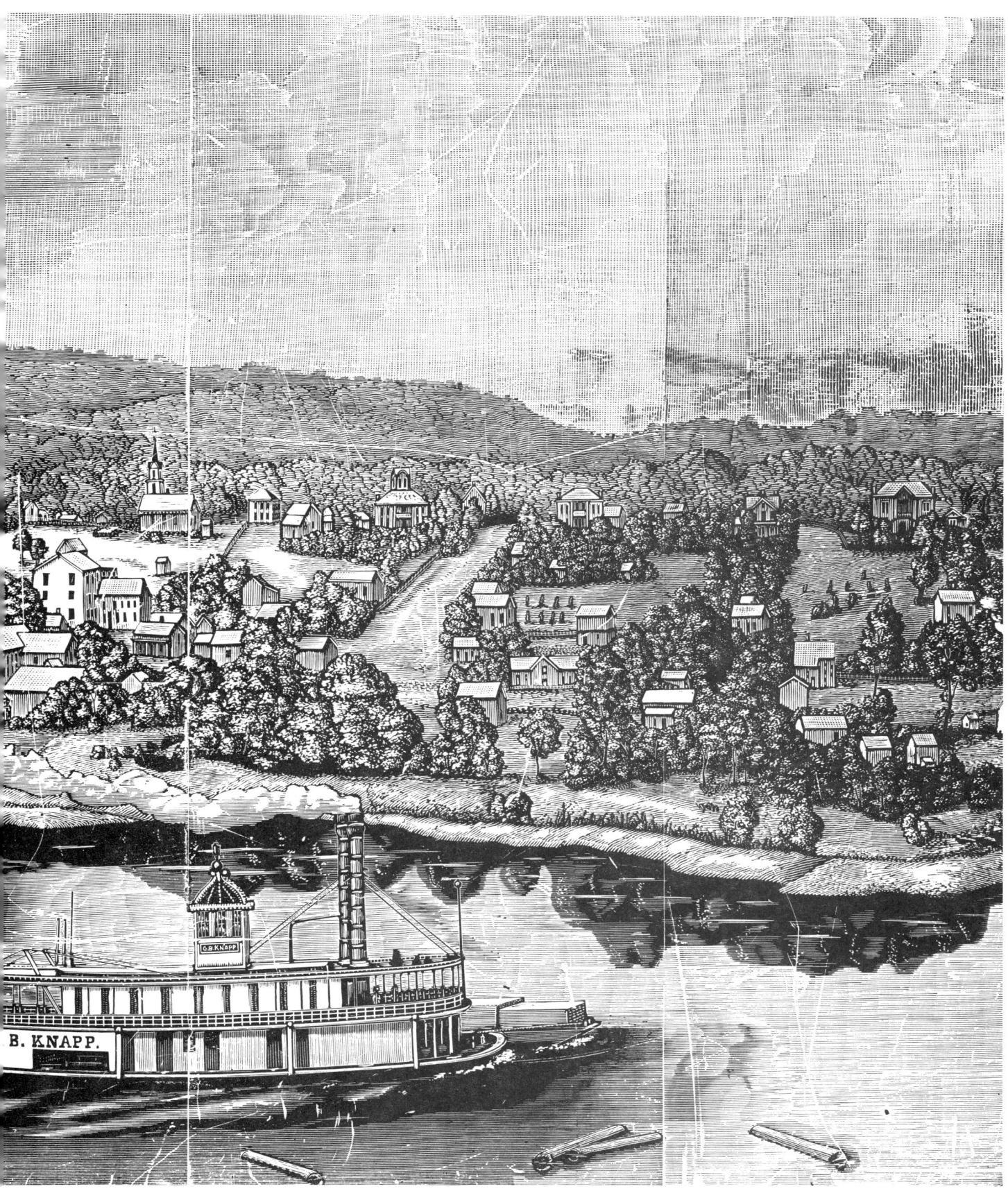

was occasioned in worming in and out." The boat passed over logs with a rumbling, grating, jarring sound. The *Nellie* called at the intermediate ports of Arcola, Marine, Sam Wall's kiln, Osceola, and Mineral Springs, where everybody rushed ashore to get a life-giving drink. Boatmen filled all possible containers with water at the Springs. Wrote a reporter of the day,

> The main attraction at Osceola was the old mill, standing solitary and alone, grand, gloomy and peculiar. Osceola is on a hill, and since the hacks quit running, people must walk up. A plank walk leads up 40 feet, then there are stairs for 100 feet or so. Then Osceola proper in all its splendor and gorgeous magnificence bursts upon the astounded vision of the dazzled beholder.

The passengers made their way up the hill while the *Nellie Kent* steamed on to Taylors Falls. At 8:00 p.m. the packet returned and sounded her warning whistle. The excursionists gathered their baskets and pails, boarded the boat, and headed for Stillwater, arriving about 11:00 p.m.

Opening the river officially in 1875 was the steamer *James Means*, which was the first boat through Lake Pepin that season, and first to get to Stillwater, arriving on Sunday, April 25. The *Nellie Kent* had come up from Prescott with the *Means*, but stopped briefly at Hudson, allowing the *Means* to take the honors. That year, the *G. B. Knapp* had been overhauled. Some of the staterooms near the stern had been removed, and a comfortable and pleasant sitting room built in the space. A new wheel was installed at the same time.

Later that spring, a gentle battle took place on the river. The *G. B. Knapp* and the *Nellie Kent* were again offering reduced fares in an effort to put each other out of business. The *Knapp* seemed to be the favorite of people on the upper part of the river, possibly because Captain Knapp was one of the pioneer steamboat men in the area. As the rate feud continued, businessmen of Taylors Falls and other points up the St. Croix were contemplating the purchase of the *G. B. Knapp*. They discussed the formation of the People's Independent Steamboat Line. Smith Ellison of Taylors Falls, "a gentleman of means and sufficient energy," was at the head of the movement. One of the provisions of the charter was that stock could not be sold to William F. Davidson, owner of the *Nellie Kent*, nor to Stillwater lumber baron, Isaac Staples.

As the rate war continued, this mythical conversation was reported in the Stillwater *Gazette* of June 30, 1875:

> Agent for the *Nellie:* "I will give you a passage on my boat to Taylors Falls and return for twenty-five cents, twelve-and-a-half cents each way."
>
> Agent for the *G. B. Knapp:* "I will make you a present of a ticket up and back; it shan't cost you a cent."
>
> Agent for the *Nellie:* "I will give you your fare up and back and furnish your meals."
>
> Agent for the *Knapp:* "I will see that offer and raise him one. I will give you your passage up and back, furnish your meals, and give you a berth."

The two packets competed in another way, namely racing. The boats would leave the Stillwater levee at unpredictable times, race up the river making only token stops, and race back in the afternoon. The winner would tie a broomstick to its smokestack, symbol of "sweeping the river." Typical was a Sunday in late June 1875. Two parties of excursionists, one on the *Nellie Kent*, the other on the *G. B. Knapp*, left the Stillwater landing at the same time. For the first half mile, the *Nellie* led the way to Taylors Falls. Suddenly, the crew aboard the *Knapp* decided to make a race of it. After much trouble and several unimportant collisions, the *Knapp* got ahead of the *Nellie* and stayed there all the way to the Falls.

A month later, the steamer *Knapp* was sunk. The boat ran into a snag in West Slough near Cedar Bend, five miles above Marine. It went to the bottom in water three feet deep. Passengers were taken to the shore, where they waited for and boarded the *Nellie Kent*. Although the *Knapp* was running again in a few days, the accident made its mark on the fares. The *Nellie*, with competition knocked out—at least temporarily—jumped fares from 25¢ to $1.50. As a result of the exhorbitant rates, liveries in towns along the river did a big business.

It wasn't long before the shoe was on the other foot. A group of celebrants for the Fourth of July holiday went from Minneapolis to Taylors Falls aboard the *Nellie Kent*. The trip up was uneventful. Excursionists happily viewed the spectacular scenery of the Dalles. On the return trip, the *Nellie* stuck fast on the infernal Arcola sand bar a few miles above Stillwater. All efforts to remove it were unavailing, so the passengers were forced to remain overnight. The next morning, the *G. B. Knapp* went to the spot, hitched on, and jerked the *Nellie* into deep water. That event marked the beginning of low water. By August the river was so shallow that Smith Ellison put in a line of bateaux to carry passengers between Stillwater and Taylors Falls. The dozen bateaux made several trips in the same manner as they had 25 years earlier before steamboats began running on the St. Croix.

As the river season ended in 1875, the steam was blown off the *Nellie Kent*, the close of her ninth season on the St. Croix. She was moored in front of Butler's warehouse in Stillwater, which would be her winter quarters. During the off-season, her furniture was stored in the warehouse while her saloons and state rooms were dismantled, and refurbished. The *G. B. Knapp* continued her upstream trips into November, at imminent risk of being frozen in, but "the continuously pouring in of large quantities of freight is tempting to the hazardous undertaking."

A new destination for the packets opened near Osceola in May 1876. The Riverside Hotel, two miles south of town, was located on a rocky promontory 200 feet above the river. The two-story structure, painted gray with green trimming, had two wide piazzas, topped by a large cupola, from which could be seen a panorama of the valley. A large elaborate hotel, it was supposed to be a health resort because of the mineral springs. Its dining room seated 200 guests. Landscaped grounds featured a driving park for horse races, large trout pond, deer park, decorative peacocks—even a black bear. Both the *Nellie Kent* and the *G. B. Knapp* scheduled regular stops at the landing there, even though the public did not patronize the hotel.

On opening day, the *Knapp* conveyed a party of guests to the Riverside. Enroute, the packet ran into a jam of logs in the vicinity of the boom, where the passage left for boats was very narrow, and the current swift. According to a newspaper report of the event,

> Employees of the boat, assisted by a few of the passengers, swarmed out on the imprisoned logs armed with pick poles and cant hooks. After a good deal of prying and lifting and prodding and stabbing and a little swearing, they broke the jam, and the boat sped on her way.

At Mineral Springs, a party of six or eight people climbed the steep stairs to Riverside House, where they were welcomed by A. L. Stephen, one of the gentlemanly proprietors of the hotel. Stephen said that if the boat had given the proper signal, he would have sent carriages to convey the party up the hill. The new hotel was beautiful. An elegant piano in the ladies' parlor stood invitingly for the use of those musically inclined; while in another apartment, a billiard table of the latest design awaited the pleasure of those inclined to worldly sports. Healing water from mineral springs was brought by hydraulic pressure up to the house and grounds. After the festivities, the visitors availed themselves of Stephen's offer. Hearing the whistle of the boat from 1½ miles away at Osceola, they were conveyed by hacks down to the lower landing at the old lime kiln.

The clockwork regularity of the *Nellie Kent*'s schedule gave it the nickname "Old Reliable." In spite of the grueling schedule, the boat held to it until 1878. Then she was taken to the La Crosse dry dock for rebuilding. During the winter she was lengthened by 25 feet. (This may have been a case of "catch-up," for in 1878, the *G. B. Knapp* was lengthened by 20 feet at Osceola.)

But the *Nellie Kent* did not return to the St. Croix. She was renamed the *Mary Barnes*. Sold to the United States government a few years later, the *Barnes* was taken to the upper Missouri River. In the winter of 1884-85, she sank to the bottom and was frozen in. Only part of her machinery was saved.

Meanwhile, the *G. B. Knapp* continued on the St. Croix. In 1879, she was tied up at Marine while being redecorated to become "the handsomest boat on the river." The *Knapp* had to spend the winter of 1880-81 at Marine because she didn't go south before the river froze over. Early in 1881, Sam Judd bought out Ellison and overhauled the boat for excursions, and for transporting lumber to St. Paul. New boilers and a new engine were installed by the new owner. During the winter months, Judd built two barges at Marine, each 116 feet by 24 feet, to be used by the *Knapp*.

Because of the arrival of railroads in the St. Croix Valley, packet boats were no longer profitable, so the *Knapp* was used primarily as a tow boat. Early in 1885, the sawmill at Marine, of which Judd was a partner, was forced into bankruptcy. Several causes were listed. The firm never fully recovered from the depression that followed the panic of 1873. Log jams on the river at Taylors Falls in 1877, 1878, and 1882 caused a lack of work at the mill. A huge jam at the Falls in 1883 kept logs back for 57 days, and the sawmill was unable to fulfill its contracts. The following spring, water was so low that the logs weren't even able to float over the falls and down to the mill. The final blow was a tornado on September 4, 1884. It ripped through Marine and demolished the mill's smokestack. It carried away a million feet of lumber. Eventually, in 1888, James S. O'Brien, acting for Anderson & O'Brien Lumber Company of Stillwater, concluded negotiations to buy the Marine lumber company, including the mill, lumber, real estate—and the steamer G. B. Knapp. An inspection revealed that the boilers on the packet were badly worn, and the boat's license for carrying passengers was revoked. A month later, new boilers were in place, and the Knapp was back in service.

Finally, on March 24, 1889, after 22 years in the St. Croix trade, the Knapp was retired. She was floated to Stillwater to be dismantled. Her machinery went into the steamboat Ravenna. A few months later, it was reported the the hull of the Knapp was being used as a floating boarding house for rafting crews on Lake St. Croix.

The Stillwater Messenger mourned the demise of the Knapp, and carried notice of her passing, stating that the Knapp was "the longest in service on these waters, and a craft that has carried more people up and down the St. Croix than any other three boats combined."

The Red Wing-Stillwater Boat Race

Although the principal water craft in this story were racing sculls, steamboats did figure in the events of the time.

Back in the 1870s, Red Wing, Minnesota, had a boat club, members of which were devoted to sculling on the Mississippi.

In June 1875 a mysterious stranger arrived in Red Wing aboard a north-bound steamboat. His name, he said, was John B. Fox. Fox quickly found a job at the grocery store owned by Hi Parks. A keen observer would have noticed that Fox did little work. He spent a lot of time just loitering along the river front. Yet Hi made no complaint. One day Fox happened to remark that he knew one end of a racing shell from the other. Someone handed him an oar. Within five minutes, he proved that he knew more about racing than all the members of the Red Wing boat club combined. Of course, he was made a member of the crew.

Both the Stillwater and St. Paul clubs sent a challenge to what they thought was a somewhat inferior Red Wing club. The downriver club accepted. June 28 was the date set for two contests—a single man race, and a four-oared contest.

The Stillwater crew bragged a lot. To stir up interest, the Red Wing club selected the most powerfully-built man in town— the village blacksmith—and took a photograph of him, stripped to the waist. The picture was sent to Stillwater as an example of its crew. (The Village Smithy had never been in a boat.)

Stillwater sent a spy to Red Wing. He was recognized. The Red Wing crew purposely put on a miserable performance. The spy returned to Stillwater and reported that everyone should bet all the money he could on the local team.

On the fateful day, the *James Means* of the Northern Line carried hundreds of passengers from Stillwater and St. Paul, along with the St. Paul Cornet Band, down to Red Wing. The St. Paul scullers rowed down in their shell. Everyone caught the gambling fever; one old-timer said that by noon only $50 was left in the First National Bank. Estimates of the total wagers ranged from $10,000 to $75,000.

The first race, the single man race, was set for 2:30 p.m. Contestants were Norman Wright of St. Paul and John B. Fox, the grocery clerk from Red Wing. The course of the race was one mile up river, then one mile down. Quickly after the start, Fox outdistanced his opponent. He stopped rowing, splashed water over his face and arms, then sucked a lemon while waiting for Wright. Fox finally won the race by one boat length.

Then came the four-oared race. Most of the money had been bet on that contest. Rowing for Stillwater were T. Scully, J. Morarity, John Cain, and John McGrath. Red Wing scullers were Charles Lent, Joseph Harrison, E. B. Phille, and, of course, John B. Fox.

The starting gun roared. Stillwater "caught a crab" on the first stroke and never recovered from that bad start. They were so badly beaten that they didn't even return to the start at all. Instead they rowed to the steamboat, yielding the race to Red Wing.

The upper river men were broke. It was said even the steamboat was unable to buy coal for the return trip until one of the heavy winners turned over $1,500 to the captain so he could feed his passengers and take them home.

There is a sequel to the story. The Tennessee Jubilee Singers, a black minstrel show, happened to be in Red Wing that day. One of the performers recognized the mysterious store clerk/oarsman. "That's no John B. Fox," he said. "That's Ellis Ward, the most famous rower in the world." Not even the Red Wing club members had recognized Ward.

Eventually, it was revealed that there were three conspirators in Red Wing—grocery man Hi Parks; Captain E. L. Baker, a miller and prominent hardware man; and Frank Sterrett, grain dealer and Red Wing agent for the Diamond Jo Steamboat Line. The trio connived to make the home town team look good. The St. Paul and Stillwater bettors were truly out-Foxed.

Excursion boat *Ben Hur* at Red Wing, Minnesota. (Courtesy of the Washington County Historical Society)

Chapter 11

Captain Stephen B. Hanks

Steamboats on the St. Croix were many and varied, with stories unique to each boat. The same is true of the men who ran and built the steamboats. From a variety of backgrounds, they came to the valley.

One of the best of the pilots was Stephen B. Hanks. He is credited with being the first riverman to use a steamboat to raft logs downriver to the mills. Hanks was a first cousin of Abe Lincoln. Stephen's father, Thomas Hanks, was a brother of Nancy Hanks, Abe's mother. Although Steve Hanks never knew Abe until he was grown, his family considered it a poor match when Nancy married Abe's father, Thomas Lincoln.

Stephen was born in Hopkinsville, Kentucky, on October 9, 1821. He was raised on a 1,300-acre farm, 400 acres of which were under cultivation. The varied home industries of the self-sustaining frontier family included a handloom for spinning woolen clothing, a grist mill, a still for making peach and apple brandy, and a tobacco warehouse. Work was done by slaves.

All the children in the family were educated, and Stephen must have looked forward to a promising career as a plantation owner. The death of Stephen's father changed the course of his life. In settling his estate, all the Hanks' personal properties were disposed of, including the slaves. The Widow Hanks tried to operate the farm with the help of friends and relatives. Unsuccessful, she traded that farm for a smaller one in Hopkins County, Kentucky. The home was broken again when a brother of Mrs. Hanks, Alfred Beck, took Stephen north to White County, Illinois.

It was there, in 1833, that Stephen got his first look at a steamboat. In his memoirs, Hanks wrote, "That night I saw a steamboat for the first time, two of them, in fact. I cannot explain the impression they made upon me. They were side-wheelers, and the pounding of the paddles on the water and the beautiful white appearance they presented made a picture never effaced from my memory."

That was the beginning of a life-long love affair with rivers, and the boats that plied the waterways. While living in White County, Hanks served as an apprentice to a builder of flatboats that floated on the Little Wabash River, down to the Wabash, the Ohio, and the Mississippi.

During the next few years, Stephen moved further north in Illinois, finally settling with his uncle at Albany, on the Mississippi. Although Hanks was busy helping his uncle clear and fence his land, he had plenty of time to observe the steamboat traffic on the Mississippi. The first few dollars Hanks earned he received for watching a loaded barge all night.

It was not until he was twenty years old that Stephen, tired of farm work, was able to break away and get off on his own. A representative of a St. Louis lumber firm stopped in Albany. He was buying livestock, and needed someone to drive it west. So it was that Hanks arrived in the St. Croix Valley in 1841, as a cattle driver. One source said he brought eighty head of livestock which were used as food in a lumber camp operated by Franklin Steele. Another reference said that Hanks worked with a crew of men that drove one hundred horses, mules, and oxen to St. Croix Falls for delivery to Governor Holcombe. Whatever the circumstances, Hanks apparently arrived in the St. Croix Valley in November 1841, stopping en route at the home of Lydia Brown Carli, the only white woman at that time in the tiny settlement that would become Stillwater.

Hanks delivered the cattle. He was then assigned to the St. Croix Falls Lumber Company, since his terms of hire stated that he would receive $200, providing he finished out the year in the employ of the lumber camp. Hanks worked in the woods during the winter 1841-42. In the spring he became assistant cook on the lumber rafts. He used his memory to advantage, learning the contours of the St. Croix. In 1842, Hanks was deemed competent to pilot a raft for the St. Croix Lumber Company from the Falls to St. Louis. After a long and exhausting trip, he returned to Albany, Illinois, expecting to get a job and settle down. But with the coming of spring, the call of the river reached Hanks. He returned to the St. Croix, and in 1843, sawed logs at Taylors Falls. He then took the first log raft down the river. Rafts before that time were lumber rafts, which were taken to St. Louis. They were propelled by oars and sweeps. Log rafts were much more practical than the high lumber rafts which were hard to handle. On that first trip, there were actually two rafts. Hanks employed Severe Brule to run one of them while Hanks piloted the other.

The next year, Hanks stayed all winter on the Snake River, waiting for rain to bring enough water to float the logs. A downpour came in May. The boom holding the winter harvest of timber broke. Away went the logs. Hanks managed to salvage some of them from the banks of the stream. These logs were among the first to be sawed at the new McKusick mill at Stillwater.

Hanks became a "real" pilot in 1844, running rafts of logs from the St. Croix to St. Louis. Known as one of the strongest and firmest raft pilots on the upper river, Hanks proved his mettle on several occasions. Once, a long oar of one of his lumber rafts was torn from its lock by a leaning tree. Four members of the crew tried unsuccessfully to put the oar back in place. Hanks waved them aside. With one tug, he yanked in the 39-foot oar and slipped it firmly into its lock.

In late fall of 1844, ice was already running downstream, endangering the raft Hanks was towing. During a night stop at Dubuque, three of the crew members went into town and had several drinks. They returned to the boat, determined to travel no further. They demanded that Hanks lay up the raft in Dubuque and pay them off. One of the crew drew a knife and threatened Hanks. As the rafter lunged, the skipper knocked the knife from his hand, and subdued him. The mutiny was ended. The next day, the raft continued downstream.

The first boat piloted by Hanks, a stern-wheeler, was open like a rowboat. Named the *Amulet*, it was brought to Stillwater in 1846. Sometimes, in fair weather, Hanks used sails improvised from tents, blankets, even boards, to propel rafts through lakes St. Croix and Pepin. In rough weather or extreme calm, he caught the rafts in a tow line, which was pulled by all hands from shore. He ran lumber for the mills at Stillwater until 1854. The only other pilot running logs was Capt. James "Sandy" McPhail.

In 1850, Captain Hanks achieved fame as pilot of the excursion steamer, *Anthony Wayne,* from St. Louis to St. Paul. He was the first

A steamboat and a bowboat taking a log raft to the mills on the lower river at Muscatine, Davenport, Clinton and St. Louis. The first log rafts were taken down the St. Croix into the Mississippi, then down to St. Louis in 1841. For 75 years log rafting flourished as a gigantic business on the St. Croix.

The bowboat (at the head of the raft) was secured fast to the bow of the raft and, by pushing ahead or in reverse as directed by the pilot of the steamboat in the rear of the raft, moved the raft to the right or left to stay on course.

The steamboat pictured is the *Lydia Van Sant*, built in 1890. The St. Croix, the Mississippi, and the Chippewa rivers were the great log rafting rivers of the North. (Courtesy of the Washington County Historical Society)

Mississippi pilot who dared steer his boat to the very base of the Falls of St. Anthony, where rapids made navigation dangerous. The arrival of the *Wayne* made citizens of St. Anthony and Minneapolis boast that their towns were the logical places for the steamer terminals of the upper Mississippi.

Captain Hanks took the *Anthony Wayne* up the Minnesota as well. He went far beyond the Sioux Indian village of Little Six (Shakopee), setting a new record for navigation of the Minnesota River.

Several times, Hanks saw all his earnings wiped out by the loss of his tows. Running rafts was a risky business. Any shortage of logs delivered to the mill was deducted from the contract of the pilot. Any accident was charged to him. In 1854, high water and tornados damaged four of Hanks' rafts. The Stillwater owner of the logs hearing of the destruction, seized all property belonging to Hanks. That amounted to two houses, a store, and half a million feet of timber. The loss was nearly $10,000, a fortune in those days. Hanks was left with only the $75 he had in his pocket. In addition to that, a warehouse fire destroyed all of Hanks' rafting kit in Albany. That was his last year as a floating raft pilot.

Stephen B. Hanks turned to steamboating. He needed to recoup his fortune in a hurry, for a girl in Albany was anxious to become Mrs. Hanks. His first job plunged him into the most strenuous steamboat race of his career. At St. Paul, he shipped as pilot under Capt. Smith Harris on the *Dr. Franklin No. 2*. The captain's brother-in-law, Orrin Smith, captained the *Nominee*, a rival packet which had been muscling in on the business previously served exclusively by the *Dr. Franklin*. Both boats ran between Galena, Illinois, and St. Paul.

On a recent trip south, the *Nominee* put out first from St. Paul, followed by the *Dr. Franklin*. About seven miles below Reeds Landing on the Mississippi, the *Nominee* was sighted lying in wait below a jutting peninsula. When the *Dr. Franklin* passed, the *Nominee* swung in behind. This was clearly the challenge to a race. It was not so much a sporting event as a business endeavor. It was a chance for the captains to demonstrate which was the faster boat, and so insure more business in the future.

"With true Mississippi River chivalry," the *Dr. Franklin* slowed enough to allow the *Nominee* an equal start. Rather scornfully, the *Nominee* held back. Captain Smith had reason to be confident. Two years previously, the *Nominee* had made the run from Galena to St. Paul and back in 55 hours and 49 minutes, an average rate of 12½ miles an hour. That was spectacular speed for that era.

Glad of the head start, Captain Harris ordered his crew to toss more wood into the furnaces. The race was on. Pilot Stephen Hanks was at the wheel, keeping the *Dr. Franklin* in mid-channel.

While the *Nominee* was really the faster boat, her skipper made one tactical error. He tried to make a short cut through a supposedly navigable slough. Because of low water, he almost ran aground. by the time he returned to the main channel, Captain Harris' packet was way in the lead.

The race continued. At times the boats were so close that passengers and crews jeered back and forth. But the *Dr. Franklin* held the lead continuously after she passed Guttenburg, Iowa. At times, passengers joined the crew ashore to help "wood up." They helped throw off sacks of mail and express at regular landings. Although it was a race, neither boat neglected its business calls. New freight was refused, except for the smallest bundles that could be loaded with no loss of time.

After 22 hours, the *Dr. Franklin* steamed into Galena, winner of the race, holder of a new record between St. Paul and Galena. Her twin smokestacks were white hot, her engines almost out of commission, her crew exhausted. And in the pilot house for all 22 hours of the race was Stephen B. Hanks.

Following the race, owners of the two boats consolidated to form the Minnesota Packet Company. Hanks became pilot of the *Galena*, pride of the new company's fleet.

Finally, in December 1856, Pilot Hanks had accumulated enough money to marry his sweetheart, Emily Bennett of Kingsburg, Illinois.

The following spring, Hanks, still assigned to the *Galena*, waited with a dozen other boats at Reeds landing for the ice to go out of Lake Pepin. All were ready for the spring rush to St. Paul. In addition to the honor of being the first boat to reach the saintly city, the winner would be awarded free wharfage for the year. Also waiting to enter the Lake was the *War Eagle*, sister packet to the *Galena*. It was considered the faster boat.

At last, the ice pack broke. The race was under way. Early on, the *War Eagle* took the lead with the *Galena* close behind. Captain Hanks was well aware of one principle of navigation which could give him an advantage in the race. When two boats were running side by side, they were drawn together. The slower boat could act as a drag on the speedier one.

Hanks knew that a few miles north of Reeds Landing at Sturgeon Bend there was a sand bar shaped like a flat-iron with its nose pointing downstream. He knew, too, that the deeper, more favorable channel was to the right of the point. He planned to force the *War Eagle* to take the shallow left channel. As the boats neared the bar, the *Galena* came abreast of the *War Eagle* to starboard. The *War Eagle* was crowded to the left of the jutting point of the flat-iron bar. As soon as the *Galena* felt the deep water of the right channel, she leaped ahead and was around the bar in a matter of minutes. When she straightened up, she was three full lengths ahead of the *War Eagle*. Leading the pack from then on, the *Galena* pulled into St. Paul at 2:00 a.m. on May 1, winner of the race—and won free wharfage for the year. Hank's skill as a pilot saved the owners of the boat $1,000 that trip.

From then on, Pilot Hanks was the favorite and most expert tutor of young pilots on the upper Mississippi and St. Croix rivers. He was known as the man who could "drive a nail with the stem of a steamer."

Skilled pilots were urgently needed, as the number of boats was increasing rapidly. More than 400 steamboats plied the upper Mississippi and St. Croix rivers between 1823 and 1863.

During the Civil War, Hanks was pilot of the *War Eagle*. Hundreds of Minnesota troops were carried to battle aboard the *War Eagle*. After the war, many discharged soldiers learned the pilot's art under Hanks.

In 1868, Hanks was hired by the newly-formed "Diamond Jo" line, established by Joseph Reynolds. Hanks was promoted to captain. For a while, Hanks doubled as pilot and captain, but found the double duties too arduous. He preferred the role of pilot. On several trips, the Diamond Jo steamers towed as many as five heavily-loaded grain and cargo barges, which made piloting especially difficult.

In 1870, Stephen B. Hanks returned to driving lumber. The old floating rafts were gone. Now, steamers nudged the rafts downstream at a faster pace. Hanks spent his last 15 years on the river as rafter-pilot for C. Lamb and Sons. Although the rafting business continued to grow, Hanks was aware that the decline of steamboating was inevitable.

At the close of the season of 1890, Captain Hanks decided he would quit the river. However, the lure of the boats kept him at his much-loved work until 1892, when he finally retired to his home in Albany, Illinois.

Stephen B. Hanks was known as "one of the few strictly temperate rivermen of pioneer days." Capt. Walter A. Blair of Davenport, Iowa, said of Hanks, "He was a genial, evenly-balanced character. He took the reverses in life as he stood the hard night watches, without a murmur or a kick, and always had a big, warm, kindly smile to greet the new morning, no matter how hard the night had been."

Fourth of July, circa 1906, from the roof of the Minnesota Mercantile. Note the log rafts in the background. Frank T. Wilson, photographer. (Courtesy of the Washington County Historical Society)

Chapter 12

Captain David M. Swain

Born in 1841 at Golden Prairie, Illinois, David M. Swain was primarily a foundryman and machinist, and best known along the rivers for his shop and yard at Stillwater, which was listed in city directories as "D. M. Swain's Marine Engine Works." David started the shop in 1867 when he was 26. Before that, he served as an engineer on Mississippi side-wheelers out of St. Paul. As an engineer, he was appalled and contemptuous of the archaic side-wheel engines which could, and did, hang up on center, usually at a moment of crisis when most needed. He resolved to design and market a new style of side-wheel engine that would not have this fault. Swain was also disenchanted with the inefficiency of the standard river return-flue boiler because of its waste of fuel and chronic infirmities.

His opinion of stern-wheel machinery was hardly fit to print. He thought outside cams, valve gears, clumsy and overweight cylinder castings and fittings were abominable. He decided that D. M. Swain's Marine Engine works would change all this. To learn more about machinery, David went to Chicago in winter and got a job with Crane Brothers, then returned to Stillwater and his own shop.

Swain's Foundry and Machine Shop, located at 106 S. Third Street, in a building just south of the Presbyterian Church, did a flourishing business as the lumber industry boomed. Keystone of its early success was not marine work, but construction of sawmill rigs, then in great demand. Somewhere along the way, David married Juliana Ainsworth. The couple was blessed with seven children: Arthur, who died in infancy; Earl who died at age four; Percy, Gertrude, Maude, Verne, and Fred.

The first family steamboat was a rafter named *Percy Swain*. The *Percy* was built on a second-hand hull, originally constructed at Reed's Landing, Minnesota, in 1882. The boat was stripped of its machinery and moved to the Red River of the North. From there, it was purchased by David M. Swain. The hull measured 129.8 by 19.7 feet.

When the *Percy* was completed, it incorporated many of David's revolutionary engineering ideas. The engines were cross-compound, the first of that sort on the Upper Mississippi network. She was the first stern-wheeler with a high pressure engine on one side, and a low pressure engine on the other. The low pressure engine operated with exhaust steam from the high power engine. As David did not believe in surface condensers, he developed a light-weight jet condenser, which occupied minimal space. The *Percy Swain* became the pacesetter for Swain's revolutionary achievements.

The boat was sold to E. H. Kirchner and Sons of Fountain City, Wisconsin. This was a river-contracting firm engaged in building wing dams. Eventually, the *Percy* was sold to a Memphis firm, the Tennessee Hoop Company, and renamed *Progress*.

The next boat built by David was the stern-wheeler *Verne Swain*, constructed in South Stillwater in 1886. According to the Taylors Falls *Journal*, the boat was "admirably fitted for passenger trade." On August 26, 1886, David was granted his original master's license by George Hayes, supervising inspector. The *Verne*, which also had a cross-compound engine, had cylinders 12 inches and 24 inches in diameter, and a 6-foot stroke. The hull was 122 by 22.5 feet. It had a pronounced upsweep in the stern hull design, and carried a very large paddle wheel. The multi-flue single boiler, called a "locomotive boiler" by rivermen, and a fan blower for better stack draft, made the *Verne* a good, practical, sensible boat. In 1886, the *Verne Swain* was taken down the Mississippi to run in passenger service out of Rock Island. She was later purchased by Capt. John Streckfus. From 1899 to 1900, she ran daily routes, leaving Clinton, Iowa, at 7:00 a.m. and arriving at Davenport at 10:30 a.m. She left Rock Island, Illinois, at 3:20 p.m. and was back in Clinton at 8:15 p.m. In 1900, she was sold and renamed *Speed*.

Later, *Speed* was registered at Greenville, Mississippi, owned by the Lyon Brothers. In 1911, she became a Green River regular, owned by Evansville & Bowling Green Packet Company. That firm swapped her off to Capt. Lewis Tanner in 1919, and she ran briefly between Gallipolis and Huntington on the Ohio, the last packet in that trade. Her final service was on the Ouachita River between New Orleans and Monroe, Louisiana, with some trips to Camden, Arkansas.

Two years after he finished the *Verne Swain*, David built another such packet, a bit smaller—125.5 feet long, 163 tons—but completely unorthodox. Designed for excursion work, the stern-wheeler *Borealis Rex* was used between Stillwater and St. Paul. It had a high, narrow stern paddle wheel, 20 feet in diameter, with buckets about 10 feet wide. The *Rex* was another boat with cross-compound engines built on a hull 121.5 by 22 feet.

This was the boat that started the Swains in business on the Illinois River between Peoria and La Salle. In 1890, businessmen of several towns along the river persuaded David Swain to go there. The *Borealis Rex*, with Capt. Charles Ebaugh as master, went into competition with Capt. Sol York, who had the daily Peoria-Henry trade, running his stern-wheeler *Rescue*. Apparently, the *Borealis Rex* ran into debt the first season. Still, Swain decided to stay in business there. David's son Percy, himself a steamboat captain, became general manager of the Illinois River operations.

Another mechanical innovation was the *Fred Swain,* built in autumn 1900 by George Godfrey for Captain Swain. It was named for the captain's son, a recent graduate of Macalester College in St. Paul. At the christening of the boat, Fred's colors were added to the usual national colors. This was Swain's first side-wheeler. Captained by Percy and Verne Swain, she was destined for Illinois trade. The interior of the cabin was finished in mahogany, with leather lounges and wicker rocking chairs providing comfort for passengers. The office was on the starboard side, with a confectionery directly opposite. The floor was carpeted. Passengers went down the central stairway to a dining room on the main deck, aft of the engines. The *Fred,* as all Swain boats, usually carried an orchestra in the summertime.

Each paddle wheel was turned by a high and a low pressure engine, inclined and facing each other. The piston rods were connected directly to the paddle-wheel shaft crank, which required each engine to oscillate through a considerable arc with each revolution of the paddle wheel. Fourteen cam rods were needed. The cylinders were set so that a centering or "hang up" was impossible. After this initial experiment on the *Fred Swain,* other similar engines were built at Stillwater for Swain side-wheelers.

On August 9, 1909, about 3:15 p.m., the *Fred Swain* was on a regular trip with seventy-nine people on board, including twenty-five children. Upbound about twenty-five minutes out of Peoria, she caught fire. The boat was immediately landed. Everyone left in safety, but the *Fred Swain* was demolished.

Launched June 28, 1900, the *Fred Swain* was built by George Godfrey for David Swain of Stillwater, but destined for use on the Illinois River. It was the first side-wheeler built by Swain. (Courtesy of Jim Johnson)

Two of the Swain sons, Fred and Verne, were brilliant mechanics. Fred stayed at the Stillwater shops, while Verne worked on the Illinois River, eventually becoming the master of the *Fred Swain*.

Although David Swain's revolutionary engine was better than any other on the river, engineers had to be trained to run it. They were required to have a condensing license, and very few men had one, so the innovative idea was slow to catch on. In spite of this drawback, the Swain Iron Works furnished machinery for nearly all the boats built at Stillwater.

In 1903, on order from Rufus F. Learned of Natchez, Mississippi, the Swains built a stern-wheel packet, *Little Rufus*. One of the few boats other than those owned by the Swains with cross-compound engines, the *Little Rufus* eventually burned.

The smallest side-wheeler with oscillating engines built by Swain was the *Kabekona*, on a hull 112 by 22.4 feet. The name *Kabekona* is said to be Indian for Stillwater. Actually, the *Kabekona* was a private yacht, with leaded fleur-de-lis in each skylight, and six staterooms, each with a private bath. She was operated by St. Paul millionaire lumberman and railroad contractor Archibald Guthrie. The craft had one tubular boiler 40 inches in diameter by 14 feet long. Eventually the *Kabekona* was sold to St. Louis millionaire Edward C. Koenig. For two-and-a-half years, she carried private excursions. On board were many important personages of St. Paul, St. Louis, and Peoria. At one time, the *Kabekona* was under charter to Mayor Thompson of Chicago. During World War I, the paddle boat was engaged by the Dubuque Boat and Boiler Company to deliver sub-chasers to New Orleans. Eventually, the *Kabekona* was purchased by a sand and gravel firm, Miller and Butterworth who operated on the Arkansas River at Little Rock. The *Kabekona* was cut up and made into a towboat, and was so used until 1919. That year, her hull and other parts were used at Augusta, Arkansas, to build the towboat, *Bonner*.

Other boats built by Swain were the *Plough Boy*, a passenger packet which plied between Stillwater and Taylors Falls, and the *Joseph Long*.

The trademark "The Royal Route" was adopted by the Swains when they first started running packet operations. Their diamond emblem showed up on the first *Verne Swain*, and was used in the St. Paul-St. Croix trade, as well as in the Iowa and the Illinois river trade. When the *Borealis Rex* was sold to new owners in 1903, the purchaser, Capt. George Prince of Vicksburg, adopted the trademark. He also became the best customer for second-hand Swain steamboats.

The excitement of the St. Louis World's Fair prompted the Swains to build a handsome stern-wheeler named *Verne Swain II*. She was 131.2 by 28.5 feet. This boat ran between Peoria and the Fair City during the summer of 1904. She was sold immediately thereafter to the Royal Route at Vicksburg. In later years, she carried the United States mail between Memphis and Rosedale, Tennessee. When the contract was cancelled in August 1924, it was announced as the last U.S. Mail contract carried by a western steam boat.

The side-wheeler *David Swain* glided into the St. Croix in May

The steamer *Kabekona* was built at Stillwater by Josiah Batchelder (far right on the deck) for Archibald Guthrie, railroad contractor of St. Paul. The boat was under construction for a year. (Courtesy of Jim Johnson)

1906 in spite of heavy rain and cold wind. D. W. Swain decided to go on with the affair regardless of the weather, saying "A wedding or launching should never be postponed." Among the honored guests at the occasion was ex-governor Samuel R. Van Sant, a steamboat owner himself. Spokesman for the affair was Stillwater Mayor James G. Armson. Hazel Farmer did the christening.

The steamer *David Swain* was one of the finest built in Stillwater. She was 136 feet long, 26.5 feet wide, and 4.75 feet in depth. The boat had a hull designed by Joseph Batchelder, was equipped with a modern oscillating engine, and had two tubular external heading boilers, and thirteen steam cylinders.

An out-and-out excursion boat, she had a central dance floor the length of the cabin, with an oak stairway leading down to a dining room on the main desk. The combination packet-excursion boat had a ladies' cabin, fitted with mahogany bulkheads and wicker furniture. She also had staterooms.

In 1907 when United States President Theodore Roosevelt made his journey down the Mississippi River to Memphis aboard the *Peoria*, the *David Swain* was *Peoria's* flagship. Of the trip, David Swain later recalled,

> Before reaching Memphis, the flotilla encountered a severe windstorm about 2:00 a.m. blowing from the Arkansas shore. Every stern-wheel steamer went to the Tennessee side, among snags, stumps, and caving banks to wait out the storm, while the *David Swain* kept right on her course. We passed the U.S. side-wheel steamer *Col. A. MacKenzie* about crossways of the river with her stern in the wind, battling with the storm. The next was the side-wheel steamer *Alton*, stern to the wind fighting the elements; the snorting and panting of her ponderous engines, of the old type, adding terror to the darkness, thunder, lightning and pelting rain. Through all, the *David Swain* kept on her way to a regular harbor, and there awaited the flotilla to come up, taking her place among them. You can readily see that the oscillating type of engines, dead centers eliminated, in the sidewheel boat, is the reliable power. The *David* made the trip from Peoria and return, 1,400 miles, with a consumption of fuel 82 pounds per mile." Afterward, the *David* was used almost exclusively for excursions.

The *David Swain* was the last side-wheel packet on the Illinois River in regular trade. Later she became the last steam packet in the Natchez and Vicksburg trade. The *David Swain* was dismantled in the early 1930s at Vidalia, Louisiana.

Percy Swain II came out new from Stillwater in 1910, and took over the packet trade between Peoria and La Salle on the Illinois River. The second *Percy* was a cross-compound stern-wheeler. Measuring 146 by 27.6 feet, the hull was of fir, as were all Swain hulls. The *Percy* was sold in 1913 to the Royal Route at Vicksburg. The boat sank on July 22, 1922, at Rifle Point, Louisiana. Her machinery was recovered and went into a steel hull, the *George Prince*.

A third *Verne Swain* appeared on the scene in 1913. This was a side-wheeler while its predecessors were stern-wheelers. *Verne III* was designed as an excursion boat. She was the largest of the Swain

Built in Stillwater in 1906, the *David Swain* was used in trade on the Illinois River. The boat is pictured at the bank of the river at Rome, Illinois. The photo was taken by Walter Kutz, clerk of the boat, on the afternoon of June 30, 1919. The men are unloading beer on the last day before prohibition went into effect. (Author's collection)

fleet to that date, 196 gross tons, and measuring 186.4 by 31 feet. She was built for the Ohio River trade.

The popularity of steamboat excursions led the Swains to procure the *Cessna* from Pensacola, Florida, in the fall of 1916. In Illinois they rebuilt her into their last and largest steamboat. Renamed *Julia Belle Swain* for David's granddaughter (Percy's daughter), the boat was brought out in the spring of 1917. The *Julia*, along with *Verne III*, operated as an excursion boat on the St. Croix. The *David Swain* was the Peoria-LaSalle packet.

World War I changed the picture. The development of hard-surfaced roads diverted freight traffic away from the river, and onto trucks. The *David Swain* at Peoria was hardly making ends meet. The decision was made to close the Stillwater plant of the D. M. Swain Marine Engine works and to sell the *Verne Swain*. Renamed the *Roosevelt*, then *Rose Island*, and finally *City of Memphis*, the boat sank on August 17, 1932, at the lower approach to the Louisville-Portland Canal locks. Although there were 781 passengers aboard, no one was hurt.

When the *Verne* was sold, Capt. David Swain, now seventy-seven, decided to go to Pittsburgh aboard the boat, where she was being taken by her new owners. He became ill en route and was admitted to the West Penn Hospital in Pittsburgh where he died July 3, 1918. Surviving were his wife; three sons, Percy, Verne, and Fred; and two daughters, Mrs. Charles Fey and Maude Swain, both of Peoria.

The boat *Percy Swain* sank in 1922. Capt. George Prince bought the *David Swain* as a replacement and took her to Vicksburg. That left the *Julia Belle* as the only boat owned by the Swain family. In May 1924 she, too, was sold. She burned on December 2, 1931, in winter quarters on the Monongahela River near Pittsburgh.

Oddly enough the last survivor of the Swain fleet on the Illinois River was the first one they brought to Peoria, the *Borealis Rex*. When a modern highway was built, the *Rex* was no longer needed as a packet, and was laid up in St. Charles. In 1938, she was sold for taxes and dismantled.

As for the Swain sons, Percy moved to Los Angeles, California. He died in 1938, at sixty-six years of age. Verne lived for many years at Grand Prairie, Illinois, on the farm bought by his grandfather, Isaac Swain, in 1835.

Chapter 13

All Aboard: Meet the Crew

Mark Twain wrote that the pilot of a steamboat was "the only unfettered and totally independent human being alive." He was the best paid of the crew. He was navigator and steersman combined.

The captain often had less skill at handling a steamboat than did his officers. Sometimes, though, he was knowledgeable enough to double as pilot. Generally, where there were both officers, the captain directed the business enterprise of the steamboat, while the pilot ran the boat.

The captain of a river boat was usually a big-hearted, honest man of good report. Fearless and masculine, he was prompt to take the part of the weak and oppressed. He was welcomed at both ends of the social scale when ashore. He enjoyed socializing in the finest of homes and in the roughest of saloons.

On the boat, he was absolute autocrat. For example, one religious captain insisted his boat be tied up from midnight Saturday until midnight Sunday to observe the Sabbath. In true naval tradition, the captain was the last to leave the boat in case of a sinking or burning. When a boat nosed in to shore, the captain, very likely clad in a long coat and top hat, could be seen watching austerely from the hurricane roof.

The pilot, while less toasted, was unique in that special society of rivermen. A pilot usually trained under an old pilot, and had to pay for the privilege. When he assumed command of his own boat, his salary ranged between $150 and $250 a month. Wages for raft and steamboat pilots were somewhat higher, from $300 to $500 a month. Pilots frequently were engaged by contract for an entire season.

Piloting was a difficult occupation. Snags, sand bars, floods and droughts changed the river from day to day. A pilot not only had to learn the usual channels of the St. Croix and Mississippi, but had to be able to read the changes which occurred between each trip up or down. A storm on the Kettle River on the Upper St. Croix would send a runoff into the lower river, digging out banks and building new sand bars.

White waters or mirror surfaces, the pilot watched the face of the river like the face of a lover. Generally, the channel ran directly from bend to bend. Dark blue meant deep water, light blue or sandy color indicated shallow waters. The pilot predicted sand bars and snags which appeared only as swirls and eddies on the surface. Going upstream, the pilot hung to the inner bank for easy water. Coming downstream, he stayed well out in the center, or held to the outside bank to ride the current. This offered a savings on fuel. It also enabled the steamboat to make the best time possible.

Reading the water was a pilot's success story. He could fairly estimate the speed of current in a bend. He decided from surface swirls and ripples whether the river concealed snags, bars, or rocks. Wind sometimes helped the pilot by ruffling deep water dramatically. On the other hand, rain dappled the whole surface, and blurred the river's mysteries. When the sun lay low, surface glare masked snags. On windy days, blowing sand hid the face of the water.

"Starboard" and "larboard" (meaning right and left) were terms used only on the river. Because the descending boat was at the mercy of the current, her pilot signaled his choice of side for passing an approaching boat. One blast of the whistle meant he would keep to the right; two blasts signaled left. The pilot of the ascending boat answered with the same signal to confirm the choice.

Sand bars always plagued pilots on the St. Croix River. They shifted constantly with the seasons. Frequently the pilot of a larger steamboat sent out a yawl to take soundings. When the deepest point of water over the sand bar was determined, the pilot drove the vessel over it at full power. A grating sound was the only inconvenience. At times, this maneuver was not successful. The packet scrunched to a sluggish halt on the sand bar. Passengers unloaded while the steamer

Piloting a steamboat was a genuine science, especially on the St. Croix and upper Mississippi. Not only did the pilot have to know every channel on the river, but he also had to know every bend in the river. The pilot was absolute master when in the pilot house, and his word was law. All bridges had to open when he signaled them. Years of experience was necessary to become a pilot, and he was highly paid. In meeting another steamboat midstream, the pilot had to know the rules of the river to avoid accidents. Many pilots made their headquarters in Stillwater. This photo was taken in 1912. (Courtesy of the Stillwater Gazette)

was hauled off. In time of extreme drought, the river became shallow to the point of non-navigability.

By contrast, storms and rains flooded the St. Croix over its banks, creating swift rapids, new shoals and sand bars. Trees washed in at each storm and formed snags which were deadly to river boats. Rising waters covered rocks, creating further obstacles to navigation, and challenging the ability of a pilot. Since the pilot memorized the channel, he quickly recognized whether any landmarks had washed away or changed since he last saw them through the wheelhouse window.

A good pilot depended on the feel of his boat. The vessel behaved differently as water grew shallow, or as the speed of the current increased. If water level was high, and the moon full, a boat might run at night. A trick pilots used was to "eat up the lights." They placed lighted candles in cylindrical paper shields on pieces of scrap lumber. Anchoring these crude floats along a stretch of water ahead, the pilots churned triumphantly over them to shore.

No radar was available to early St. Croix pilots, yet any pilot worthy of his command could pull the rope, get a blast from the whistle, and determine his location by the length of time it took for the echo to return from the bluffs along the river.

Those were the days of huge gold watch chains, velvet coat collars and cuffs. When ladies visited the pilothouse, the pilot donned kid gloves. Windows of many pilothouses were ornamented with the signatures and addresses of many fair visitors. "Costume de rigueur" of the raft pilot consisted of French calf boots, black cassionere trousers, red flannel shirt of extra fine goods, large black silk necktie tied in a square knot with flowing ends, and a soft wide-brimmed black or white hat.

The mate, lowest paid officer aboard, was directly under the captain in overall management of the boat. On larger packets, the second mate was the go-between for captain and crew.

The cabin boy was aide to the captain. He washed and pressed the captain's clothes, shined his shoes, ran his errands, and put the lantern out after the captain fell asleep. The cabin boy slept an average of four hours a night. At the end of the week, he got a sack of licorice if he was good, a boot in the seat of his pants if not.

The chief clerk sold tickets, and supervised the freight check. Junior officers were a mate and a mud clerk. The mate drove the crew, and stood watch from noon to 6:00 p.m., and again from midnight to 6:00 a.m. The mud clerk kept accounts, and usually worked the same hours as the mate. The name "mud clerk" derived from the fact that most levees were unfinished, and the clerk's boots got muddy as he checked freight aboard.

The chief engineer had command of the boiler room, while the second engineer handled the machinery when the chief was off duty. In *The Rivermen* published by Time-Life books of New York, Paul O'Neil records that steamboat engineers had no way of telling how much horsepower they had at hand. For decades, there was no means of gauging steam pressure, or even the limits imposed by their crude safety valves. In times of stress they simply ordered extra fuel into the fireboxes, tuned their senses to the resultant vibration, and with their

The dining room of the *Isaac Staples*. Present are Everet Johnson, the cabin boy; Thomas McAloon, the cook; and Jean Reed, the clerk. (Courtesy of the Washington County Historical Society)

ears estimated both the power output and strain on the boilers. The single-cylinder, high-pressure engines of the day exhausted steam with a sound like slow cannonading, a cacophony that could be heard for miles, even under normal operating conditions. This attained a howitzer-like intensity as pressure mounted. The racket sometimes culminated in the hideous roar of exploding boilers. Passengers seemed as exhilarated as the steersmen and engineer when a boat labored noisily through fast water with the safety valve tied down.

Most boats had a blacksmith's forge on board. All river engineers were good blacksmiths, able to make anything from wrought iron bars, with a forge and anvil and a two-pound shaper. They turned out such things as double bolts which clamped the "buckets" to the paddle wheel arms, chains, and chimney guys, as well as making repairs to the engines and boilers.

Supervising and preparing meals was the duty of the steward. On small packets, he also served the food. On larger boats, he had assistants as needed.

The boat's carpenter kept a stock of wheel arms and buckets on hand. If the boat bumped a log, or the paddle wheel picked up drift wood, he was on deck, even in the middle of the night, to make repairs.

How many crew members there were was determined by the size of the boat. Stokers and roustabouts were necessary to keep boilers fired, take soundings, load firewood, stow freight, and see to the needs of the passengers.

Countless immigrants found their first jobs on the river. In the 1850s, more than half of steamboat deck crews were German or Irish. "Rousters," forty or more to a packet, turned out night and day to the mate's call. For $20 a month, they carried wood; unloaded horses, cattle, wagons, plows, bales and barrels; manned pumps and capstans; handled mooring lines and landing stages.

Rousters lived on the lower deck like cattle. They slept when and where they could amid the freight. They were on call night and day. They ate leftovers from the cabin tables. When the steward cried, "Grub pile," the "rousters" put their portions on wooden shingles to eat.

Theirs was a perilous life. They lived close to the boiler heat. Roustabouts were burned by bursting steam pipes, crushed by falling cargo, drowned in the river. A packet seldom stopped to rescue a rouster. "Bully boys" charged with keeping the roustabouts working, managed them with fists and profanity. Some used clubs. There were bully boys who were not above shooting. The roustabout's job was a young man's job, full of violence and change.

Rousters had one recourse. They could desert a boat when she needed them most. By striking during the harvest season, when other jobs were available, they were able to win higher wages and better working conditions—for one trip at least.

Among the hazards faced by steamboat captains, in addition to the river itself, were river pirates, Indians, and "skeeters."

Geologist David Dale Owen was hired by the United States General Land Office to do a mineral survey of the St. Croix Valley.

He wrote to his wife from Stillwater on July 21, 1847, about the "swarms of mosquitoes, buffalo gnats, gadflies and a host of other small but excessively annoying insects which infest these regions during the last two weeks of June, all of July, and the first two weeks of August. Only by dint of the greatest perseverance and resorting to every imaginable means of repelling their attacks we are enabled to get sufficient sleep." That complaint still is voiced by river afficionados.

Steamboat racing was as much a part of the St. Croix River pilot's life as were whiskey and women. A filler in the *Stillwater Gazette*, dated December 1, 1875, reads, "If the ark had been manned by a steamboat captain, he would have been unhappy during the entire voyage, because there was no opposition on the river to race with."

There were tricks to getting the best speed out of a paddle-wheeler. Going downstream, a wise captain had his crew weight the side which led into the current most frequently. Going upstream, they did the reverse. Skippers were known to throw casks of bacon and pitch into the roaring furnaces, tie down the safety valve, and begin the race.

Limber boats were faster, so some crews sawed half way through the framing timbers to loosen a hull. Generally, racing was done for the sheer sport of it. In the spring of the year, however, racing became serious business. The first boat into port at Stillwater or St. Paul after the ice went out got the best freight contracts for the season. With such an incentive, steamboat pilots braved floating ice, which was hard on hull and paddle-wheel alike, to be the first boat at the levee.

In later years, when towboats took over most of the commerce on the river, two raft boats sometimes raced. Clumsy craft at best, they stayed in wide reaches of the river to race. One writer compared such a contest to two turtles competing.

When fog shrouded the river, pilots tied up in port, or anchored along the bank. Sometimes boats just drifted. Storms occasionally blew boats ashore, or toppled the tall pilothouses. The only real danger to the boat existed when the direction of the river and of the wind coincided. Relief from a gale was found as soon as the boat rounded a bend.

In the 1860s and 1870s, the majority of boats on the St. Croix were engaged as towboats. The average lumber raft moved at four miles an hour. Log rafts averaged 275 feet by 600 feet in size, some four acres of logs, weighing 3,500 tons. Although boats usually towed single layer rafts, some were made up in double layers.

It took the skill of an expert pilot to raft logs downriver to mills along the St. Croix and Mississippi. In spite of the fact they were called "towboats," the steamers in reality pushed the log rafts. The bow of the steamer was made fast to the stern boom of the log raft. The stern of the towboat was swung by means of guy lines running from the corners of the raft to a double-spooled engine on the boat. As the line was paid out on one side, it was reeled in on the other, giving the towboat mobility and control over the raft. Sometimes a smaller "bow-boat" was attached to the front of the raft, as well.

To take a tow through a bend, the pilot engaged in "flanking." He threw the engine into reverse to check the tow and give it time for the turn. At the same time, he backed the paddle wheel to drive the current under the raft and let it drift with the stream.

According to the Winona *Independent* newspaper of May 14, 1901, the many attempts to install feminine pilots on raft boats on the river was a hopeless failure. "The management of raft boats, like locomotives, was meant for men, not women," concluded the article. However, it was reported shortly thereafter that the last woman pilot on the upper river had retired. One woman was left on the lower river, piloting a circus boat below St. Louis. These brief references indicated that there were indeed several female river pilots on the upper Mississippi, who most probably also worked on the St. Croix.

Boatmen depended on the river for their livelihood, so the time of breakup and freeze of the river were very important to them. An early breakup of ice in the spring, and a late freeze in fall meant extra trips, with added profits from cargo and passengers. A late spring and early fall cut into their revenue. Rivermen watched nature for signs to try to predict the seasons.

Thin bark on trees meant a mild winter and an early breakup, so said the pilots. If muskrats built their houses on the banks of the river instead of in the adjoining lowlands, rivermen expected a mild winter. On the other hand, if muskrat houses were large and numerous, the boatmen counted on a rugged winter. They had a saying, too, that the river would not freeze until after the last full moon of the year.

Although they were for the most part practical, level-headed men, the crews of the St. Croix riverboats had superstitions. White cats were considered a bad omen, but black cats were welcomed aboard as harmless. A white horse or mule on board brought bad luck. Rats were considered good luck, but a preacher on board made some captains uneasy.

Names of boats came under very careful scrutiny. Names beginning with "M" were suspect because it is the 13th letter of the alphabet. Six-letter names were considered risky for steamboats. That resulted in such practices as adding an "h" to the "*Dakota*" to give her the seven-letter name "*Dakotah*," and subsequent good luck.

Coffins were regarded as mere freight, with no stigma of bad luck. It is said that many a coffin with corpse inside, transported down the St. Croix to bring a loved one home, made a convenient card or lunch table for the crew.

Pilots, captains, and crew of the steamboats relied on their own common sense, and their river sense, to navigate the St. Croix safely. It was not until boating neared its end in the early 1900s that a government guide book was issued, with charts of the channel and rules for navigation. It came too late to be much use to men who lived by, for, on, and with the river for their entire lives.

Chapter 14

Laws, Lights, Whistles and Mail

As early as 1830, the federal government, realizing the importance of the Mississippi River and its tributaries in opening the West and in providing transportation for freight and passengers, began work on the river. Snags and sand bars were removed. Rapids were dynamited. Sloughs and backwaters were closed off to confine the flow of the channel, assuring deep water. The work continued through the next half century. And in 1880, Congress authorized a four-and-one-half foot channel on the Mississippi.

In 1858, a memorial was introduced to Congress by W. H. C. Folsom of Taylors Falls asking for improvement of the St. Croix River. Twenty years passed before any significant action was taken. Thaddeus C. Pound, representing the St. Croix Valley in Congress in 1878, secured the first appropriation for river improvement. The six-year schedule of allotments was as follows: 1878—$8,000; 1879—$10,000; 1880—$8,000; 1881—$10,000; 1882—$30,000; and 1883—$7,500. The money was expended under the supervision of Major Farquier and Charles J. Allen of the United States Engineering Corps, headquartered in St. Paul. The improvements were concentrated in removing snags, deepening the channel, building wing dams, and riprapping the shores.

In spite of the delay in getting funds specifically for the St. Croix, work on the Mississippi was extended to include the border river in the 1850s. Government steamers deepened the channel and installed channel markers.

On August 12, 1873, the U.S. steamer *Montana*, which had been deepening the channel on the Mississippi, arrived at the port of Stillwater. John B. Davis was in command of the boat. At Stillwater, Captain Davis purchased piling with which to improve the Mississippi near Beef Slough and Rolling Stone sand bars. Davis and his crew examined Catfish Bar near Afton, and the Willow River

Bar just off Hudson in the St. Croix, and said that material improvement in the depth of the water could be made at very little expense.

The following summer, Captain Davis proved his point. On July 26, he invited a limited number of valley area residents aboard the *Montana* to show them how a sandbar could be demolished.

For years, Catfish Bar had been an annoyance and difficulty to riverboat captains and to towboats rafting logs. The *Montana* cruised around the sand bar, while the group aboard observed it from every angle. The bar projected straight out into Lake St. Croix from the Wisconsin shore. There was an abrupt descent on the lower side of the bar with the water reaching a depth of 50 to 60 feet.

After the survey, the *Montana* was spun in below the bar, and run up to shallow water. Captain Davis lowered iron scoops, then backed down into deep water, bringing away five or six cart loads of earth. The mud was deposited in deep water. "The work on the sand bar will be continued until a free and untrammeled passage for rafts and boats is effected," Davis announced.

Another annoyance on the river was a man-made obstacle. To lumbermen, the St. Croix Boom was the heartbeat of the valley, for it controlled all the timber that floated from the upper tributaries to the mills downstream. To pilots and navigators, the St. Croix Boom was the headache of the river. The company continued to drive piles where it pleased. Sheer booms, cribs, and boom clogs were installed at the whim of the lumbermen, without regard for what was happening to the river. The cribs and booms changed the current of the river. New sand bars formed around the pilings, obstructing navigation in every conceivable manner. Through the years, there was a continuing battle between lumbermen and rivermen for their rights on the St. Croix.

In 1885, a waterways convention was called by Minnesota Governor Lucius F. Hubbard. Some one thousand delegates from the midwestern states met in St. Paul. Result was the passage of a resolution recommending a liberal policy of improvements for waterway transportation. Of paramount importance was the immediate and permanent improvement of the Mississippi and Missouri rivers and their tributaries, including the St. Croix.

Edward W. Durant of Stillwater made a valuable statement to the convention regarding the resources and commerce of the valleys of the St. Croix and Mississippi. Mr. Durant said that there had been a cry that the days of steamboating were over. "I think that if they are, the only cause for it is the extremely short and uncertain season for steamboating resulting from neglected and filled up channels," he was quoted as saying. If the rivers were improved, said Durant, steamers could operate five months a year, and be one of the most important means of transportation to the upper Mississippi valley. Following the conference, government boats continued to work in the valley, making the river navigable.

In 1906, there was a movement urging the improvement of the river channel of the St. Croix to a depth of four feet between Stillwater and Taylors Falls. Major Derby of the U.S. Corps of Engineers solicited letters from citizens of the valley, asking their opinion. Many

The tug *Edwin C*, built by George Muller in 1897-98 for the Bronson & Folsom Company. It was in the process of towing a brail of logs through the pontoon draw by means of a long line. (Courtesy of the Washington County Historical Society)

strong letters were written in response to Derby's request. Typical of the replies was one from Capt. W. C. Smith of St. Paul, who had built the steamer *Lora* and had used the boat for trade between Prescott and Taylors Falls.

> From 1881 to 1885, I ran a boat and fleet of barges in trade between this city and Taylors Falls, carrying thousands of cords of wood, lumber, railroad ties and laths, shingles and tons of brick each year, which traffic gave me a profit while done at a rate two-thirds less than current railroad rates.
>
> In 1900, I built a fine excursion boat for that trade, but had to give it up as I could not get any guaranty that the Boom Company would allow me the natural flow of water.
>
> What is needed, it seems to me, is that the river be surveyed with a view of giving four feet of water in the channel from the mouth of the river to Taylors Falls. It may not be improper for me to suggest that in case a four-foot channel could be established, I would gladly put a packet in the trade, as soon as I was assured of the fact.
>
> As you are doubtless aware, the scenery along the St. Croix River is in places of surpassing loveliness and is almost its whole length very beautiful. When the fact became known that a line would be established, passengers would avail themselves in great number of the opportunity to visit the Dalles of the St. Croix, as well as the Interstate Park, established at that point.

No definite decision is recorded regarding the channel of the St. Croix. A six-foot channel was authorized for the Mississippi in 1907, and maintenance work was continued on the St. Croix. On the Father of Waters, wing dams of rock and brush were built along

The government boats, *Minnesota, Iowa, Illinois, Missouri,* and *Muscatine* at Stillwater. The first four were also built at Stillwater. (Courtesy of the Washington County Historical Society)

sloughs and lowlands to divert the water into the center channel. A clear, deep passage was assured for boats.

In 1930 Congress authorized a nine-foot channel, four hundred feet wide, on the Mississippi. By that time, the application of diesel power to boats brought an end to the glamorous age of the steamboat. Towboats and barges, the workhorses of the river, were the only ones to benefit from the improvements.

On January 22, 1930, an order was issued by the War Department relative to the St. Croix. While no depth was specified, it was ordered that the channel be kept open from Taylors Falls to Stillwater.

Rules and Regulations

The Steamboat Act of 1838 offered the first regulations regarding river craft. The law asked for inspection of all boilers and machinery, replacement of tiller ropes with iron rods or chains, and the use of running lights. The act was vague, and soon became a dead issue.

A much more comprehensive law was passed in 1852. It defined rules for passing in the channel, required fire hose and fire pumps, and established a limit to allowable steam pressure for the boilers of the steamboats. The measure regulated stowing of fuel and cargo on the packets, and called for escape routes for all passengers in case of emergency. Escape stairways had to be provided from the main deck to the upper levels. Life preservers were mandatory.

Inspection of equipment in major river districts was provided for. The law was extended to include inspection of manufacturers of steamboat boilers.

Boats were checked regularly by United States War Department inspectors. The St. Croix River was in the fifth inspection district. Offices of the district supervisor were in the Custom House in St. Paul. Two men from the St. Croix Valley held offices in the inspection service. Capt. George Hayes, an Osceola resident since 1855 and an outspoken Democrat, was appointed to the position of district supervisor by Pres. Grover Cleveland in May 1885. Four years later, when the Republican party was in power, he was removed by Pres. Benjamin Harris. A few months later, Capt. George B. Knapp, also of Osceola and a man of the right political persuasion, was appointed inspector of hulls for the Galena district.

The act of 1852 demanded the examination and licensing of both engineers and pilots of steamboats. Previously, any man who could get himself hired became a pilot or engineer as vacancies on the crew demanded.

The reform measure made it mandatory that sufficient floor space be provided for each passenger "in a sheltered and ventilated common room." The law established a quota for the number of deck passengers allowed on a steamboat. However, this limit applied only to people traveling more than five hundred miles, so immigrants still were crowded into any space available aboard the boats.

Reform came too late. The high tide of immigration was passing in the mid-1850s. Many people had lost their lives in the pre-regulation boiler explosions and overcrowded steerage of steamboats.

The *Juniata,* one of the scores of packets that connected the towns of the St. Croix Valley during the heyday of steamboating, from the late 1830s until the turn of the new century. (Courtesy of the Washington County Historical Society)

The act was ineffective for two reasons: the law applied only to new steamboat construction, and there was no machinery for enforcement of the law.

The effect of the Steamboat Act of 1852 was noted on the St. Croix some twenty years after its passage. It was reported that the steamer *G. B. Knapp* was being renovated. Since the law required that any passenger steamer provide for all possible emergencies, Capt. Oscar Knapp ordered fifty pieces of board of the proper size, and that these so-called "life-preservers" be located in the staterooms.

He further announced that an attachment was made to the engine of the boat by which any part of the steamer could be flooded should a fire occur. Before that time, the usual solution of a fire on board was a bucket brigade. Crew and passengers passed pails of water from the river to the site of the blaze in an attempt to extinguish it.

In August of 1872, Captain Gordan and Captain McMurchy of the United States government team were at work inspecting steamboats on the St. Croix. Craft were checked for compliance with marine law. Under those provisions, passenger boats were prohibited from using kerosene oil on board. Life preservers were to weigh not less than six pounds each. Fire extinguishers had to be provided on every boat. A few pilots and engineers had their licenses revoked for a short time for non-compliance with the marine laws. Generally, though, captains, pilots, and engineers of the steamers were men of good reputation and responsibility who complied with regulations.

Whistles and Lights

Whistles were part and parcel of boat traffic throughout the history of the craft. A steamboat whistle had frightened the Indians when the first boat up the St. Croix, the *Palmyra*, entered the Dalles of the river in 1838.

Whistles were regulated in 1855. The law not only required the use of whistles, it also set a system of signals. A boat descending the river signaled with one blast of its whistle to keep to the right; two to keep to the left. The ascending boat acknowledged the signal by answering in the same way.

Lights came to the St. Croix River because of an act of Congress in 1874. It provided that beacon lamps, day beacons, and buoys be installed on all inland rivers.

Old-time river pilots resented the markers. They feared that the addition of lights and lamps would diminish the importance of their knowledge and skill, and open the doors of the the pilothouse to ignorant and inexperienced men.

May 1875 found a boat at work marking the channel of the St. Croix. The crew placed lights on poles, or hung them from trees. Depending on the location, the poles were from six to sixty feet high.

People living along the river were hired to tend the lanterns. Pay for lamplighting ranged from $12 to $20 a month, according to how difficult it was to service the lamp. Each night at dusk, the lightkeeper climbed up the pole or tree to fill the lamp with coal oil. Each morning, he repeated his climb to extinguish the flame. Beacons were

The Golden Bugles of the *Jonathan Padelford*. (Courtesy of the Stillwater *Gazette*)

The *Wakerobin* on the Mississippi River near Genoa, Wisconsin. A government boat, the *Wakerobin* worked on the Mississippi and St. Croix rivers. Here a channel marker is being installed on the banks of the river. (Courtesy of the Washington County Historical Society)

large lanterns with Fresnel reflectors to amplify the light.

Each light keeper received the following equipment: ten gallons of oil, fourteen envelopes, two quires of letter paper, two dozen steel pens, one pint of ink, three lead pencils, one memo book, three pen holders, and one ink stand. Then, as now, there was a lot of paper work connected with government jobs.

At some locations along the St. Croix, an "A" board, painted white, guided pilots during the day. Each board supported a brass lantern which burned for a week with one fill of kerosene. The lanterns cost about $10 a month to maintain. They were not permanent installations. The boards had movable poles so they were easily relocated in time of flood. A government boat tended the lamps, trimmed wicks, and inspected the lanterns. On regularly scheduled visits, the boat captain distributed the supply of oil to light keepers along the stream.

A proposal in the 1880s to use electric beacons drew a storm of protest. Old time rivermen were sure that the electric lights would blind the eyes of anyone looking at them. There were also some protests from the light keepers, for they saw the end of their jobs. In spite of the objections, battery-powered beacons replaced hand-lighted lanterns, and the lamp keepers were retired, phasing out another aspect of steamboating on the St. Croix.

Mailmen of the River

In early days of steamboating, mail was carried on board the boats as a service. It reached its destination during the summer at the whim of the captain. With the cessation of steamer travel in fall, mail deliveries stopped until a spring thaw opened the river again.

Henry W. Crosby, a settler at Lakeland, was perhaps the first St. Croix postman. In 1841, he received the contract to carry mail which arrived at Prescott by canoe from Prairie Du Chien. Crosby delivered letters all along the river from Prescott to St. Croix Falls. The cost of mailing a letter was 25 cents.

At the end of the decade, in 1849, Dr. Phillip Aldrich of Hudson was given the mail contract between Point Douglas and St. Croix Falls. Making the trip twice each month, Aldrich boarded a packet and sorted out the Willow River (Hudson) mail from that bound for Stillwater and above. The honor of being Hudson's first postmaster goes to Dr. Aldrich. He received that appointment on November 21, 1849, a post he held until November 17, 1851. The first post office was in the home of the doctor's son, Paschal, on Buckeye Street. Mrs. Paschal Aldrich (Martha) often tended the post office for her father-in-law. In view of the fact that she could not read, people were invited to help themselves to their mail.

In 1858, a regular mail service was established to St. Paul from points south and east. From the saintly city, letters were delivered to Stillwater by stagecoach. Apparently this was not satisfactory. The Stillwater *Messenger* late in 1858 complained, "Instead of sending our mail direct from the junction of the Mississippi and the St. Croix, a distance of 30 miles traversed by daily steamer, our mail is sent to St. Paul, making a circuit of some 60 miles." And causing additional delay, no doubt.

Early the next year, the steamboat *Equator* made a few trips with mail to and from Stillwater. The mission failed as a result of a disastrous storm on Lake St. Croix, which completely wrecked the boat.

Eventually, in 1860, the stern-wheeler *H. S. Allen*, captained by Isaac Gray, established a regular service between Prescott and Taylors Falls. The *Allen* was described as "the regular St. Croix River U.S. Mail Packet." Even this official boat made just two mail deliveries a week.

In 1862, the *Enterprise*, owned by Capt. Oscar Knapp, joined the *Allen* on the mail route. On alternate days, the two packets churned up and down delivering correspondence between villages and towns along the river. "The mail must go through" in spite of frequent delays caused by low water, log jams, sand bars, and accidents. During the summer, at least, a daily mail delivery was established by boat. The summers of 1863 and 1864 were extremely dry, resulting in low water on the river. Captain Knapp said that his boat could no longer jump over the sand bars, so mail delivery by boat was discontinued. The next report of a mail boat on the St. Croix was in 1871. Then the *Wyman X* took over the service because the river road was so poor that the stage coach ceased its runs. In winter, deliveries were reduced to three a week. When it froze over, the St. Croix River provided a good highway for both mail and passengers.

In 1875, the *G. B. Knapp* was designated as official mail boat. With "U.S. Mail" painted in white letters on her bulkheads, she made daily runs upriver from Stillwater.

As roads improved, and steamboating decreased, mails took to the land.

Often over winter when travel on the northern rivers was impossible due to ice, steamboats were dry docked. Winter was the time for making major overhauls and repairs. This is the United States Engineering Department tow boat *Coal Bluff* at Keokuk, Iowa, in 1922. (Courtesy of Durand Blanding)

Chapter 15

Winter Tales

Navigation on the St. Croix was usually good for eight months of the year. From the April arrival of the first boat through the hot months of summer, steamboat traffic was a routine part of daily life in the St. Croix Valley. By late October or early November, ice started forming in the upper reaches of the river. By mid-November the river, including Lake St. Croix, was frozen over.

A typical report was printed in the St. Croix *Union* in November 1857. "The Steamer *H. S. Allen* had attempted to make a final trip to Taylors Falls, but was unable even to get to the head of Lake St. Croix. The *Eolian* made her way into port at Stillwater on November 12 with much difficulty. After discharging her freight, she returned to Prescott to go into winter quarters."

Although snags were perhaps the primary cause of boat losses on the river, with fire the second cause, ice in spring and fall was dreaded by boat captains. In fall, new ice cut like a knife. The *Fanny Harris* was cut down by floating ice and sank in twenty feet of water opposite Point Douglas. The *Alex. Gordon*, a side-wheel rafter built at La Crosse in 1867, met a similar fate in 1880. It was sunk by ice a little north of Marine in December. The boat belonged to Haycock and Company, wood dealers of St. Paul, who raised her and put her into shape for the next season's business.

Usually, packets intending to make a late trip north were strengthened by spiking on sheathing of four-inch oak plank at the bow of the boat.

By early April the ice broke up, allowing the first boats to race to port, setting new records, and beating out the competition to get the biggest share of trade for the season. They faced the danger of shifting ice. When the wind changed, ice rafts turned and often crushed steamers.

The first spring trips were not easy. In 1848, Edward W. Durant boarded the *Senator,* earliest boat to traverse the river that year. The trip from Galena to St. Paul took nine days. The boat was cast ashore on Lake Pepin by ice. The *Senator* was unable to ascend the St. Croix because of ice, so passengers were landed at St. Paul, and walked to Stillwater.

The *Nellie Kent,* first steamer through Lake St. Croix in 1872, arrived at Stillwater at 10:30 a.m. on Tuesday, April 23. Capt. Russell Ruley had left St. Paul at 3:00 p.m. a day earlier. He found some ice between Afton and Hudson, but made good time nonetheless.

Before roads were cut through the wilderness, communities along the St. Croix were isolated in winter. The need for communication and transportation between river towns inspired several attempts to navigate the frozen river by means of ice boats.

Norman Wiard, an inventor of some renown, made such a vehicle in 1856. He placed it on the Mississippi River at Prairie du Chien, having the intentions of running it to St. Paul, with side trips on the St. Croix.

The ice boat resembled the palace car of a railroad, mounted on steel runners. Unfortunately, the unique vehicle didn't make a single trip. It failed because of the roughness of the ice. It was put on display at Prairie du Chien for some time.

Boat builder Martin Mower of Arcola tried twice to solve the riddle of winter navigation of the St. Croix. His first effort was in 1868-69. Mower invented a boat intended to run on the ice between Stillwater and Taylors Falls to provide much-needed communication between the two points. The ice craft did indeed make several trips, carrying both passengers and freight. Mower encountered the same problem that had been Wiard's undoing—rough ice.

Despite the failure of the first attempt, Mower was undaunted. He tried again. The winter of 1876-77 was a busy one at Mower's Arcola boatworks. His crew, headed by John S. Irish of Taylors Falls, was hard at work on the *Ada B.,* a 105-foot stern-wheel packet. At the same time, they were constructing Martin's newest invention—an ice steamboat. Valley area residents had first read about the project in the Polk County *Press.* In December, the Taylors Falls *Journal* noted that the "ice steamboat or steam iceboat" would carry only the crew and fuel. Passengers and freight would be carried in covered sleighs or cars linked on behind.

The vehicle had a superstructure 30 feet by 7 feet, mounted on four ordinary sled runners. Two small engines provided power for the miniature craft. Locomotion was furnished by two iron-spiked wheels, near the rear runners. Spurs three inches long dug into the ice as the wheels revolved, pulling the strange vehicle ahead. There was a screw arrangement which permitted the raising and lowering of the driving shoes.

To steer the ice boat, Mower installed a wire tiller rope which extended from the pilot's wheel to the front runners. This peculiar engine was designed to pull a 28-foot passenger car.

The ice steamboat was named *Queen Piajuk,* after the daughter of a Cross Lake Chippewa chieftan who was said to have participated in the War of 1812.

The *Queen Piajuk*, an ice steamboat constructed by Martin Mower of Arcola to solve the riddle of winter navigation. The *Queen Piajuk* ran on ordinary sled runners, with locomotion furnished by two iron spiked wheels. (Courtesy of the Washington County Historical Society)

The *Queen* was described in the Stillwater *Gazette* as having a single smoke stack. "A handsome jack staff ornaments the bow, while perched jauntily on the pilot house is the figure of a swan with its wings outstretched as if eager to retain the graceful position on the bosom of the lake." The figure was symbolic of the ability of the craft to run over the ice and, if necessary, to float on the waters as gracefully and buoyantly as a swan.

The passenger car which trailed behind was elegant. Walls of the ladies' sitting room were handsomely paneled in rich yellow ash, black and French walnut, and birdseye maple. The windows were similar to those used in the new palace cars then in vogue on the railroads. Men had a smoker in the coach, and the ladies had a retiring room, which was said to be a perfect model of its kind. The floor was carpeted with the finest grade of Axminster, which matched the design and color of the crimson brocatel upholstery of the high-backed, two-seated divans. Two large mirrors, which had been taken from the bridal chamber of a Fulton City, Illinois, hotel, hung on the wall.

A trial run was scheduled for January 28, 1877. The big day arrived. Some two hundred spectators assembled. Steam was built up in the boilers to 110 pounds of pressure. The crowd waited. The craft remained stationary. Four horses were hitched to the ice steamer. The engine pounded; the horses strained. The craft remained in position. Finally, all the men in Arcola were enlisted to help. Armed with crowbars, they tried to move the boat, but it would not budge.

Charles E. Mears, editor of the Polk County *Press*, commented that the engine needed to be five times as large to be effective.

For a week, Mower and his crew worked on the *Queen Piajuk*. On Sunday, February 4, it finally made its maiden voyage—or slide—to Stillwater. Repeated whistles echoed through the early afternoon stillness. Crowds gathered at the elevator docks and on the ice at the waterfront. The iceboat and its crowded palace car came crawling down the river at the rate of seven miles an hour. Martin Mower himself followed behind, driving a team of horses.

Pilot of the remarkable vehicle was Jack Kent, who felt that the steam ice boat, or ice steamboat, was a "big thing on ice."

During the balance of the year 1877, Mower worked to get the kinks out, and was partially successful. The following winter, he tried again to perfect the mechanical problems of his ice boat. He launched it again in February of that year. Apparently everything worked satisfactorily. Unfortunately, a proposed test run to Stillwater was postponed because of thin ice. There were no further trips that season.

With the coming of another winter, Captain Mower announced that he would start up his steam iceboat and run regular packet trips between Stillwater and Taylors Falls. In 1879, Mower made one trip. During the second week in January, the *Queen Piajuk* arrived at Stillwater "whistling a lively tune." By the end of January, Mower was ready to make the twenty-six mile run to Taylors Falls. The packet averaged a speed of ten miles an hour. He made the trip in four hours, which included stops at Marine Mills, Osceola and Franconia.

The *Queen*, which scuttled and jumped across the ice on the points of its spiked wheels, was nicknamed "St. Croix Grasshopper." The Polk County *Press* predicted the establishment of regular water stations along the river to service the ice boat.

Apparently Mower himself had doubts about his pet project. On February 5, 1879, the St. Croix Grasshopper left the Stillwater levee for the upper river. The following day, the weather turned warm and ice became treacherous.

Historian James Taylor Dunn speculated that the *Queen* probably reached its home port of Arcola safely, but perhaps was dismantled there. The oak timbers from the ice craft may have been used to build the pile driver *Arcola*.

So ended the dream of a regular steam ice boat (or ice steamboat) to ply the St. Croix in winter.

Perhaps in hope of competition with the *Queen*, Captains Knapp and Erskine Smith of Osceola built an ice velocipede in 1877. Its first trip, in February, proved a success. It was a "bow wheeler," run by hand. It, too, had the motion of a "grasshopper goin' for a granger's field." Faster than the *Queen Piajuk*, it traveled about ten miles an hour on its first run, and speculation was that with a little work, twice the speed could be obtained on glare ice.

The ice velocipede was made of the hind runners of a pair of bob sleds. It had a platform on top, with two wheel timbers five feet long attached in front. A buggy wheel was hung on a small shaft between the timbers. Cranks were attached to the wheel shaft, fastened to connecting rods which in turn were attached to levers. A chair was placed between the levers. The operator sat on the chair, and worked the levers by hand, moving the machine. It was steered by the feet which rested on a beam attached to the nose of the sled. The runners moved right or left at a slight touch of the foot. Information about the winter craft appeared in both the Stillwater *Lumberman*, and the Polk County *Press*. However, there was no further mention of the ice velocipede, possibly because of an early breakup of ice that year.

What happened to the summer craft in winter? With the coming of the freezeup, steamboats were taken out of the water. Many were rebuilt during the off-season. There were times when packets were iced in at the waterfront before they could be taken to winter quarters.

The *G. B. Knapp* suffered a loss while iced-in. In 1868, it wintered in Coon Slough, fifteen miles below La Crosse, with a guard on duty. The watchman was given an order which supposedly came from Captain Knapp. It read that the goods were to be stored in a city warehouse. Although the paper was a forgery, it fooled the watchman. He let the furnishings be taken off the boat. They were sold at auction in La Crosse, a thousand dollar loss for the captain.

In 1875, several steamboats were locked in at the levee at Stillwater, causing much concern for the owners and captains of the boats. Children had easy access to the craft, and scrambled aboard to play. They built fires on the decks, and "did other depredations," according to the Stillwater *Gazette*. The boat captains asked for and received the necessary law enforcement to prevent further vandalism.

The year 1909 found at least three boats wintering on the levee at Stillwater—the steamer *Roamer* owned by Dr. Rudolph J. Schiffman of St. Paul, the *Baby* of Bronson and Folsom Towing Company, and the *Edwin C* of the St. Croix Timber Company. All had been scheduled for overhauling during the cold months. In mid-January, work was quickly finished, and the boats were launched. Normally launching would wait until spring. However, Stillwater was building a park on the levee. The new retaining wall was completed almost to the place where the boats were stored, so they had to go into the water, winter or no.

On February 2, 1875, a most unusual sight greeted citizens of Stillwater. The following, reprinted from the *Gazette*, records the incident:

> It is seldom that we see a steamer sailing through our streets in mid-winter, but that sort of spectacle dawned upon the crowd yesterday when the hull of the steamer *Swallow* came careening gaily up Chestnut Street drawn on several sleds by several horses. At the junction of Chestnut and Main this cumbersome and somewhat vast equipage halted. It isn't in the nature of a steamboat which is acknowledged to be 85 feet in length to sail along the streets of a densely populated metropolis, and make all the zigzags with the utmost ease and fluency. Consequently, all the teams and men, as well as the hastily-congregated gamins and other fellows, decided that a halt was in order.
>
> There was a brisk snow storm prevailing at that time, but people accumulated faster on that corner than the snow did. Everybody had a different plan for making a successful riffle, but the engineer was possessed with an idea that he was entitled to say. And the word "go" was given by the engineer, and the vast cavalcade hawed ship down the main street. They obeyed orders so literally that Gatchell's nigh horse was drawn under the projecting bow of the oncoming boat, and crushed down by its resistless force.
>
> Hundreds of wierd shouts rent the air. There was another brief halt while the prostrate horse was extricated.

Happily, the horse was not hurt. The *Swallow* was then moved to the St. Paul, Stillwater, and Taylors Falls railroad, and loaded on a flat car. She was taken to Breckenridge, Minnesota. According to the St. Paul *Dispatch*, "It is the first instance, in Minnesota at least, of transporting a steamboat bodily by rail." The stern-wheeler *Swallow*

The *Aquila* at Wabasha, Minnesota, on January 2, 1932. An open winter allowed the towboat to continue in service most of that year. Master of the boat was William G. Peters; captain was William Henning; engineer, Milt Roundy; mate, Edd Hudson; fireman, Ben Ogaly; cook, J. T. Hudson; and deck hand, Henry Sachpell. (Courtesy of the Washington County Historical Society)

belonged to Capt. Josiah Staples. During 1871 and 1872, Joe Perro was the pilot. For two years, the *Swallow* ran between Stillwater and Taylors Falls. It was one of the boats which took part in the "Battle of the Piles." The *Swallow* had been sold the preceding fall to parties who planned to use her on the Red River.

In late April 1875, the *Swallow* was at the levee in Breckenridge, and was scheduled to leave on April 30 for her first trip to Fort Garry. No trip, surely, was as sensational as the one she made through Stillwater in a snowstorm.

Every once in a while, freak warm spells turned winter into summer on the St. Croix. Once such season was the winter of 1870. On December 2, a week and a half after the 120-foot stern-wheeler *Wyman X. Folsom* was put into winter quarters, the idea was born to celebrate Captain Wyman's twenty-sixth birthday with a cruise. A crew was assembled. The *Wyman X* was brought back into service. More than two hundred excursionists started from the upper levee at the head of the Dalles. They took on Captain Folsom's model barge and passengers at the Chisago Mills landing at Taylors Falls. They stopped for another group at Franconia. At Osceola Mills, the levee was crowded with gay and happy people who joined the excursion. Marine Mills, too, contributed its share of passengers.

During the trip to Stillwater, valley bigwigs pontificated on the mildness of St. Croix Valley winter weather. Passengers stood on the hurricane deck without overcoats. At Stillwater, the Cornet Band joined the *Wyman X* and its barge to furnish music for dancing and to lead group singing. The *Wyman X* steamed up and down the lake near Stillwater. The boat started its return trip to Taylors Falls at 5:00 p.m.

Another mild winter was that of 1877-78. The river was virtually free of ice. Several excursions were run both on the Mississippi and between the ports of Stillwater and Taylors Falls on the St. Croix. On Christmas Day 1877, and again on New Year's Day, the sidewheeler *Aunt Betsey* and the Osceola-built *Maggie Reaney* carried passengers for a water cruise from Jackson Street levee in St. Paul for the benefit of the Orphan Asylum.

A shipment of flour was made by boat from Osceola to Stillwater on Christmas Day, 1877.

On December 28, the 165-foot *Ida Fulton* carried an excursion to the Dalles of the St. Croix from Stillwater. On board were a crew of ten men and sixty-five passengers. The boat left at 10:00 a.m. while a large party was on hand to see the excursionists off with a great waving of handkerchiefs. Some of the ladies carried straw fans and parasols. Some of the men wore pantaloons, linen dusters, and straw hats. The *Ida Fulton* returned to Stillwater the following morning. (The *Fulton* was later dismantled at Dubuque. Her engines were put into the new boat *Glenmont*.)

On New Year's Day, the freak weather ceased. A boat started down the St. Croix from Stillwater, again with several men wearing linen dusters and straw hats. It turned very cold and the boat returned to town, having gone no more than a mile or two down the lake. King Winter returned to close the river once again.

Chapter 16

High Water, Low Water

Even today, with all the flood control, diking, and system of dams along the upper Mississippi and its tributaries, the St. Croix River is subject to seasonal highs and lows. In years of heavy snowfall, the St. Croix floods its banks. In years of little spring melt and lack of rain, the waters drop to reveal snags, deadheads, and especially sand bars. Both high water and low provided special challenges for the steamboat men in years past.

Typically, hot dry spells in July and August lowered the level of the river, exposing sandbars, and draining the channel. Boats were delayed, sometimes for days, waiting for rain and a rising river.

James W. Goodhue, Minnesota's first newspaper editor of the *Minnesota Pioneer*, was on an excursion in August 1849. He boarded the 158-ton side-wheeler *Highland Mary* in St. Louis. Later, after leaving Stillwater for Taylors Falls, the boat made its scheduled stop at Marine Mills. Shortly after leaving Marine landing, the boat ground to a halt on the Marine bar. Passengers helped the crew unload the boat, which included 11,500 bushels of Indian corn. Freight was transferred to a flat boat in pouring rain. When freed, the *Highland Mary* headed back downstream.

Shortly thereafter, Dick McLagen's boat stuck fast on a bar at Osceola. In spite of efforts to extricate the craft, it remained there for seven days. McLagen threatened to lay claim to the land, but said it was mighty poor soil.

By contrast, due to heavy snows on the upper St. Croix, and long rains in the spring and summer of 1850, a great flood occurred. In those years, Main Street in Stillwater was about ten feet lower than it is today, so the heart of the city was inundated.

On a warm June day, the side-wheel steamer *Lamartine* brought an excursion party up the St. Croix. It stopped at Stillwater, where some of the local people boarded the boat. The excursion continued north to the Apple River. Because of high water, the *Lamartine* was able to ascend that stream. Later in the day, when the boat returned to Stillwater, passengers found the levee there completely submerged.

The steamer sailed right into town. It crossed Main Street half a block south of Chestnut where the water was about five feet deep. It maneuvered close to the corner of the Minnesota House. The crew ran out the gang plank, and passengers walked into the hotel without getting their feet wet.

The *Anthony Wayne* landed passengers on a platform in front of the Minnesota House, 200 yards inland from the normal shoreline of the river.

In Hudson, J. D. Putman owned the Hudson Hotel, located at First and Buckeye streets. During high water, river boats regularly docked at its porch. Once, an over-eager steamer rammed the building and knocked the porch off.

The *Blackhawk*, first of three steamers to carry the name, was 130 feet long, "handsome, neat, and safe." The boat went up the St. Croix in 1852 and stuck on sand bars a dozen times. There was a delay of several hours at each grounding. The packet had to be maneuvered off the bars by sending out a boat with men and ropes. The ropes were tied around trees to haul the *Blackhawk* over the bars.

Not just the St. Croix suffered during the dry spells. The whole Mississippi River system was affected. In 1860 there was little river traffic anywhere in the upper Midwest. Low water prevented boats from ascending the Keokuk Rapids.

That August, the *H. S. Allen* was stranded on the Arcola bar three miles above Stillwater. The crew dug a channel through the sand bar with six yoke of cattle and heavy plows.

The years of 1863 and 1864 were also times of extremely low water. Travel was very difficult for steamboats. Capt. Oscar Knapp complained, "The legislature should pass an act prohibiting the use of water in the channel to catfish. A good-sized pickerel, lying crosswise in the channel, interrupts navigation." Boats were reported leaving a trail of dust behind them. If caught on a sand bar, they had to wait for the morning dew to get off.

For one week in August 1863, river traffic stopped altogether. The next year, from early June until the end of July, only one boat, the *Enterprise*, traversed the St. Croix. Needed freight was transported by bateaux. Eventually, Capt. H. H. Herrick, piloting the *Spray*, a very light draft side-wheel boat from La Crosse, made regular trips until the close of the 1864 navigation season.

Capt. E. W. Durant piloted the stern-wheeler *Alone* in 1863. (The first owner of the boat said his wife ran away, and left him *Alone*.) The boat drew 20 inches of water. That summer, the capricious St. Croix was so low that Durant had to employ a yoke of four oxen to pull the boat over the Willow River bar at Hudson.

The following year, an excursion packet left Stillwater in mid-June carrying a group of people to Taylors Falls to see a circus. When they arrived, they discovered that, because of low water, the circus had been prevented from making the trip upriver. It was performing instead at Hudson.

The *Mike Davis* was a 105-foot steamer used as an excursion boat and for government work. In June 1891, the craft was left on the bottom of the river at Taylors Falls because of the closing of the gates of the Nevers Dam, which stopped the flow of water. This was not the first time the *Mike* was grounded by the dam. Her captain, George Hayes, said, "This dam is a terrible nuisance to steam navigation, managed as it is."

The levee at Stillwater was also a victim of high waters. Built in 1858, it was made of stone, earth, and logs. According to the Stillwater *Gazette* of January 15, 1879, "the stone was to be taken from lots purchased from Socrates Nelson and from Second Street in front of said property. The earth was to be taken from Third Street north of and near Myrtle Street. It wasn't so stated, but it was tacitly understood that the contractor should steal the logs as a matter of course." The levee was built some 230 feet east of Main Street. Cost was $10,000. In spring, the floods came. Water rose higher than it had ever risen before. The sandy portion of the levee began to wash away. Logs loosened, and one by one, floated away. Many of them were corralled by quick-thinking entrepreneurs, and sold at reduced rates.

In the mid-1870s, the Mississippi was so low that steamboats brought goods to Stillwater for transport to Minneapolis and St. Paul by rail. That was cheaper and quicker than to try to run the sand bars in the Mississippi.

The *Helen Mar* had taken three weeks to get to the lower rapids on the Mississippi in October, one of the longest passages on record. With such slow going it was doubtful that the *Helen* could reach St. Louis and return before the St. Croix froze over. Low water in fall was a constant concern to steamboat captains. They did not want to be caught at freeze-up time. Some years, rather than risk being frozen in, they stayed below and didn't deliver adequate winter stores to settlers along the river.

In mid-August 1900, the stern-wheel paddle-wheeler *Lotus Lily*, then belonging to Capt. Oscar Knapp, was the only boat that reached Taylors Falls. It was hung up for several days on the Marine sand bar. It probably would have remained longer, but rain swelled the stream to float the boat off. A few years later, the *Lotus Lily* sank to the bottom below the Hudson bridge. That year, the water was so deep that none of the boat was visible. Capt. Henry C. Doughty of Prescott said he would raise the *Lotus Lily* with the *Purchase* when waters receded enough to show the boat's exact location.

After a dry spring of low waters in 1905, the rains came. Captain Doughty said there was plenty of water, and there would be no trouble in taking the steamer *Purchase* from Stillwater to Taylors Falls.

The following spring, the St. Croix was unusually low. The new steamer *Clyde* and the bow boat *Mary B.* of the Bronson and Folsom fleet arrived on the first trip of the season on May 10. The steamer *Lizzie Gardner* and her bow boat departed with a big tow of lumber. They reported some difficulty because of three new sand bars which had formed in recent years.

As logging continued and lands along the river were denuded of trees, erosion filled in the St. Croix above Stillwater. The channel

The *Ben Hur* tied up on Water Street in Stillwater during the flood of 1891. During spring floods steamboats were sometimes able to discharge their passengers right at the doors of hotels simply by means of a gangplank. The *Ben Hur* sank in 1916 in Louisiana. (Courtesy of Dick Anderson)

The steamer *Lizzie Gardner* of La Crosse and tugboat *Baby* of Stillwater on the levee on the St. Croix. (Courtesy of the Washington County Historical Society)

Two famous old Stillwater rafters—the *Juniata*, built in Winona (on the right), and the *Clyde*, a steel-hulled boat built in Dubuque (on the left). Both belonged to the Bronson Folsom Line and worked out of the St. Croix to the sawmills on the lower river. (Courtesy of the Washington County Historical Society)

become too shallow for steamboats to continue the trip between Stillwater and the Falls. The lower river benefitted when the system of locks and dams was initiated on the Mississippi River during the 1920s and 1930s, and a constant nine-foot channel was maintained by the U.S. Army Corps of Engineers.

In 1978, a modern steamer fell victim to the lure of high water on the St. Croix. Tuesday, June 13, saw the excursion boat *Jubilee I* leave the Stillwater levee and head north. More than 200 passengers were looking forward to a special trip, because high water would allow the stern-wheeler to navigate the narrow channel north of Lake St. Croix. The paddle wheel churned the river to foam as the *Jubilee I* passed Muller Boat Works and the old St. Croix Boom site. Passengers were unwrapping their bag lunches when the boat steamed between piers of the abandoned Wisconsin Railroad bridge. Lunches were forgotten as the boat glided under the High Bridge for a spectacular view of that remarkable structure.

As the river became shallower, Capt. A. Carr Griffith enlisted the aid of people on two pontoon boats to sound the depth of the river to insure safe passage of the *Jubilee*. Although the paddle-wheeler scraped on sand in one place, it plowed ahead, and safely crossed the Arcola sand bar.

Steamers *Lizzie Gardner*, *Juniata*, and *Clyde*, tied up at the levee at Stillwater during the rafting days. Steamers *Clyde* and *Juniata* belonged to the Bronson Folsom Line, one of the best known rafting firms on the upper rivers. The small boat to the right is the tugboat *Baby*, built by George Muller, also of the Bronson Folsom Line. The *Baby* was used to tow log rafts from the St. Croix Boom to the various rafting grounds and sawmills that lined the St. Croix Lake for a distance of nine miles. The *Juniata* was built in Winona; the *Clyde*, a steel-hulled boat, was built in Dubuque. The *Baby* originated in Stillwater. (Courtesy of the Washington County Historical Society)

A short distance beyond the bar, the *Jubilee I* turned around for the return trip to Stillwater. Moments later, she was stuck fast on the infamous sand bar.

From then until 11:00 p.m., efforts were made to release the boat from the sandy trap. The two stern wheels were run forward and back, then in opposite directions in an attempt to fishtail out of the sand. A power boat offered assistance. First it sped by close to the *Jubilee* in the hope that the waves would float the boat. Later, the power boat tied up alongside, and revved its motors in an attempt to churn away sand from under the bow of the vessel.

As daylight faded, small pleasure craft arrived to evacuate passengers from the *Jubilee*. The last of them left the boat about 11:00 p.m. The following day, the *Jubilee* was finally towed off the sand bar. Despite the inconvenience to many of the passengers, they retained a special feeling of experiencing firsthand a bit of life on the river as known a century earlier.

The steamer *Kalitan* with the barge *Markatana* at Lowell Park in Stillwater. (Courtesy of the Washington County Historical Society)

Chapter 17

Good Times While the Boats Ran

For Newsmen

Steamboat news was regularly covered in the press. The Taylors Falls *Reporter*, a newspaper first published in 1860 by Frank H. Pratt, carried stories about the boats, crews, passengers, and freight. Accidents and schedules were written up, as were news items about the launching of new boats, and the sinkings, explorations, and sales of the old. In return, crewmen brought downriver newspapers to the editor, enabling him to have the latest outside news, often before exchange newspapers reached him through the mails.

The Stillwater *Gazette* for many years carried a column of river news, listing boats arriving and departing from the levee, and the cargo they carried. Many of the items in this chapter were gleaned from steamboating columns in newspapers.

For Gamblers

The image of the Mississippi River gambler was pretty much confined to the lower reaches of the Father of Waters. There was not much gambling on the upper river. However, there were reports that the stern-wheel passenger packet *Fanny Harris*, which plied the St. Croix as well as the Mississippi, was frequented by a gambling quartet—Bill Mallen, Bill and Sam Dove, and Napoleon Bonaparte "Boney" Trader. These men did their best to separate other travelers from their money.

Usually the gamblers went on board in pairs, but separately, pretending not to know each other. Of course, they worked together in the "friendly" game that happened to start. After the stakes were won and split, one of the pair went ashore at Prescott, Hastings, or

Stillwater, while the other went on to St. Paul—until time for their next scam.

The gamblers assumed different roles each time they traveled. They dressed, talked, and acted the parts of Indian agents, merchants, lumbermen, or settlers to con their victims. They relied on marked cards to guarantee their good luck.

For Excursionists

Even in the early years of steamboating on the St. Croix, people from the east came to "explore" the frontier states. In August 1852, Mrs. Elizabeth Ellet, author of "Summer Rambles in the West," traveled up the St. Croix on the 30-stateroom side-wheeler *Blackhawk*. At Marine, the well-known writer of the day was joined by a group of ladies for the remainder of the trip to Taylors Falls.

Fourth of July in 1859 was a 24-hour celebration at Stillwater. The customary morning parade was just ending when a cannon blast announced the arrival of the steamer *Itasca*. She bore celebrants from St. Paul and other points along the Mississippi River.

The steamer *Gracie Kent* at Millville, Louisianna, January 9, 1898. Built by George Muller at Stillwater in 1896-97 for the Interstate Navigation Company. (Courtesy of the Washington County Historical Society)

An 1898 handbill advertising the steamer *Henrietta* which cruised "between St. Paul and all points of interest or attraction on the Mississippi, Minnesota and St. Croix rivers." (Courtesy of the Stillwater *Gazette*)

The *Henrietta*, a steamboat owned by Captain and Mrs. Edward White Durant. It was named for Mrs. Durant. In 1872, Captain Durant became a partner in Durant, Wheeler and Company, dealers in lumber. (Courtesy of Jim Johnson)

Once the boat docked and the passengers disembarked, tumblers of the Turner Society performed. The German Singing Society presented a program. Members of the military marched. Finally, "the multitude adjourned to the armory for a cold supper. In the evening, a ball was held at the Sawyer House. The nightlong celebration was interrupted only by the whistle and bell of the impatient steamer *Itasca*, calling her guests for a return trip home."

One show that was seen by hundreds and hundreds of people was P. A. Older's Museum, Circus, and Menagerie. Setting up first in St. Paul, then in Stillwater, the circus carried the famed Cardiff Giant. The mammoth stone statue, touted as a petrified human, was over 10 feet and weighed 2,990 pounds. Actually, the Cardiff Giant was made in Chicago from Iowa gypsum. The show was well worth the price of admission, for it also contained a living horned horse, and a "wild, uncouth sea cow."

Seven years later, residents of Osceola and Marine boarded the 148-ton stern-wheeler *Maggie Reany* en route to Stillwater. The attraction that June day was W. W. Coles' Great New York and New Orleans Circus, Menagerie, Museum, and Congress of Living Wonders.

Although in the 1890s, steamboating was winding down as a profitable business, there were pleasure boats on the river. In June 1897, the 110-foot *Gracie Kent* made an excursion to Taylors Falls under the sponsorship of the Marine Mills Cornet Band. A week later, in 96-degree heat, the steamer took a large crowd from upriver villages to attend the Barnum and Bailey Circus, which was playing in Stillwater. The street parade was said to be "the most brilliant pageant of the kind ever seen here." The next month, the *Gracie Kent* carried an excursion as a benefit for a crippled Marine child.

In 1898, a ten-coach train brought an excursion from Minneapolis to the St. Croix Valley. The train went to Otisville, and at Log House Landing, 400 excursionists boarded the 110-foot stern-wheel towboat *Park Bluff* for a trip to Taylors Falls.

A Stillwater dancing party chartered the 110-foot stern-wheel rafter *Pauline* in June 1899. After a thorough overhauling and remodeling, William Sauntry's *Pauline* presented a "decidedly noble appearance." The steamer left the Stillwater levee at 8:30 p.m., headed for a ball at the Marine Village Hall. The passengers must have enjoyed themselves, for they didn't begin the return trip from Marine until 4:00 a.m.

One of the biggest and best-equipped boats ever to run on the St. Croix was the *Lora*, designed by Capt. John A. Kent. On October 3, 1900, the *Lora* carried a large party of excursionists from Taylors Falls to Stillwater to hear one of the great orators of the day. Campaigning for the second time against President William McKinley was Democratic political leader and presidential aspirant William Jennings Bryant. The paddleboat stopped at Marine to take on passengers, who paid fifty cents for the round trip. At Stillwater the passengers stayed on board the *Lora* to hear Bryant expound for an hour on "Republic Not Empire," and "Equal Rights to All."

Shortly after the turn of the century, a Scandinavian organization in Hudson sponsored an excursion to Red Wing. About 600 people boarded the boat, which had a dance barge tied alongside. The morning was calm and delightful. After lunch, however, a terrific storm of almost tornado force developed. Five-foot waves threatened the boiler room. The boat creaked and moaned. The captain maneuvered the boat alongside a steep bank, out of the storm's reach, and the boat and barge both survived.

Perhaps the biggest of any excursion ever on the St. Croix took place during the first week of June 1901. Twenty-eight coaches of the Soo Line Railroad brought some 2,000 railroad conductors to St. Croix Falls from a convention being held in St. Paul. After spending a few hours touring the Interstate Park at Taylors Falls, about 2,000 men crowded onto two steamboats, William Sauntry's *Columbia* and the *Lora*, and traveled to Stillwater. This was ironic, for the railroads were the main reason for the demise of steamboating.

A thousand men, women, and children enjoyed the Retail Grocers' excursion on the St. Croix in July 1905. The excursionists aboard the steamer *Purchase* and its barge the *Twin Cities* were unable to get beyond Log House Landing at Otisville because of low water. Many families went ashore and ate lunch, and had their program of athletic sports. The *Purchase* was owned by Capt. E. C. Anthony of Hastings. The steamer, earlier known as the *Mountain Belle,* had run to St. Louis during the World's Fair, towing a passenger barge.

One of the first excursions of the 1906 season was held on Sunday, May 13, aboard the *Purchase*. The *Purchase* made only one more excursion to Taylors Falls. That was in 1914, when the boat and its

The *Pauline* was built in Stillwater in 1879 for the rafting firm of Durant, Wheeler and Company. This famous rafting concern operated steamboats out of Stillwater for many years between the St. Croix and points on the river to St. Louis. Many of the best known steamboats on the St. Croix were built by the boat building works at Stillwater. (Courtesy of the Washington County Historical Society)

barge carried 800 passengers. Loaded to capacity, the *Purchase* failed to stop at Marine, where a number of passengers waited to board the boat for the trip to Taylors Falls. Other smaller passenger boats bypassed the village that day too, all loaded to capacity.

St. Paul columnist and cartoonist Frank Wing took a trip on George Muller's stern-wheeler *Olive S.* in August 1917. With Capt. James T. Teare at the wheel, the boat made the journey from Stillwater to Taylors Falls.

Even though the river became unnavigable above Arcola for steamboats, excursions were held in the lower reaches of the river. In 1914, a company of 1,100 people, young and old, arrived at Lowell Park in Stillwater at 2:00 p.m. June 11. Under the auspices of the Potter Association from Red Wing, the excursion was aboard the steamer *G. W. Hill.*

Two weeks later, members of the Elks Club of Hudson made an excursion to Red Wing. Stillwater Elks and their families had been invited to join the party.

A pleasure boat which docked at the Stillwater levee during the 1920s was the showboat *Goldenrod*. Actually, the craft was more of a barge, which was towed to Stillwater by the steamer *Crown Hill.* The *Goldenrod* burned at the St. Louis waterfront June 1, 1962.

The excursion steamer *J. S.* made trips on the St. Croix during

The steamer *Purchase*, a rafter rebuilt by Swain, shown here on the St. Croix taking W. H. Pankonin's Excursion from Stillwater to Taylor's Falls. (Courtesy of the Washington County Historical Society)

The excursion boat *Sidney* seen from the St. Croix River at Stillwater, 1913. (Courtesy of the Washington County Historical Society)

The steamer *Crown Hill* with the barge *Goldenrod*. They came to Stillwater on September 23, 1926. This floating theater visited the cities along the rivers and gave shows. (Courtesy of the Washington County Historical Society)

the 1920s. It, too, burned, and was replaced by the largest boat ever to dock at Stillwater up to that time. The boat was operated by the Strekfus line out of St. Louis—the steamer *Capitol*.

The steamer *Capitol,* one of the largest boats on the upper river and the largest of any type at Stillwater, June 12, 1931. The *Capitol* had a capacity of 2,500 passengers and was one of many excursion boats operated by the Streckfus Line of St. Louis. It traveled as far north as Stillwater and down to New Orleans in the south. (Courtesy of the Washington County Historical Society, top; bottom, Jim Johnson)

Chapter 18

Bad Times

Cholera on the River

Many happenings affected steamboating on the St. Croix. Whims of nature, of the gods, and of man himself shaped and molded what should have been a routine way of life.

In 1849 a cholera epidemic swept through the whole Mississippi River Valley. Popular Capt. John Atchison of the *Highland Mary* died suddenly on his boat of cholera at the landing at St. Louis. Boats on the St. Croix were hit by the disease. Tar and sulfur were burned to purify the air in an effort to keep the epidemic from spreading.

Disputes

At one time, the St. Croix River was involved in a dispute between St. Paul and Minneapolis for the use of the Mississippi between the Falls of St. Anthony and Fort Snelling.

Minneapolitans believed that the river could be navigated to the Falls in spite of the fact that it was shallow and very rocky. In 1850 the two communities of Minneapolis and St. Anthony embarked on a crusade to snatch from St. Paul its position as head of Mississippi travel.

One of the ways in which businessmen hoped to induce steamboats to travel beyond St. Paul was to form a company to run boats from falls to falls—those of the St. Croix to those of St. Anthony. Of course, several Stillwater businessmen believed this was a good investment. They hoped to use shallow draft boats, such as those that navigated the St. Croix, to maneuver through the shallows near St. Anthony. Despite much planning and sizable investments, the service did not materialize.

Showboat Problems

During the summer 1852, the showboats *Banjo* and *James Raymond* brought an exhibition by Spaulding and Rogers to the city of Stillwater. The steamers tied up at the lower levee. Many young men were anxious to see the play. They were out of money because they had not been paid by the mills. Some brought bundles of shingles, which were accepted as admission. Others were not admitted, and became angry. Just at the close of the program, there was a demonstration on shore by the disgruntled young men. Stones and other convenient missiles were thrown at the boats. The men on board responded with musket and rifle shots. Fortunately, no one was injured. You can well imagine that the departing crowd left the levee without delay.

A similar incident occurred in Stillwater one summer day in the 1860s. A showboat pulled up to the levee. Many local citizens went on board to see the play. On shore were men who did not have the required admission. When they attempted to board the boat, they were met with strong resistance. Angry at being refused, the men started throwing rocks. The captain gave orders for the boat to back out into the river. It did, with Stillwater residents still on board. The boat refused to return to the levee. At length, skiffs and bateaux were sent out to rescue the Stillwaterites. And no one saw the show.

Showboats returned in other years without incident. The *Banjo* brought the Ned Davis Minstrels to the St. Croix in 1857. In June the following year, the *Banjo* and the *James Raymond* arrived with calliope playing. The circus had come to the Valley. The Twin boats presented afternoon and evening performances of the Great Monkey Circus and the Burlesque Dramatic Troupe in the audience chamber, which seated 800 people. When the circus moved to Hudson, a banker in that city paid the admission for the whole village with the currency of the day—pine shingles.

Wedding Delays

May 22, 1855, was to be the wedding day of William Kent and Ellen Kidder, and of Isaac Freeland and Agnes Kent of Osceola. The Rev. T. M. Fullerton of Stillwater was invited to perform the ceremony. When he didn't show up, the suggestion was made that the ceremony be postponed. That idea was voted down, and a justice of the peace was called to marry the couples. Fullerton finally arrived, just in time to make the closing prayer. The steamboat on which Fullerton had traveled was late because it had been hung up on a sand bar.

Mechanical Difficulties

Spring came early in 1858. Capt. Asa B. Green of the *Equator* planned a grand excursion on March 29. He had an ulterior motive. He was competing with the *H. S. Allen* for the business of St. Croix

Valley residents. At any rate, 200 guests accepted Captain Green's invitation for the trip. Music and refreshments were provided. The crowd was in high spirits. Enthusiasm was dampened when a careless deckhand fell overboard, and was lost despite an hour's fruitless search. After the delay, the excursion continued. Early in the afternoon, just above Marine Mills, the engine broke down, and the boat was stranded in midstream. What to do? While some of the passengers worried, others danced. About that time, the rival *H. S. Allen*, on a homeward trip from the Dalles of the St. Croix, rescued most of the passengers and returned them to Stillwater. The *Equator* was repaired, and followed the next day.

The steamer *Ravenna* (top), built in 1888-89 at Stillwater by George Muller for Anderson & O'Brien Lumber Company and equipped with machinery taken from the famous *G. B. Knapp*. It was later owned and operated by Bronson & Folsom. On June 12, 1902, it capsized (bottom) in a cyclone near Dubuque, Iowa, Capt. John Hoy, Byron Trask, Louis Walker and Dell Munson lost their lives in the accident. Ernest Hoy, son of the captain, was in his stateroom, partly dressed, when the storm struck. He found himself in water to his neck but managed to break open a window and crawl up onto the side of the hull. With several others, he clung there 45 minutes before being rescued by the steamer *Teal*. (Courtesy of the Washington County Historical Society)

Bad Weather

Bayard Taylor, world traveler, poet, and lyceum lecturer, spoke at Stillwater in April 1858. His topic was "Life in the North." Sponsors of the lyceum, the St. Paul Young Men's Christian Association, were expecting a huge crowd because the lake had opened early that year, and boats were running. Only 200 people were in the audience because cold and stormy weather held up the steamboats.

On the day of the lecture, the stern-wheeler *Equator*, under Captain Green, left Prescott with more than 300 people on board. As the packet passed Catfish Bar just across from Afton, a storm struck. Because this is a wide stretch of lake, the wind raised a great sea. Forty-mile gale winds and rain struck the boat broadside. The boat crawled into the teeth of a blizzard as rain turned to snow. Water poured across the deck. The engines stopped. They were restarted, and the boat headed north again. It went about three of the twelve miles toward Stillwater when a rod broke, and the paddle wheel stopped. The boat fell off into the seas. The first surge turned her sideways. The second wave struck broadside. Tables had just been set for dinner. The boat rolled. Tables were thrown over. Glass and china smashed. Children screamed. Women fainted. Men turned white and began scrambling and fighting for life preservers.

The mate acted quickly. He fashioned a sea anchor from two spars, and tossed it overboard. The action soon brought the boat around to head into the waves. It took more than an hour to drive the *Equator* stern-first across the lake to the shore above Glenmont on the Wisconsin side of the St. Croix. The hull was crushed, and the boat foundered. Captain Green and his crew removed the terrified passengers. Men carried women and children ashore through four feet of water. Just in time, for the winds then blew the cabin off of the sunken hull, and the boat was a total loss. Fires were built from the wreckage. Runners were sent to farm houses and to Hudson to get help. Many of the men walked to their homes in Prescott and Hastings.

Fear of Attack

Early in August 1862, the *Fred Lorenz* docked at Stillwater levee. Aboard was the the body of Stillwater's own Capt. Gold T. Curtis. He had assembled a full company of the Fifth Regiment, Minnesota Infantry, for service during the Civil War. The troops joined Gen. Henry W. Halleck's Union forces as part of Gen. John Pole's Army of the Mississippi near Corinth. Curtis died on July 24 at St. Louis while en route home on furlough because of ill health.

Later that month, word of the Sioux uprising on the Minnesota River reached St. Croix Valley residents. It was rumored that Hole-in-the-Day, chief of the Chippewa, would join the Sioux to massacre Valley settlers.

All the citizens were jittery. In Osceola, townspeople asked the captain of the steamer *H. S. Allen* to sound his boat whistle loud and clear if he found any evidence along the river of danger from the

Indians. At 2:00 a.m. one August morning, several long, shrill whistle screams startled the entire village out of its sleep. Some of the residents armed themselves to resist the expected Indian attack. Others packed their belongings and got ready to run. Later it was discovered that the commotion was caused not by the *H. S. Allen*, but by the steamer *Enterprise*. The captain blew his boat whistle as a well-meant courteous greeting to the city, even at 2:00 a.m.

Sometimes the best-laid plans went awry. A delightful excursion was planned for the latter part of May 1872. Some forty ladies and gentlemen, including the Stillwater band, left town at 1:00 p.m. on the steamer *Helen Mar*, with Capt. William Kent at the helm. The group was taking a trip to Prescott. They stopped at Hudson briefly, then continued downstream.

About eight miles below Hudson, something happened to the furnace. The steam was shut off and the big paddle wheel stopped turning. Helmsman David Swain had his hand still on the throttle. In a bold voice, he said, "I'll hold her nozzel agin' the bank till the last gallot's ashore."

Swain nosed the *Helen Mar* to the bank. A gang plank was shoved out. Many of the passengers went ashore, but quite a number of the men remained on board. At length the fire in the furnace was quenched, and it was determined that the damage was not too serious. The boiler was repaired.

While all this was going on, the passengers were stranded on shore for four hours. According to a report in the Stillwater *Gazette* of that time, they "walked along the shore, gathered bouquets, talked politics and other kinds of nonsense."

Shortly after 6:00 p.m., the *Helen Mar* steamed away for Prescott. After a short visit in that city, the group returned to Stillwater, making the return trip in three hours and fifteen minutes, without further incident.

Pirates

The steamboat *Henrietta*, which appeared on the St. Croix during the summer of 1854, was a piratical craft, a terror to people along the river. (She is not to be confused with another *Henrietta*, a most reputable boat, which appeared on the river at a later date.) This early steamer had a crew of the roughest men, engaged mainly for their fighting ability. The boat bought supplies in various ports, then left without paying. Needless to say, it was not a popular vessel. The crew fought with sheriffs and constables who tried to collect the bad debts.

S. S. Denton, who was once a passenger on the *Henrietta*, said that at McGregor, Iowa, a sheriff came on board to serve a writ of attachment. A crew member struck the lawman with a stick of cord wood, knocking him senseless. The boat set sail, with the wounded sheriff on board. The *Henrietta* made a landing a few miles below the city, deposited the sheriff, and sailed away.

The pirate craft was indebted to dealers and merchants in nearly every port between St. Paul and St. Louis. Officers in St. Paul were alerted to the situation. They awaited the arrival of the guerilla craft, armed with legal writs. When they failed in their purpose, Rensselaer R. Nelson, a young, aspiring attorney in St. Paul, was employed to follow the *Henrietta* to Stillwater and collect the debts. Nelson enlisted the help of Washington County Sheriff A. B. Green. The men were at the city levee in Stillwater when the boat landed. Papers were served by Deputy Fred Curtis. Deputy Michael Kilty was at the snubbing post, with strict orders to "hold the fort." The pirate crew decided to set sail to avoid being served the writs. In trying to convince Kilty to cast off the line, someone threw a rock, which hit him in the head. He sank down, but the line remained on the post. The boat backed off, in the hope that the line would break. When it didn't, one of the *Henrietta*'s crew cut the big rope. The line was hauled in, and became the property of the attorney, who later became Judge Rensselaer R. Nelson. The rope was the first fee he collected in Minnesota.

Later, Curtis recalled that a number of citizens were attracted to the waterfront when the *Henrietta* docked. The levee had just been covered with broken rock. As Curtis was stoned, he held to his post because he thought he had a lot of backers, "good husky stalwart fellows" who agreed to help him. When the crew rushed ashore and attacked him, he knocked down a few of the boat crew. However, when pressed by overwhelming numbers, Curtis deceded to retreat. When he turned around, he found himself all alone. All his "stalwart" backers had vanished.

Accidents

No serious steamboat accidents were reported on the St. Croix. Usually there were problems with machinery on the boats. Most of the deaths were drownings.

In October 1868, the stern-wheel packet *Pioneer*, built in Osceola, broke her shaft above Stillwater and had to be towed to the Osceola levee by the *G. B. Knapp*. The extra load was too much for the *Knapp*. A cylinder exploded, sending the pitman from its fastenings into the river. Luckily, no one was hurt. After Capt. Oscar Knapp cleaned up the wreck, he took the steamboat to Taylors Falls on one engine.

That same month, officers of the *Nellie Kent* tried in vain to save a drunken passenger who fell overboard. Later that year, in May 1873, Minnesota State Senator Jonas Lindell fell off the *Knapp* and drowned. It was around midnight and the Senator was helping to work an oar on the bow when the oar turned quickly and threw him into the river. Searchers were unable to locate him in the dark.

On Saturday, September 25, 1875, the stern-wheel rafter *Mark Bradley*, built in Prescott in 1872, had a narrow escape from destruction by fire. The companionway leading to the forward part of the saloon deck caught fire from an ash pan fronting the boilers. Two men and three women on board succeeded in arresting the blaze, but not before the companionway was destroyed.

The *G. B. Knapp* hit a snag going down river near the lime kiln south of Osceola early in August 1880. The deadhead knocked a hole in her bow, which caused her hold to fill with water. The boat sank. In only four weeks, the damage was repaired and the boat was back in service. A year later, the Knapp ran into rocks while towing a large barge loaded with lumber. The barge was wrecked and the lumber just floated away.

On May 15, 1881, two men fell off an excursion barge towed by the Knapp. The steamer was returning from an upriver trip, when she struck the rock at Cedar Bend, below Osceola. As she rounded Slough Island heading down river, the wind and current forced first the barge, then the boat into the rocks on the Wisconsin shore. Two passengers, Ole Opsahl and Jacob Jacobi, were sitting on the edge of the barge. The impact threw them into the river. A small child also fell off, but was saved. No one placed the blame on the boat's officer. However, the license of Capt. Marcus Thompson was revoked because the Knapp at the time of the accident was carrying only one lifeboat.

In 1884, the Osceola-built Cleon blew out the throttle valve, which damaged the cabin and the piano. Two years later, an explosion on the Cleon severely injured a deck hand. The head of the steam capstan burst, and a piece of metal weighing about twenty-five pounds hit the deck hand in the stomach. The Cleon took the injured man to Osceola immediately. Dr. H. E. Combacker was called to attend him.

In June of 1886, a huge log jam occurred at Taylors Falls. Two steamboats, along with two engines, several teams of horses, and over 200 men, were employed in efforts to break the jam. Six weeks elapsed before it was broken.

Victim of one of the frequent steamboat mishaps, the *Abner Gile* lies on its side near the main channel of the river. (Courtesy of Jim Johnson)

The steamer *Red Wing* and a barge taking out a passenger excursion on the St. Croix from the levee at Stillwater. The small launch in the foreground was the boat of John Jeremy, noted character "Fisherman John," an old riverman who made a national reputation as a finder of drowned bodies. He had a mysterious method of recovering drowned persons that succeeded when all other methods failed. (Courtesy of the Washington County Historical Society)

The pile driver *Arcola* was passing Marine Mills on June 29, 1897. Waves from the boat washed a little girl off a plank on the levee. The child drowned.

During the years of steamboating on the St. Croix, many boats were struck by lightning, but few burned as a result. The electrical bolt was diffused through the iron of the boilers and machinery, and escaped into the river through the water wheel shafts.

Chapter 19

End of an Era

Although the railroads became a threat to steamboats during the 1870s, there still was plenty of activity on the St. Croix during that decade.

In 1872, the steamer *Dowler's Humbug*, a nondescript craft, docked at the lower levee in Stillwater. The landing, known as "Nelson's Point," was located near Butler and Gray's warehouse. The levee above the city, located near the present-day Soo Line bridge, was called "Titcomb's Landing."

Dowler's Humbug was said to be "a three-cornered, diversified, rectangular, octagon-shaped hexagon with sharp obtuse angles on her sides and a thin-shaped wide prow, gracefully tapered from 1¾ inches at her bow to 16 or 23 feet amidships." Joseph Perro was captain of the odd-shaped craft. Despite her peculiar design, the *Humbug* was "capable of jerking a raft of logs in more directions at a given time than anything else that ever floated."

To celebrate the Fourth of July in 1872, two special excursions took place on the St. Croix. The *May Queen* left Stillwater on July 3 and steamed to Frontenac to see the great regatta held on Lake Pepin. The St. Paul Band was engaged to go along and play for entertainment and dancing. To accommodate dancing, a large barge decorated with evergreen bows was attached to the steamer. Fare for the two-day trip was $2 per person. Another boat, the *Bill Henderson*, made a one-day trip to the regatta. The *Henderson*, a small stern-wheeler packet, ran in the wheat trade between Prescott and Taylors Falls, connecting with trains to Stillwater.

River news in 1873 told that Captain Joseph Perro had left the area in March for Le Claire. There he would fit up the tow boat *Moonstone* for the summer trade. This boat would replace the *Pioneer* which had outlived her usefulness. The *Pioneer* had been brought to the Osceola levee in November 1872 to be rebuilt. By January,

Captain David B. Hayes decided that the project was too expensive. He had the machinery removed and sold. It was taken to Breckenridge, Minnesota, where it was installed in a steamboat built to run on the Red River of the North. The hull of the *Pioneer* lay on the Osceola levee for a year longer, then was made into a boat for hauling wood.

The Matt Clark Company was one of the largest transportation firms engaged in rafting logs down the St. Croix. The company employed as many as 150 men during the season. It operated seven boats: the *J. K. Graves, David Bronson, Isaac Staples, Menominee, Evansville, Jennie Hayes,* and *Bun Hersey.* (Note: the *Bun Hersey* and the *B. Hershey* were two different boats.) The first six boats took rafts all the way to their destinations on the Mississippi, some as far south as Dubuque, Iowa, which was a principal market for logs. Towing a raft, the steamboats took as long as a week to make the trip. Some kind of record was made by the *Isaac Staples* working together with the *George S.* in 1904. They towed a raft of logs and lumber cut by the East Side Lumber Company to Dubuque in four days' time. The return trip took just two days.

The *Bun Hersey*, a side-wheeler built in South Stillwater in 1883, was employed in the rafting trade, mainly on Lake St. Croix, although it made a number of trips to Marine Mills and Taylors Falls. One of the last boats in service, it burned at the Stillwater waterfront. Each of the Clark Company steamboats made fifteen to twenty trips every season. They were furnished with electric lights in 1886, which enabled them to run day and night.

The famous steamer *Isaac Staples* of Stillwater. Built by Morgan and used by lumberman Isaac Staples to haul out part of his enormous log output on the St. Croix, the *Staples* was later rebuilt by George Muller for Bronson and Folsom. This photo was taken in 1902. (Courtesy of the Washington County Historical Society)

Harper and Gillespie was another Stillwater boat firm. Among the boats in its fleet was the *Nina*.

Other boats working out of Stillwater were the *Glenmount, J. W. Van Sant* (which was owned by Minnesota governor Samuel R. Van Sant), the *Chauncey Lamb, Eclipse,* and *Frontenac*. The *Penn Wright,* owned and operated by H. L. Peavey of Stillwater, was a raft boat. It, too, burned at Stillwater.

A diminutive boat, the *Nettie,* made its appearance on the run between Prescott and Hastings. The *Nettie* was termed "a marvel of smallness, about as large as a sack of flour."

The *A. T. Jenks* was a stern-wheeler built in Cincinnati in 1880. The boat was 113.6 feet by 22 feet by 3.7 feet. It was built for Durant, Wheeler and Company of Stillwater. James Newcomb of Pepin, Wisconsin, was pilot and captain, with Frank Clemmons of La Crosse as mate. The *Jenks* burned in winter quarters in Stillwater in 1883. It was rebuilt in 1884 as the *Ed Durant Jr.*

The *Blue Goose* did a brisk business along the river in the 1880s, working primarily near the St. Croix Boom north of Stillwater. Known as "the floating palace of sin," the brothel on water served about five hundred men in the area. "They had a hell of a business going up there," said Ralph DuPae, engineer at Northern Engraving in La Crosse. He apparently spoke from first-hand experience. "First they gave you a cake of soap and told you to jump in the river. Afterward, both you and the girl jumped in the river and took a bath," he said.

An end-of-the-year report in 1887 stated that three steamers and twenty-four barges had engaged in freight and passenger traffic on the St. Croix. The steamers had made 141 round trips between Stillwater and Taylors Falls, 75 between Marine and St. Paul, and 20 between Franconia and St. Paul. Fifty-one steamers had engaged in towing logs and lumber on the border river during the year.

The excursion boat *Vernie Mac* was purchased by Captain Jack Kent and other investors of Osceola in 1898. Built in Wabasha, Minnesota, in 1892 by Samuel Peters and Sons for Captain Duncan McKenzie, the *Vernie Mac* was a stern-wheeler, 127 feet by 24 feet with a 20-inch draw. She was first used for the rafting trade. Her new owners had the boat repainted and refitted in first class condition for the St. Croix trade. She made her first trip on April 20, 1898, for the short-lived Interstate Park Navigation Company, composed of H. C. Doughty, H. C. Combacker, C. H. Oakey, and C. W. Staples. The *Vernie Mac* was sold to Anderson Tully towing Company of Memphis, Tennessee, in 1900.

Another excursion steamer on the St. Croix in 1898 was the stern-wheeler *Henrietta*. A poster published by the Rapid Transit Company, over the signature of E. W. Durant, manager, read:

> Excursion Steamer *Henrietta* with her double-decked dancing and observation barge will ply during the summer season of 1898 between St. Paul, and all points of interest or attraction on the Mississippi, Minnesota, and St. Croix rivers.
>
> The Steamer *Henrietta* and barge have been refitted and in a manner that will be appreciated by the public.

The steamer *Purchase* at the Stillwater levee on Lake St. Croix. The tugboat in the foreground is the *Baby*. (Courtesy of the Washington County Historical Society)

Liberal charters will be made to lodges and societies for trips, excursions. I invite inspection of boat and barge to insure your patronage. For further particulars, address E. W. Durant, Stillwater.

Durant and Wheeler had offices on the second floor of the Opera House in Stillwater. The *Henrietta* was named for Captain Druant's wife. The boat had originally been a raft boat, then was changed into an excursion boat. It was the last big steamer to take an excursion to Taylors Falls in 1916. Soon afterward, the *Henrietta* was sold to William MacCraney of Winona, and renamed the *Purchase*. This was the fourth name change for the paddle boat. Originally, it was the *I. E. Staples*, then the *David Bronson*, next the *Henrietta*, and finally the *Purchase*. A few years later, just before the boat was to be put up for the season, it hit a bridge near Winona and sank.

Also owned by Durant and Wheeler was the steamer *Louisville*, operated by Capt. R. J. Wheeler. Subsequently, the steamer was purchased by Knapp, Stout, and Co. of Dubuque, Iowa.

That steamboating was of prime importance on the river is evident by excerpts from the Stillwater *Gazette* during the spring of 1901.

On April 18, "The levee presented an appearance of activity this morning. Steamboats were thick in sight, and during the day others arrived. Five raft boats left yesterday, several today." The *City of Hudson* (originally the *Comet*) was scheduled to serve as bow boat for the *Lizzie Gardner*. The *Lora* had gone to St. Paul to make bookings for excursions, stopping at Hudson to pick up a concert barge.

A few days later it was noted that William Kaiser inaugurated a big log and lumber shipping business with Stillwater as the base of operations. He had a contract with Northern Pacific Railroad to bring in an average of fourteen cars full of lumber daily. The logs came from northern Minnesota, including the Bemidji area. In Stillwater, they were unloaded, then rafted on the St. Croix to be towed down the Mississippi.

On April 28, the *Gazette* editor speculated that the disappearance of the pineries along the St. Croix made it almost impossible to forecast the state of water for the season. Usually a high state of water at the beginning of the season would remain through the rafting season. He predicted that the time was not far distant when high water on the river above Stillwater would be practically unknown. Before they were logged off, the pine forests had held the rains, and prevented the silting-off of the banks into the stream.

The following month, the *Gazette* reported that the *General McKenzie*, a new government snag boat, was on the river. It replaced the *General Barnard*, which went out the previous year. One of the finest rafters, the *Wanderer*, owned by the Lamb Lumber Company, was to be used for pleasure purposes only in the future.

About the turn of the century, the steamers *Baby* and *Edwin C* were seen frequently on the St. Croix. The *Baby* was actually a tug. After the fire of 1904 practically destroyed the old wooden pontoon bridge at Stillwater, the East Side Lumber Company, located on the Wisconsin side of the span, used the *Baby* to haul rafts from the mill to Stillwater, carrying horses and loads of lumber across the river.

In 1906, Capt. Oscar F. Knapp was making plans for regular trips to and from Taylors Falls. The small steamer *Lorene* arrived from Dubuque, Iowa, where she was built for Knapp, and was taken to Osceola. Knapp had operated steamboats on the St. Croix for thirty-five years and knew the river intimately. He had operated the larger steamer *G. B. Knapp* for many years. With his expertise, he designed the *Lorene* for use in low water. The steamer had a draw of only two feet. Captain Knapp ordered a barge built to be used with the *Lorene*, giving a combined capacity of fifty passengers. At first, the craft was used only between Osceola and Taylors Falls. As conditions improved, trips were extended to daily runs between Stillwater and Taylors Falls.

One of the first excursions of the 1906 season was held on Sunday, May 13, aboard the steamer *Purchase*. The boat left the Stillwater levee at 8:30 a.m. In the years since lumbermen denuded the land along the banks of the river, silting had filled in the channel and caused the formation of sand bars. However, Capt. H. C. Doughty found plenty of water in the river due to the melting and runoff. He was able to reach Taylors Falls with no trouble.

The same year, the firm of Bronson and Folsom added two new boats, the steamer *Clyde* and the bow boat *Mary B.* to its fleet. Because

The steamer *Clyde*, best known of all steamboats in the log rafting trade on the St. Croix. The steel hull was built in Dubuque in 1870 for the firm of Ingram and Kennedy. It was later owned by Bronson and Folsom. (Courtesy of the Washington County Historical Society)

of high water, the river was reported excellent for navigation. Still, there were a few bad spots. The wing dam below Osceola was causing some hindrance to navigation. Three sand bars had formed. It was believed that, with dredging, the St. Croix could again be suitable for large steamers even as far north as Taylors Falls.

One of the towboats on the river in the early 1900s was the *Ravenna*. On June 12, 1902, she capsized in a sudden squall near Dubuque. Capt. John Hoy and clerk Bryon Trask drowned in the accident. The boat was raised. In 1906, she was badly damaged in a windstorm on May 21, near Hastings. The boat was going through the bridge with the bow steamer *Bun Hersey* helping with a raft of logs when the wind swept the *Ravenna* against the middle pier of the drawbridge. The guards on the larboard side of the steamer, on the boiler deck, and on the cabin deck were broken. Hull seams opened enough to cause some leakage. The steamer returned to Stillwater for repairs.

The boat *Ben Hur*, under Capt. John T. Smith, took excursions out of Stillwater for several years. In the fall of 1911, the *Ben Hur* was

The steamer *Ben Hur* at Hastings, Minnesota, on the Mississippi River. This boat took excursions out of Stillwater during the summer of 1911 and is shown here on just such a trip. The captain was John T. Smith. In the fall of 1911 the boat was taken to New Orleans and sold to a packet firm where she remained in service until 1914 when she sank after backing into a piling. One life was lost. (Courtesy of the Washington County Historical Society)

End of an Era / 139

This is the first boat to carry the name *Polly* (top). It summered on the St. Croix and Mississippi and wintered in the south. Nicknamed "The Candy Boat," the *Polly* carried a doctor on board as well as vaccines, quinine sulfate, bolts of cloth, and candy for the people in the bayous. In the spring of 1928, this *Polly* (bottom) rested on the shores of the Mississippi near Wabasha, Minnesota. When the river opened, the boat journeyed up the St. Croix to St. Croix Falls with owners Mr. and Mrs. Anderson Gratz of New York and pilot Capt. A. Carr Griffith, now retired, of Marine on St. Croix. On the afterdeck is a Pierce Arrow automobile. (Courtesy of A. Carr Griffith)

taken to New Orleans and sold to a packet company there. She served until 1914, when she sank after backing into a piling, with the loss of one life.

The last Taylors Falls-to-Stillwater passenger boat to operate on the St. Croix was the *Atlantis*. The boat was piloted by its owner, Charles Christensen. It made daily trips to the Falls.

A popular boat on the Mississippi and St. Croix rivers was the *Polly*, known as the *Candy Boat*. The first *Polly* was a stern-wheeler of wooden construction. That was replaced by an all-steel boat, with propellers in tunnels, and constructed with five water-tight compartments for safety. The paddle-boat was 135 feet long with a 21-foot beam. It had a 20-inch draft fully loaded. It was called the "candy boat" because during its winter tour in the south, it delivered red and white peppermint sticks to children in the bayous of Louisiana. They weighed a quarter of a pound each, were wrapped in waxed paper for dry keeping, and aerated for floating. Crew members also gave medicines, magazines, bolts of bright calicoes, books, and aid to all in sickness and distress. During floods, the *Polly* was used to rescue people and animals. After the death of the boat's owner, Anderson Gratz, in 1935, the *Polly* was taken over by the U.S. Army Corps of Engineers. Renamed *Surveyor*, she was used as an inspection boat on the Mississippi and St. Croix. The *Surveyor* was working as late as 1965.

The steamer *Kalitan* with the barge *Markatana* in Lake St. Croix, July 12, 1931. The *Kalitan* and the barge were privately owned and were frequent visitors to Stillwater. (Courtesy of the Washington County Historical Society)

The Army Corps of Engineers operated the *U.S. Wakerobin*, a stern-wheeler, as a snag boat on the Upper Mississippi and St. Croix rivers. The *Wakerobin* was in Stillwater July 1, 1931, for the opening of the interstate bridge.

Small privately-owned pleasure boats began visiting the St. Croix in the 1900s. Among them was the steamer *Kalitan* with the barge *Markatana*. The *North Star*, owned by Dr. Charles Mayo, was seen at the Stillwater levee in the 1920s.

Another pleasure boat which docked at the Stillwater levee was the showboat *Goldenrod*. That craft was more of a barge, and was towed to Stillwater by the steamer *Crown Hill*.

An excursion steamer, the *J. S.*, made trips on the St. Croix in the 1920s. It burned in 1925 and was replaced by the largest boat ever to dock at Stillwater, the steamer *Capitol*. The *Capitol*, operated by the Strekfus line out of St. Louis, had a capacity of 2,500 passengers. The *Capital* continued to make seasonal visits to the St. Croix once or twice a summer through the 1930s.

With the outbreak of World War II, the large pleasure steamboats withdrew from the river. For the next two decades the waters of the St. Croix served as playground for small boats, canoes, motorboats, sailboats, and launches. The heyday of steamboating was ended.

The steamer *Capitol* tied up at the levee at Stillwater, June 12, 1931. A well-known excursion boat, one of the finest on the river, the *Capitol* visited cities from St. Louis to Stillwater. (Courtesy of the Washington County Historical Society)

A Capitol Excursion

On August 31, 1921, 377 men, women, and children of the area boarded the *Capitol* for a moonlight excursion down the St. Croix River with Hudson as their destination. The trip downriver was splendid. The Catfish Point sand bar was passed safely. Ahead lay a big sand bar near the Northwestern draw bridge. Would that hold up the palatial steamer? No. The passengers breathed more easily when that obstruction was passed.

The *Capitol* continued to the high bridge, and started to swing around for Hudson. A bump. The boat lost momentum, then quit moving altogether. According to a newspaper report of the day, "The powerful engines of the *Capitol* tried time and again to push the vessel off the bar and after several attempts gave up."

Captian Verne Strekfus directed that two ropes, each two and one-half inches thick, be taken ashore and fastened to some piling. The capstan was used to pull the ropes, towing the boat shoreward into deeper water. The scheme worked fine for a little while. Then, without warning, the piling caved in. The maneuver was repeated . . . and repeated.

Finally, after five and one-half hours, the boat was worked off the sand bar, and headed for Hudson, arriving at 2:45 a.m. Sunday morning, almost six hours late. Word of the hangup must have reached Stillwater, for about the time the *Capitol* docked, automobiles arrived from the upriver town. Many of the passengers returned home by car.

The rest of the excursionists waited two hours until Captain Strekfus announced it would be impossible for the *Capitol* to pass over the sand bar for the return trip to Stillwater. Instead, he had made arrangements with the Omaha Railroad dispatcher for a special train to take the passengers home.

The crowd left the brilliantly lit steamboat and started up the dark beach to find the train. After following the railroad tracks for half an hour, the people located the depot. There, they waited for the special. Some younger members of the party sang, picking such appropriate tunes as "We Won't Get Home 'Til Morning," "Where Do We Go From Here," and "The Long, Long Trail." Despite the lateness (or earliness) of the hour, the singers must have been enthusiastic, for it was reported that the songs "being wafted across the lake . . . were re-echoed against the Wisconsin hills, [and] some of the citizens of Hudson being so impressed with the singing . . . awoke and stood at a respectful distance no doubt wondering for the time being where the crowd came from."

Made up in Stillwater of a switch engine, one coach, and a combination baggage and passenger car, the special finally arrived about 4:00 a.m. Everyone crowded on board. The excursionists waited another three-quarters of an hour before orders arrived permitting the train to cross the bridge. At last, they were en route toward home.

Sponsors of the excursion were members of American Legion Post 48 of Stillwater. They cleared about $98. The cost of the special train was met by the Strekfus Company, owners of the *Capitol*.

"Taken altogether," concluded the newspaper report, "it was a great experience—one that will not be forgotten for some time by the participants—all treating the adventure, so to speak, as one to which no blame could be attached to anyone."

(Photo courtesy of Durand Blanding)

Steamboat 'Round the Bend

Residents of St. Croix Falls, Wisconsin, saw an unusual sight in August 1941. Jim Miller opened a restaurant built in the shape of a steamboat. The 134-foot land-locked boat was located near U.S. Highway B and Wisconsin Highway 35. The "Steamboat 'Round the Bend" was designed as a paddlewheeler, a replica typical of the old boats on the river.

Miller's connection with St. Croix River history went back three generations. His grandfather, James Campbell, began as a logging boss back in 1852 and settled in Taylors Falls. Campbell's daughter Katie married Carl Muller, who operated excursion boats out of Taylors Falls. Jim Miller's mother was Muller's sister. Miller earned his pilot's license in the late 1920s. During his high school years, and for several years afterwards, he piloted excursion boats for his uncle Carl.

Miller began building "Steamboat 'Round the Bend" in 1940. It opened in the fall of 1941. Shortly afterward, Miller went into service during World War II. His wife, Regina, operated the restaurant for a few months, but, because of gas rationing, customers were few. She closed it early in 1942.

On his discharge in 1945, Jim Miller returned to the St. Croix valley and reopened the Steamboat. In the mid 1950s, Miller remodeled the building. Because the Dalles House in Taylors Falls ceased operations, that name became available, and Miller adopted it for his restaurant.

Many people along the St. Croix River still remember the "Steamboat 'Round the Bend." The restaurant had a 20-foot plate glass window in the deck bar. The upper deck, with 2,300 feet of floor space, offered shuffleboard, deck tennis, sun lounges, and chairs. Forward on the upper deck was a large pilot wheel and ship's bell. Miller's living quarters were in the pilothouse. The stern wheel, nine feet in circumference, actually churned in a pool of water. While it lasted, "Steamboat 'Round the Bend" was a fitting tribute to its departed sisters, the steamboats on the St. Croix.

(Photo courtesy of Jim Miller)

Capt. William D. Bowell aboard the *Jonathan Padelford* (top). Originally 105 feet in length, the *Padelford* was cut in two and a 20-foot section inserted. The *Padelford* is cruising past St. Paul. (Courtesy of William D. Bowell [top] and the Stillwater *Gazette* [bottom])

Chapter 20

The Steamboats Return

The romance of steamboating returned to the St. Croix Valley in 1970. Capt. William D. Bowell of Stillwater brought in the *Jonathan Padelford*, which cost a quarter of a million dollars. The stern-wheeler was built for Bowell at the Dubuque Boat Works of Iowa. Originally, she was a 105-foot, diesel-driven boat with a capacity of 250 passengers. The *Padelford* cruised five to six miles per hour upstream, seven to eight downstream. During the winter of 1972-73, the *Padelford* was cut in two and a 20-foot section inserted. The work of expanding the boat from 250 to 400 passenger capacity was done at LaMont, Illinois. At the same time, the boat was refurbished from stern to bow. New carpet and drapes were installed. Added were the Golden Bugles—four ships' horns of cast bronze and brass. They weighed 350 pounds and sounded four tones. The horns were made by Kahlenberg Company of Two Rivers, Wisconsin, a firm which makes whistles for river and ocean boats all over the world. After operating the expanded excursion boat on the St. Croix for a season, Captain Bowell moved the *Padelford* to the Mississippi, docking at St. Paul.

The sternwheeler *Jubilee I* appeared on the St. Croix River in the spring of 1973. Owner was Captain A. Carr Griffith of Griffith Marine Engineering and Manufacturing Company of Stillwater. As a young man, Griffith had worked on the St. Croix River. From March 1928, until October 1929, he worked on the *Polly*, also known as "The Candy Boat." He was on the Mayo brothers boat, the *North Star*, when it steamed under the newly-opened interstate bridge at Stillwater in 1931. Griffith purchased the *Jubilee I* from Sunline of Cincinnati. The paddle-wheel boat was built by the Dubuque Boat and Boiler works, and was launched in 1963. It had operated out of Cincinnati, and wintered on the upper Tennessee River. The 78-ton craft is 106 feet long, has a 32-foot beam and a five-foot depth, with a draw of two and one-half feet. It can accommodate 350 passengers,

The *Polly* in dry dock for repairs to damage amidships. The boat was constructed so that the canvas, search light and pilot wheel could be removed to allow it to pass under low trees during its winter operations on the bayous of the south. (Courtesy of A. Carr Griffith)

Built by the Dubuque Boat and Boiler Works, the *Jubilee I* was launched in 1963. It was purchased by Capt. A. Carr Griffith and brought to the St. Croix River in 1973. (Courtesy of A. Carr Griffith)

and features an 18-by-21 foot dance floor. Of all-steel construction, the boat is operated by twin diesel engines. It is a bank boat, which means it can be run right up to the shore to board passengers. The *Jubilee I* operated out of Stillwater and Hudson for several seasons. The boat was sold and is now operating on southern rivers.

On July 21, 1977, residents of Stillwater were startled to hear the strident sounds of a calliope wafting across the city. It was the *Delta Queen*, probably the largest steamboat ever to ply the St. Croix. It tied up at the levee for about two hours, attracting admirers from many miles around. The *Delta Queen* is truly the last of the old time steamboats. She is listed in the National Register of Historic places, and is carefully preserved in her historic originality.

The triple-galvanized steel hull of the boat was fabricated at Glasgow, Scotland, on the River Clyde, in 1926. It was disassembled and sent to Stockton, California, where it was reassembled. A superstructure was added, creating the *Delta Queen*. She was the acme of riverboats in the United States. Crystal chandeliers, brass fittings, oak and mahogany ceiling beams, all help to create her elegance.

During World War II, her passenger service was halted. The *Queen* was drafted. She hauled servicemen to their ships at sea, between Oakland and San Francisco. After the war, the *Delta Queen*

The *Delta Queen* was built in Glasgow, Scotland, in 1926 and was disassembled and sent to Stockton, California. During World War II, she was drafted and hauled servicemen to their ships at sea between Oakland and San Francisco. After the war, the steamboat was put into service on the Mississippi River and its tributaries. (Author's collection)

The first official visit of the *Delta Queen* to Stillwater was in October 1977. In spite of cold rain that turned to snow, throngs of people turned out to greet the last of the old-time steamboats. (Author's collection) was abandoned, along with many other small boats. She was purchased in 1946 by Captain Tom Green of Cincinnati's Green Line, and taken to that city in July 1947. The *Queen* was put into services for cruises on the Ohio, Tennessee, and Mississippi rivers.

The *Delta Queen* is a 1,837 ton boat, 285 feet long, and 58 feet wide. She draws 7.5 feet of water and is powered by her original steam engines and a single 26-ton paddle wheel, which is 28 feet in diameter.

The *Taylors Falls Princess*, a 250-passenger excursion boat, is an authentic paddle-wheel boat, presently used on the St. Croix. (Author's collection)

The *Josiah Snelling*, companion steamboat to the *Jonathan Padelford*. Both operated by Capt. William D. Bowell, the boats are now docked at St. Paul. (Courtesy of William D. Bowell)

The boat has four decks with cabin capacity for 192 passengers. Normal crew is 75. The deck floor is of iron bar, an extremely hard wood from Siam. Her cabin deck is of Oregon cedar. Machinery of the *Queen* is from Krupp Iron Works in Germany. The deck railings are of teak wood, and the entire boat is ornamented with stained glass windows, plush carpeting, and bronze grillwork.

In 1966, Congress threatened to put the *Delta Queen* out of action by a "Safety at Sea" law, which was intended for ocean vessels. Because of her antique structure, the *Delta Queen* could not be altered to comply with the law. However, in 1969, Congress passed a special act which exempts the boat from certain provisions. All of the wooden superstructure was treated with fire retardant paint. Extensive fire safety equipment was installed, including a water sprinkler system and electronic fire and smoke detectors.

From 1973 to 1976, the *Delta Queen* was owned by Overseas National Airways. Ownership of the *Queen* passed to Coca-Cola Bottling Company in 1976, and the Delta Queen Steamboat Company was separated from Coca-Cola four years later.

After her initial visit to the St. Croix, the *Delta Queen* returned on July 31 for a short stay, then made her official visit to Stillwater on October 10, 1977. Despite heavy rain that turned to snow, some 1,500 people toured the *Queen*.

Since the 1920s, there has been no commercial river traffic on the St. Croix above Marine. Beginning in 1906, tourists have enjoyed the scenic beauty of the Dalles of the St. Croix by excursion boat operated by the Muller family. In recent years, two replica paddleboats have been added to the fleet operating there. The *Taylors Falls Queen* is 78 feet long, 20 feet wide, and has two decks. Launched in 1981, it was built at La Crosse, Wisconsin. The *Taylors Falls Queen* has a 15-inch draw, and can carry up to 150 people. Newest addition to the fleet is the *Taylors Falls Princess*. It has an ultra-light aluminum hull with a 17-inch draught. Capacity is 250 people. The *Princess* was launched in May 1985. It was most appropriate that the sesqui-

The *Taylors Falls Queen*, an 80-foot authentic paddle-wheeler, is presently used for daily excursions and dinner cruises. Its capacity is 150 passengers. (Author's collection)

centennial of the village of Marine was celebrated aboard the *Taylors Falls Princess.* A four-hour evening dinner and dancing excursion left from the Marine landing on July 8, 1989.

"The largest, most luxurious stern-wheeler on the St. Croix" is the *Andiamo Showboat,* owned and operated by Dick and Don Anderson of the St. Croix Boat and Packet Company, Stillwater. Originally the *Cumberland Princess,* the boat is 120 feet long, 31 feet wide. It is an authentic replica of an 1880s steamboat. Built in 1983 by Tucker Marine in Cincinnati, Ohio, the steamer was purchased by the Andersons in March 1985. She was remodeled to reflect all the elegance and splendor of 19th-century boats and was ready for service in May. The *Andiamo Showboat* carries five modern diesel engines—two turn the huge paddle wheels, three provide electrical power. With

The *Cumberland Princess* (top) became the *Andiamo Showboat* (bottom) after being purchased by Dick and Don Anderson of Stillwater in March 1985. Daily cruises and dinner cruises aboard the *Andiamo Showboat* are a part of summer in the St. Croix Valley. (Courtesy of the Stillwater *Gazette*)

The Steamboats Return / 151

The *Andiamo* going under the Interstate Bridge at Stillwater. The excursion boat offers daily cruises on the St. Croix during the navigational season. (Courtesy of Debra Chial)

Capt. A. Carr Griffith with the *Queen of the Lakes*, an excursion boat he designed and built for the city of Minneapolis. The *Queen* was launched in 1969 and operated on Lake Calhoun. It was designed so the stacks folded down, allowing the boat to pass under the bridges for use on Lake of the Isles and Cedar Lake. (Courtesy of A. Carr Griffith)

a capacity of 250 passengers, the *Andiamo Showboat* offers first and second decks with enclosed salons, and an open promenade deck.

A second steamboat was added to the St. Croix Boat Company fleet with the purchase of the *Andiamo* in February 1986. A sidewheeler, it was built the previous year. The *Andiamo* is 65 feet long, 26 feet wide. It has a capacity of 85 people and offers a completely enclosed main deck, covered second deck, and open top deck.

For those who cherish visions of the "Good Old Days," all of these excursion boats recreate the essence of steamboat days on the St. Croix.

Chunking paddle wheels, fluted smokestacks, and lofty boats trimmed with carpenter's lace pay tribute to the century-old memories of steamboats on the St. Croix.

Chapter 21

Steamboat Men

Many men followed the call of the river. Listed are names gleaned from various records of the steamboating years on the St. Croix. Missing, no doubt, are as many names as are included.

BALL, Spencer. Resided in St. Louis, Missouri, but was well-known in the St. Croix Valley for he had command of the light-draft stern-wheel packet *Charlie Cheever* for several seasons in the early 1870s. He was a man much esteemed by those who knew him. He died of consumption on January 18, 1875.

BATCHELDER, Josiah. Born May 30, 1833, in Wellington, Maine. He moved with his parents to Bangor, then to Exeter, Maine, where he learned the trade of ship building. He arrived in Stillwater in 1855 at age 22, and spent one season building flat boats and skiffs. The following year, he went to Maiden Rock, Wisconsin. He constructed the *Lottie Lyon*, the first locally-built packet to navigate Lake Pepin. He married Elizabeth Bowers in Red Wing in 1859. In 1866 Batchelder moved to Frontenac, where he built many luxurious yachts, sail boats, and row boats. He returned to the St. Croix Valley in 1877, and settled south of Stillwater on a farm. In October of that year, he became one of the organizers of the Stillwater Dock Co., in partnership with Durant, Wheeler and Co., and David Tozer's St. Croix Lumber Co. He built the ways and docks for the Stillwater Dock Company, of which he was named manager. The firm became a boat building center of the area. Early in its operation, Stillwater Dock Co. built the steamers *R. G. Wheeler*, *Kit Carson*, and *Pauline*. Among other boats constructed by the firm were the *Daisy*, *Dispatch*, *Cyclone*, and *Nina*. The last boat built by Batchelder was the *Fury*, in 1899. In the early years of the 20th century, the federal government took over the boat works. Batchelder was named superintendent of the U.S. Boat Yard. There, barges were built for use in dredging and cleaning the St. Croix, Mississippi, and Minnesota rivers. "Josie" worked at the yard until May 1912 when he retired at the age of 79 for health reasons. He died January 21, 1913, at his home in Baytown.

BRADLEY, Cyrus A. Born in Kaskaskia, Illinois, in 1825. Bradley moved to Osceola, Wisconsin, in 1848. Engaged in lumbering, Bradley became a

Josiah Batchelder, one of the organizers of the Stillwater Dock Company, built the steamers *R. G. Wheeler*, *Kit Carson*, *Pauline*, *Daisy*, *Dispatch*, *Cyclone*, *Nina* and *Fury*. (Courtesy of Jim Johnson)

The *Fury* pushing a barge on the St. Croix. (Courtesy of Jim Johnson)

river pilot running rafts to St. Louis with stems and blocks, called oars and sweeps, before steamboat towing was in vogue. When steamboats became useful in running rafts, he built two steamers especially for raft towing. Bradley moved to a farm near Osceola in 1874.

BRASSER, George. Born in 1833 in the province of Quebec, Canada. After sailing schooners on the St. Lawrence River, Brasser rafted logs between Quebec and Montreal. He arrived in Stillwater in 1855, and rafted and piloted between Stillwater and St. Louis. His first trip on a raft was under Capt. Joe Perro. Brasser was employed by the Schulenberg and Boeckler Lumber Company of Stillwater.

BUISSON, Cypriano. Piloted the *Clyde* in the 1870s. In 1877 he was master and chief pilot on the rafter *B. Hershey*. He was captain of the *Morning Star* from 1914 to 1917.

One of the later and faster boats on the northern rivers was the *Morning Star,* built in 1911. In 1918 she was sold to a Cincinnati firm and disappeared from the North. (Courtesy of the Washington County Historical Society)

BUTLER, Charles J. Born in Pittsburgh, Pennsylvania, in 1822. Butler arrived in Marine Mills in 1851, where he worked as a bookkeeper and general clerk for the lumber firm of Judd, Walker & Company. From 1862 to 1878, he was engaged in the towboat business with Capt. Isaac Gray.

BRYAN, Anthony H. Born in Baton Rouge, Louisiana, September 29, 1850. At age 21, Bryan went to Cincinnati, Ohio, and entered a steamboat works. After two years, he became assistant engineer on boats on the Ohio and the Mississippi rivers. He worked for the Cincinnati and New Orleans Packet Company. Two years later, he received his license as second engineer, then achieved his first engineer's license. He ran boats on the Mississippi and the St. Croix until 1879.

CHAMPLIN, H. D. Born in 1840 in Cattaraugus, New York. He moved to Hudson, Wisconsin, in 1858. Champlin ran a boat on the St. Croix for 13 years. He owned a boat for seven years, selling it in 1875. He then conducted a livery, boarding, and sale stable.

CORMACK, John W. Born in Illinois in 1816. He came to Stillwater in 1844, and began piloting on the St. Croix the following year. He lived in the city for 30 years, during which time he served as a river pilot and was in the rafting business. He died in 1885 in Princeton, Mille Lacs County, Minnesota.

DARRAH, L. W. He lived in Stillwater while he served as captain on St. Croix River boats.

DAVISON, Charles H. Born in St. Louis, Missouri, October 2, 1859. Son of veteran pilot Daniel D. Davison, Charles moved to Stillwater in 1893. He was pilot and captain of boats for the firm of Bronson and Folsom of

Stillwater. He served on the *J. G. Chapman, L. W. Van Sant, Staples,* and the *Ravenna.* In 1909 Davison retired to Florida.

DE CAMP, Ira. Born January 26, 1850, in Harrisburg, Virginia. He traveled with his family to Wabasha, Minnesota, in 1857 in a prairie schooner. De Camp was at various times master or pilot of the *Clyde, Lillie Turner, Van Sant, Buckeye, Luella, Sea Wing, Hersey, C. W. Cowles,* and the *Hartford.*

DIBBLE, William. Born in 1815. He came to the St. Croix Valley in 1839 from New York State. Dibble was one of the founders of Marine Mills. In 1844 he quit the lumber business and moved downriver to Point Douglas. He received a charter to operate a ferry to Prescott, and across the Mississippi to Hastings. He sold out and left for California in 1849 in search of gold. Dibble died in 1884.

DOTTERWEICH, George. Born in Cleveland, Ohio, in 1858. As a small boy, he moved with his parents to Winona, Minnesota. For fifteen years previous to 1902, Dotterweich served a pilot on logging boats on the St. Croix and Mississippi rivers to St. Louis. Between 1902 and 1918, he had charge of the Chicago Northwestern Railroad ferry which operated on the Missouri River between Pierre and Fort Pierre, South Dakota. Dotterweich moved to Stillwater, Minnesota, in 1918 and operated a store at 324 East Hazel Street for fifteen years. He died February 28, 1934.

DURANT, Edward White. Born April 8, 1829, in Roxbury, Massachusetts. At age nineteen, Durant journeyed to Stillwater. He was a rafter on the St. Croix for three years. Achieving his license, he was a pilot from Stillwater and St. Paul to St. Louis for the next thirteen years. From 1866 to 1880, he was general manager on the river for Hersey, Staples and Company.

EAMS, Albert. Captain of the *Queen of the Yellow Banks,* a small sternwheeler that operated on the St. Croix for three months during 1852. Called "a little pet of a steamboat," the Lilliputian boat made tri-weekly trips between Stillwater and Taylors Falls at the fare of $1.00 for the round trip.

ELLIOTT, William. Born in May 1825 in Ireland, Elliott arrived in St. Paul in 1850. He was a pilot on the Mississippi and St. Croix for several years, working primarily at rafting logs and for the lumber companies.

FIFIELD, Sam S. Born June 24, 1839, in Carmena, Penobscot County, Maine. Fifield settled in Prescott, Wisconsin, in 1854. He was a clerk until 1859, when he shipped as night watch on the steamer *Equator* between Taylors Falls and Prescott. In May the boat was wrecked. Fifield, along with other members of the crew, was transferred to the *Kate Cassel.* When the boat went into winter quarters at the end of that season, Fifield's career as a steamboat man ended.

FOLSOM, Wyman X. Elder son of W. H. C. Folsom of Taylors Falls. He was captain of the packet steamer *Wyman X* named for him. Unable to maneuver a barge between the bridge pilings at Hudson, he was one of the instigators of the famous Battle of the Piles in 1871.

GARRISON, Lemuel. Born March 27, 1839, in New Jersey. At age sixteen, he moved to the Wisconsin River. He shipped on a steamboat to learn piloting. In 1860 Garrison moved to Stillwater. He navigated both the St. Croix and Mississippi rivers as pilot and commander. He was also a practical artisan, and often looked after the details of the engine room of boats under his command.

GRADY, Asa Barlow. Born in Warren, Vermont, in 1826. Although he had only a common school education, he attained knowledge of the law. He was admitted to practice in Minnesota and Wisconsin in 1857. He was part owner and captain of the steamer *Equator* in 1859 when the boat was wrecked in Lake St. Croix. Grady served as Washington County sheriff at one time.

GRAY, Isaac. A former hotel keeper, Gray was at one time captain of the *H. S. Allen*. He boasted that if the St. Croix should entirely dry up, he would still be able to get through on a heavy dew. The *Allen* operated between Taylors Falls and Prescott as a mail packet from 1860 to 1862. Gray built and operated the steamboat *Eugene*.

HANFORD, John. Hanford was a pilot on the St. Croix during the 1840s. He married the adopted daughter of Socrates Nelson of Stillwater. Hanford died in Stillwater.

HANKS, Samuel. A brother of Stephen B., he began piloting in the 1840s and continued his career well into the 1880s.

HANKS, Stephen B. (His biography is carried in an earlier chapter.)

HAZZARD, George H. Born at Seaford, Delaware, December 5, 1846. He traveled to Taylors Falls as a youth, and became an expert log rider. He worked as a clerk on steamers for several summers and in 1895 became the first commissioner of Interstate Park.

HOEY, John. Born August 4, 1850, in West Cananda. Hoey served on board the *Petrel* on the Mississippi beginning in 1865. In 1868 Hoey moved to Stillwater and rafted on the St. Croix and Mississippi for the next five years. In 1876 he received his pilot's license, then his captain's license. He became commander of the *Isaac Staples*, a post he held well into the 1880s.

HOOPER, William H. Born in Warwick Manor, Maryland, December 25, 1813. Hooper moved to Galena, Illinois, in 1835, and engaged in mercantile business. In the panic of 1838, his business failed to the amount of $200,000. After years of struggling, he finally paid off the debt entirely. In 1843, Hooper engaged in steamboating as clerk on the *Otter*, and was well known in Stillwater. That year, his boat landed the mill irons for the McKusick and Company mill. The following year, Hooper built the steamer *Lynx* and several other boats, the last being the *Alexander Hamilton*, of which he was part owner. The steamer burned at St. Louis in 1849, which left him again penniless. Immigrating to Salt Lake in 1850, Hooper espoused Mormonism and became one of its leaders. His business enterprises prospered. He died in Salt Lake City.

JENKS, Austin T. Born October 12, 1833, in Essex County, New York. Jenks went to Albany in 1854 and was employed on the Hudson River there. In winter, he taught school. Entering the firm of Durant, Wheeler and Company of Stillwater in 1874, he served as a pilot. He built the *Brother Jonathan*, the second boat ever built specifically for rafting purposes.

JEWELL, Phillip B. Born October 25, 1816, in Hopkintown, Merimac County, New Hampshire. Jewell relocated to St. Croix Falls in 1847 and moved to Hudson in 1851. He was an active lumberman and a veteran pilot on the St. Croix.

KEECH, George W. Born April 30, 1828, in Syracuse, New York. Keech went to sea as a whaler and entered the trading business in 1844. He arrived in the St. Croix Valley in 1852, spending much of his time on western lakes and rivers as an engineer.

KENT, John (Jack). Brother of William Kent. In March 1898, he purchased the excursion boat *Vernie Mac,* a stern-wheeler, 130 feet by 24 feet with a 20-inch draw. He refitted and repainted it to first-class condition for the St. Croix trade. The boat's first trip was between Stillwater and Taylor's Falls on April 20, 1898. Jack Kent died in 1908.

KENT, William, Jr. Born in Frederickton, New Brunswick, on April 22, 1824. Kent traveled to St. Croix Falls in 1844, and shortly afterward moved to Osceola Mills. He was one of the original owners and builders of the first mill there, which was erected in 1849. Through purchase of the interests of other partners, he became sole owner of the mill and townsite. He sold the mill to B. H. Campbell in 1853. Kent engaged in lumbering until 1864, then entered steamboating until 1879. He built the *Nellie Kent, Helen Mar,* and *Maggie Reaney.* When railroads made steamboats less than profitable, Kent engaged in mercantile pursuits. He was the first treasurer of Polk County and always took an active interest in public affairs. He was once county judge. "His genial character, his vigorous, sturdy walk, his cheering words and his strong face became a part of the life of the village of Osceola." Kent died January 9, 1904.

KNAPP, Oscar F. Born in Clinton County, New York, in 1831. At age fifteen, with his parents, he went west to Oshkosh, Wisconsin. When he turned twenty-one, he moved to Osceola and entered the lumber business. In 1856, he married Angeline Hayes. The same year, he began steamboating and continued in it for more than thirty years. The first boat he owned was the *H. S. Allen,* bought in 1856 with Capt. E. B. Strong from H. S. Allen of Chippewa Falls for $5000. He ran the *Allen* for about three years. In 1861 he engaged as a pilot on the *Enterprise,* a small but serviceable boat of light draft and fair speed. The following year, he purchased the packet and ran it for three more years. Knapp was captain of the *G. H. Gray* in 1863. He and other businessmen in Osceola built the unfortunate side-wheeler *Viola* at Franconia in 1864. The stock company built the *G. B. Knapp* in 1866, and the *Jennie Hayes* in 1879. In 1877, Knapp entered government service. He worked under Major Charles J. Allen with a crew improving the St. Croix River. His two sons—Ben, born in 1857, and George, born in 1859— succeeded their father in the steamboat business. Both inherited their father's popularity as rivermen. Both were expert pilots and captains, and both spent their lives on the river.

The *G. B. Knapp* at the waterfront in Stillwater. (Courtesy of Jim Johnson)

LEACH, John. Born in 1818 in Ireland. Came to the St. Croix Valley in 1854 and made his home in Marine Mills for many years. He was engaged as a pilot on the St. Croix and Mississippi rivers. In later years, he moved to Stillwater where he died alone in a little cottage, March 7, 1896.

LEAVITT, William L. Born in 1841 in Naples, Maine. He arrived in Prescott, Wisconsin, in 1861. After 1878, he devoted his attention to steamboating.

MACCORMACK, John. Began piloting on the St. Croix River in 1845. He married Miss Jackins in 1860. The couple made their home in Stillwater during the thirty years he served as a pilot. MacCormack died in Princeton, Minnesota, in 1885.

MCCARTHY, Nelson. Born July 4, 1819, in Pike County, Pennsylvania. In 1834, he married Mary McKune. The couple moved to the St. Croix Valley in 1846 where McCarthy engaged in lumbering and piloting. In 1847, they moved to a farm on Osceola Prairie.

MCDONALD, James. Born in London, Canada, March 2, 1851. McDonald shipped on the *Belle of La Crosse* as mate in 1880 for a trip from St. Louis to St. Paul. Afterward, he shipped on the *Mary Barnes* and worked for one month on the *St. Croix*.

MCPHAIL, James. Born in Iverness, Scotland, in 1824. McPhail immigrated to Stillwater in 1848 and married Eliza Purinton the following year. "Sandy" McPhail was one of the first log pilots on the Mississippi and St. Croix. He died in St. Louis in 1857.

MASSEY, Louis. Born August 6, 1793, in Canada. Massey left home at age 17 for Michigan and worked at several trading posts. He was a captive of Indians for a time. In 1812, Massey was employed by Colonel Dickson of the British government as one of a crew to bring to Prairie du Chien five Mackinaw boats loaded with supplies. The boats started from Mackinaw, went to Green Bay, then up the Fox River to Lake Winnebago, to the site where Portage City was built. At that point, the boats and their contents were hauled overland to the Wisconsin River and continued to Prairie du Chien, a trip of three days and three nights from Portage.

In the winter of 1813, Massey engaged in freighting with small keel boats on the Mississippi from St. Louis to New Orleans. In 1818, he turned his attention north and worked for the American Fur Company at Fond du Lac and on Lake Superior near Duluth. Massey arrived at Fort Snelling in 1828 and turned to farming. Ten years later, he moved to the St. Croix Valley, locating near Hudson. He and three other settlers rafted the flooring and boards to build their houses down the St. Croix River from Marine Mills. Although Massey never engaged in active boating on the St. Croix, he is worthy of mention because he was on the rivers of the upper midwest even before steamboats made their appearance.

MEARS, Charles E. Born January 9, 1844, in East Boston, Massachusetts. When he was 13, he moved with his family to Osceola, Wisconsin. Charles engaged in rafting on both the St. Croix and Mississippi rivers. He was a clerk on steamboats until 1861.

MEEDS, Charles H. Born July 29, 1836, in Standish, Maine. Meeds journeyed to Minnesota in 1874 to navigate on the Mississippi River. He settled in St. Anthony and worked on the *Governor Ramsey*, the first boat to run above the falls of St. Anthony. In 1876, he purchased the steamboat *Ida*, the largest towing packet on Lake St. Croix.

MULLEN, James W. of Taylors Falls spent much of his early and middle life on the river. In 1846, he was a cabin boy on the *War Eagle*, traveling between St. Louis, Stillwater, and Fort Snelling.

NORTHUP, Anson. His name was borne by the first steamboat ever launched on the Red River of the North. Born in Conewango, Cattaraugus County, New York, January 4, 1817. Although Northup's education was limited, he was a man of native ability and energy. He lived in Ohio for some years and moved west in 1838. In 1841, he removed his family from Ohio to St. Croix Falls, Wisconsin. He traveled by way of St. Louis, embarking on the steamer *Indian Queen* for the Falls. The steamer was three weeks making the trip. Above Prairie du Chien, both crew and passengers were obliged to cut wood to run the boat. In the spring in 1844, Northup moved from Taylors Falls to Stillwater where he built and kept the first hotel in the city.

A restless man, Northup moved to St. Paul in 1849, to St. Anthony Falls in 1851, then to Minneapolis in 1853. At each place he built a hotel. Although his genius was chiefly toward hotels, he turned his hand to lumbering, steamboating, and statesmanship. His great steamboat enterprise was the attempted transfer of the steamer *North Star* by water from the Mississippi to the Red River of the North. The boat was 100 feet long by 20 feet wide, and of light draught.

Starting from St. Cloud in the spring of 1859, he ascended the Mississippi as far as Pokegama Falls. He hoped to ascend further and, during a high stage of water, to float the boat over the height of land into the tributaries of the Red River. However, the water never rose high enough to accomplish that scheme. The following winter, Northup took the boat to pieces and moved it overland to the Red River. There he reconstructed it and launched it opposite the mouth of the Cheyenne River. It was taken to Fort Garry and afterward sold to a Mr. Burbank (possibly James W., organizer of the Northwest Express Company; Burbank was involved in steamship and stage lines). The name of the boat was then changed to *Anson Northup*, in honor of its mover. It was the first steamboat on the waters of the Red River.

O'NEAL, Hugh. Born December 11, 1844, in St. Lawrence County, New York. O'Neal came to Stillwater in 1865. He served continuously on the St. Croix and Mississippi as engineer, then as pilot. At one time, he owned a one-third interest in the packet *Minnie Will*. The boat was wrecked on the rocks off New Boston, Illinois, and O'Neal suffered a severe financial loss. After that set back, he engaged in running log boats on the river for the St. Croix Lumber Company.

PARKER, John. An early river pilot, he came from Vermont to the St. Croix Valley in 1848 and married Susan Cover. He first located at St. Croix Falls. About 1850, he settled in Oak Park. The couple had three children. Edwin E., the eldest, was killed July 24, 1874, at the age of 25, by the explosion of the boiler of the steamer *Penn Wright*. A son John E. moved to Bemidji. Daughter Ella married river pilot Henry L. Peavey of Stillwater. Mr. Parker died in June 1867 while performing his duties as a pilot. He was caught in the coils handling a line to "snub" a raft. The injuries he received caused his death.

PEAVEY, Henry L. He was a river pilot who married the daughter of pilot John Parker. Peavey was owner of the *Penn Wright*. On March 25, 1884, the boat was sold to Martin Mower of Arcola for $5,400. Peavey was pilot of the *Henrietta* in 1890.

PERRO, Joseph. Known far and wide as "Big Joe." Of French parentage, he was a native of Kaskaskia, Illinois. Perro took up residence in Stillwater in 1844. He moved to Baytown in 1847 and purchased a great deal of property. Large of frame, big-hearted and honest, manly, of good report for courage and honesty, Perro was fearless and prompt in taking the part of the weak and oppressed. He died August 19, 1897, in South Stillwater and was buried in St. Michael's Cemetery in what is now Bayport, which was property he once owned.

PERRO, Sylvester. Born 1852, in Baytown, the first white child born in that town. At age 15, Sylvester joined his father Joe to learn what he could of river navigation. After four or five years, he boarded the *Lady Pike* to learn piloting. Perro worked two seasons on the steamboats, then went to the Red River of the North as a pilot. Until 1880, he spent his summers on the Red River and his winters in Baytown. He died January 22, 1940.

QUINLAN, John. Born January 20, 1859, in Brooklyn, New York. He came to Stillwater with his parents as a child. After learning the trade of plumber, gas and steam fitter, he opened a shop on Chestnut Street, giving employment to three mechanics. Quinlan later became captain of the *LeRoy*, then of the tug boat *Baby*. He died June 1, 1906.

John Quinlan and family. Quinlan came to the St. Croix Valley as a child. He became a dealer in gas pipe fittings, brass fixtures, pumps and similar wares. Later he was captain of the tug boat *Baby*. (Courtesy of Jim Johnson)

RAITER, Frank M. Born February 4, 1842, in Sweden. Raiter worked as a cook on St. Croix River steamboats for six years.

REGISTER, Capt. Samuel M. Born in 1827 in Dover, Delaware. Register journeyed to St. Paul in 1850 aboard the *Highland Mary No. 2*. He proceeded to Stillwater, arriving on April 21, and started to work on the river as a pilot. In 1872, he began running the *Helen Mar* and bought a one-third interest in the boat. He ran the *Mar* for about six years, then went to work for Isaac Staples. He was very prominent in navigation circles, for Register had a thorough knowledge of the river.

REYNOLDS, Joseph. Born 1819 to Quaker parents in Fallsburg, New York. After receiving a common education, he began his career as drover and butcher. He bought livestock, killed and dressed the animals, and sold the meat to customers. In New York, he built a flour mill, feed mill, and tannery. He sold all his businesses in 1856, and moved to Chicago. There, he began buying furs. In 1860, he sold out again, and moved to McGregor, Iowa, where he started a grain-buying and shipping venture. Since railroads had not yet reached the river, he moved his grain by boat. Buying a small stern-wheeler in 1862, he named it the *Lansing*, and used it for his own grain as well as freight for others. Before the end of the year, Northern Packet Company bought Reynold's boat, promising to greatly improve its service. Reynolds was not impressed by what they accomplished. In retaliation, he ordered another boat built, and named it the *Diamond Jo*. The Diamond Jo Steamer Company was established in 1867. During the next 20 years, Reynolds developed an impressive fleet of boats and signed many shrewd deals with railroads and elevators, thereby assuring his prosperity. The firm operated an average of six steamers on the Mississippi and St. Croix Rivers each year. Reynolds never allowed bars to be operated on his boats. He discouraged both drinking and gambling. His boats were always immaculately clean. Each of them carried a diamond emblem on all four sides of the pilot house. A "JO" for the company president was lettered between the chimney braces.

RHODES, Charles. Born June 5, 1828, in Kentucky. Rhodes' father was a river pilot, and Charles began to work the Mississippi as a boy. In 1852, he moved to the St. Croix, settling in Stillwater in 1863. He worked as a pilot between Stillwater and St. Louis, where he was regarded as one of the best pilots on the river. Rhodes died March 4, 1898.

ROOT, James. Born November 3, 1848, in Albany, New York. Root arrived in Stillwater in 1866, and made two trips as pilot on the steamboat *Tiger* traveling between Stillwater and Lake Pepin.

RULEY, Russell. Born at Richmond, Virginia, June 10, 1836. In 1848, Captain Ruley, then of Prescott, was employed as a cabin boy on the *Clearmont II*, running between Montrose, Iowa, and Rock Island, Illinois. He entered the St. Croix working first on the *H. S. Allen*, and later on the *Nellie Kent*. Ruley drowned in 1894 in the Mississippi River at Red Wing, weighted down with rocks (a suicide).

SHORT, Jerome E. He began on the river as a raftsman in 1867. He worked as a deckhand on the rafter *Viola* in 1868. The next year he was second pilot of the *Viola*. In succeeding years, he became master of the *Lone Star*, then pilot of the *G. B. Knapp*, the *Annie Gordon*, and the *Chauncey Lamb*. From 1874 to 1880, he was master of the *Lamb*. For the next two seasons, he was master of the *Silver Wave*. Short became master and owner of the *Abner Gile*, a stern-wheeler rafter, from 1883 to 1888. The *Gile* was built in 1872 in Le Claire, Iowa. While in the U. S. Marshall's hands for debt in 1898, the boat

The *Abner Gile*, built at LeCaire, Iowa, in 1872, was owned by Jerome E. Short for a time. It sank at South Stillwater in 1899. (Courtesy of A. Carr. Griffith)

One of the oldest rafters in the northern waters, the steamer *Mountain Belle* did not enter the rafting business until 1874, having originally been a packet boat. In later years it became an excursion steamer under the name of *Purchase* and was a frequent visitor to Stillwater and the St. Croix. It was dismantled in 1917 after a long career. (Courtesy of the Washington County Historical Society)

burned at South Stillwater. It was said to have been in rafting longer than any boat except the *Mountain Belle*. Short was one of five brothers who worked on the river.

SOULE, Jesse H. Born in Avon, Maine, in the 1820s. Soule traveled west in 1854. He took a boat from Galena to St. Paul. During the trip, the boat was wrecked. With difficulty, it reached an island, where it sank almost immediately. All who had been on board remained on the island for forty-eight hours until they were rescued by a passing boat, the *War Eagle*.

STAPLES, Josiah. Son of Samuel, brother of Isaac, Josiah was born June 20, 1826, in Brunswick, Maine. He arrived in Stillwater in 1848, and engaged in milling, lumbering, and steamboating. He married Lydia McGlaughlin in 1853, and fathered six sons and one daughter.

STREIF, John. Born in 1840 in Canton Glarus, Switzerland. When he was five years old, Streif was brought to the United States. The family located in Galena, Illinois. In 1868, John began running with steamers on the Mississippi and its tributaries, including the St. Croix. He was connected with the boats *Milwaukee*, *Dubuque*, *David Pike*, *Alex. Mitchell*, *War Eagle*, and *Granite Star*, and he worked for the Diamond Jo line for five seasons. In 1876, he went to the Red River of the North and ran boats on that stream and on the Assiniboine. He returned to Lakeland in the 1880s.

THING, William. Served as a clerk on the paddle boat G. B. Knapp in 1872.

TREADWELL, Edgar C. Born March 29, 1832, in Susquehanna County, Pennsylvania. He moved to the St. Croix Valley in 1846. Ten years later, he became a pilot on the St. Croix and worked at that position until 1863, when he enlisted to fight in the Civil War. He was wounded in fighting at the Yazoo River.

VAN SANT, A. C. Began working on the river as a cabin boy on the *War Eagle* at age fourteen.

WARD, John G. Born in Philadelphia, Pennsylvania, in 1838. He moved to Galena, Illinois, with his family when quite young. At age twelve, when his parents died, John went alone to Marine Mills on the steamer *Nominee*, arriving in 1851. He was the first white boy on the upper St. Croix. He wintered in the pineries. A Civil War veteran, he died in 1922.

WARD, Thomas E. Brother of John G., he worked as a clerk on the steamer *Knapp* in 1878. He arrived at Marine Mills in 1855. Both of the Ward brothers engaged in steamboating and river business.

WHEELER, Ralph. Born in 1829 in Chautauqua County, New York. He began piloting on the St. Croix in 1850.

WHITE, Henry. Born in 1855 at Stillwater. At age fourteen, he began life on the river. He worked on the steamboats *James Means*, *F. B. Clark*, *G. B. Knapp*, *Penn Wright*, and the *Dispatch*. He joined the crew of the *Isaac Staples* as first mate in 1880.

YOUNG, Capt. Augustus R. Born in November 1827 in Somerset, Maine. He moved to St. Anthony in 1850 and was an early navigator on the St. Croix and Mississippi rivers. Young moved to Stillwater in 1873. He was captain of the stern-wheel rafter *Minnesota*, flagship of the Stillwater fleet at the Battle of the Piles.

Bibliography

Anderson, William C. *The Headstrong Houseboat*, (New York: Crown Publishing), 1972.

Blair, Walter A. *A Raft Pilot's Log*, (Cleveland: Arthur H. Clark Co.), 1930.

Bowell, William D. Speech to Stillwater Lions Club at the St. Croix Bowl, Stillwater, April 28, 1976.

Comfort, Mildred Houghton, *Winter on the Johnny Smoker*, (New York: William Morrow & Co.), 1943.

Dalles *Visitor*, Taylors Falls, Minnesota. Helen White, Publisher. Summer 1974 and Summer 1984.

Donovan, Frank. *Riverboats of America*, (New York: Crowell Publishing), 1966.

Drago, Harry Sinclair. *The Steamboaters*, (New York: Bramhall House), 1967.

Dunn, James Taylor. *150 Years of Village Life*, (Marine on St. Croix: Marine Restoration Society), 1989.

Dunn, James Taylor. *Saving the River*, (St. Paul: St. Croix River Association), 1986.

Dunn, James Taylor. *The St. Croix, Midwest Border River*, (New York: Holt, Rinehart and Winston), 1965. Paperback reprint, (St. Paul: Minnesota Historical Society Press), 1979.

Durant, Edward White. "Steam Navigation: Lumbering and Steamboating on the St. Croix River," a paper read at a meeting of the Executive Council of the Minnesota Historical Society, April 11, 1904. Paperback updated reprint, (St. Paul: Minnesota Historical Society Press), 1979.

Easton, Augustus B. *History of the St. Croix Valley*, vol. I and II, (Chicago: H. C. Cooper, Jr.), 1909.

Eskew, Garnett Laidlow. *The Pageant of the Packets*, (New York: Henry Holt & Co.), 1929.

Folsom, W. H. C. *Fifty Years in the Northwest*, (St. Paul: Pioneer Press Company), 1888.

Gilman, Rhoda R. and Holmquist, June Drenning, co-editors. *Minnesota History—50th Anniversary Anthology*, (St. Paul: Minnesota Historical Society Press), 1965.

Griffith, A. Carr. Interviews, December 1972, June 1978 and December 1989.

Havighurst, Walter. *Voices on the River*, (New York, MacMillan), 1964.

Heyler, Walter. "Steamboat Traffic on the Upper Mississippi River," (St. Paul: Minnesota Historical Society), microfilm no. 15.

Hunter, Lewis C. *Steamboats on the Western Rivers*, (Cambridge: Harvard University Press), 1949.

Lewis, Sinclair. *The God Seekers*, (New York: Ramdom House), 1949.

Merrick, George Byron. *Old Times on the Upper Mississippi*, (St. Paul: Minnesota Historical Society Press), reprint, 1987.

Merrick, George Byron. "Steamboats and Steamboat Men of the Upper Mississippi," *Saturday Evening Post*, (Burlington, Iowa), 1913-1920.

Minneapolis *Sunday Tribune*, (Minneapolis, Minnesota), November 25, 1934.

Morrison, John E. *History of American Steam Navigation*, (New York: Argosy Press), 1967.

O'Neil, Paul. *The Rivermen*, (New York: Time/Life Publications), 1975.

Runk, John. Photographic collection: Stillwater Public Library, Washington County Historical Society (Stillwater), Minnesota Historical Society (St. Paul).

St. Paul *Dispatch*, St. Paul, December 14, 1980 and May 14, 1982.

Sampson, Henry L. "The Great Red Wing/Stillwater Boat Race," Heritage Series, WAVN Radio, Stillwater, Minnesota.

Shippee, Lester Burrell. "Steamboating on the Upper Mississippi after the Civil War," *Mississippi Valley Historical Review*, Mississippi Valley Historical Association, vol. 6.

Stillwater *Gazette*, Stillwater, Minnesota, Phil Easton, publisher.

Stillwater *Post Messenger*, Stillwater, Minnesota.

Twain, Mark. *Life on the Mississippi*, (New York: Harper & Brothers Publishers), 1874.

Villiers, Capt. Alan John. *Men, Ships and the Sea*, (Washington D.C.: National Geographic Society), 1962.

Warner, George E. and Foote, Charles M. *History of Washington County and the St. Croix Valley*, (Minneapolis: North Star Publishing Company), 1881.

Waison, Kenneth. *Paddle Steamers, an Illustrated History of Steamboats on the Mississippi and Its Tributaries*, (New York: W. W. Norton), 1985.

Waterways Journal, January 2, 1954, (Washington, D.C.: National Geographic Society).

Weatherhead. "Westward to the St. Croix," Hudson *Star Observer*, (Hudson, Wisconsin), 1978.

Winther, Oscar Osburn. *The Transportation Frontier*, (Bloomington, Indiana: Indiana University Book Store), 1942.

Winona *Daily News*, (Winona, Minnesota), Heritage Edition, October 31, 1986.

Wyman, Norbury L. *Life on the River*, (New York: Bonanza Books), 1971.

Index

Index of Boats

Abner Gile, 31, 51, 60, 131, 160, 161.
Active, 62.
Ada B, 27, 31, 47, 106.
Alert, 50.
Alexander Gordon, 105.
Alexander Hamilton, 156.
Alexander Mitchell, 161.
Alice D, 52, 57.
Alone, 112.
Altair, 40.
Alton, 89.
Amulet, 81.
Andiamo, 151, 152.
Andiamo Showboat, 150, 152.
Andiamo Too, 41.
Annie Barnes, 53.
Annie Gordon, 160.
Anson Northop, 159.
Anthony Wayne, 81, 82.
Aquilla, 109.
Arcola, piledriver, 44, 59, 108, 132.
Arcola, steamboat, 43.
Argo, 37.
Ariel, 20.
Arkansas, 31, 55.
Artemus Lamb, 30.
A. T. Jenks, 52, 135.
Atlanta, 28.
Atlantis, 140.
Aunt Betsy, 27, 31, 65, 110.

Baby, 31, 46, 54, 57, 109, 113, 115, 136, 159.
Bangor, 41.
Banjo, 39, 40, 126.
Belle Mac, 30.
Belle of La Crosse, 158.
Ben Campbell, 4, 45.
Ben Hur, 13, 32, 113, 138.
B. Hershey, 4, 31, 134, 154.
Bill Henderson, 31, 133.
Blackhawk, 112, 118.
Blue Goose, 135.
Blue Lodge, 30.
Bonner, 88.
Borealis Rex, 31, 57, 86, 88, 90.
Brother Jonathan, 31, 49, 156.
Buckeye, 155.
Bun Hersey, 31, 58, 134, 138, 155.
Burdette, 50.

Caleb Cape, 37.
Capitol Steamer, 124, 141, 142.
Candy Boat, 139, 140.
Cecelia, 23.
Cessna, 90.
Charlie Cheever, 153.
Charlotte Boeckler, 30.
Chauncey Lamb, 30, 135, 160.
City of Hudson, 52, 136.
City of Memphis, 90.

City of Prescott, 35.
City of St. Paul, 65.
City of Stillwater, 47.
City of Winona, 31.
C. J. Caffery, 30.
C. K. Peck, 31.
Clearmont II, 160.
Cleon, 32, 66, 67, 131.
Clyde, 31, 46, 113, 114, 115, 137, 154, 155.
Coal Bluff, 104.
Col. A. McKenzie, 89.
Columbia, 8, 26, 28, 57, 121.
Comet, 136.
Crown Hill, 122, 123, 141.
C. W. Cowles, 155.
Cumberland Princess, 150.
Cyclone, 53, 153.

Daisy, 53, 153.
Dakotah, 96.
Dalles, 32, 42, 45, 46, 62, 64.
D. A. McDonald, 31.
Dan Hines, 31.
Dan Thayer, 31.
David Bronson, 30, 46, 47, 50, 134.
David Pike, 161.
David Swain, 88, 89, 90.
Delta, 44.
Delta Queen, 146, 147, 148.
Dexter, 45.
Diamond Jo, 160.
Dispatch, 37, 51, 153, 162.
Dr. Franklin, 27, 37.
Dr. Franklin II, 82.
Douglas Boardman, 30.
Dowler's Humbug, 133.
Dubuque, 161.

Eclipse, 31, 135.
Ed Durant, 31.
Ed Durant Jr, 50-52, 135.
Edwin C, 31, 46, 58, 98, 109, 136.
Eldora, 37.
Ellen M, 52.
Enterprise, 4, 25, 27, 32, 41, 42, 45, 62, 64, 103, 112, 129, 157.
Eolean, 39, 105.
Equator, 39, 41, 103, 126, 128, 155, 156.
E. Rutledge, 31.
Eugene, 156.
Eva, 47.
Evansville, 30, 134.
Everett, 50, 51.
Excelsior, 17, 25, 39.

F. B. Clark, 162.
Falls City, 39.
Fannie Harris, 105, 117.
Fannie Thornton, 31, 45.
Fayette, 21, 22.
F. C. A. Denkman, 30.
Flora Clark, 31, 57.
Frontenac, 30, 135.

Flying Eagle, 31.
Frankie Folsom, 46.
Fred Lorenz, 128.
Fred Swain, 87, 88.
Fred Weyerhauser, 30.
Fury, 52, 153.

Galena, 83.
Gardie Eastman, 31, 50.
Gazelle, 31.
G. B. Knapp, 27, 28, 31, 46, 49, 55, 62, 63, 66, 68, 69-77, 101, 103, 109, 127, 130, 131, 137, 157, 160, 163.
General Allen, vi.
General Barnard, 136.
General Hyde Clark, 31.
General McKenzie, 136.
George Prince, 89.
George S, 31, 46, 134.
George Washington, 4, 5.
George Lysle, 31.
Germania, 66.
G. H. Gray, 31, 42, 45, 157.
Glemont, 110, 135.
Golden Gate, 30.
Goldenrod, 122, 123, 141.
Governor Ramsey, 158.
Gracie Kent, 16, 26, 57, 118, 120.
Gracie Mower, 47.
Granite Star, 161.
Gray Eagle, 11, 40.
G. W. Hill, 122.
Gypsy, 20, 46.

Hartford, 155.
Helen Blair, 40.
Helen Mar, 30, 64, 65, 113, 129, 130, 157, 160.
Helen Schulenburg, 31, 50.
Henrietta, 30, 50, 119, 129, 135, 159.
Highland Mary, 23, 111, 125, 160.
H. S. Allen, 32, 41, 42, 103, 105, 112, 126, 127, 128, 156, 157, 160.
Humboldt, 31, 37, 54.

Ida, 158.
Ida Clark, 31.
Ida Fulton, 110.
I. E. Staples, 31, 50.
Illinois, 99.
Indian Queen, 23, 45, 158.
Iowa, 99.
Irene, 31.
Isaac Staples, 10, 12, 30, 46, 57, 93, 134, 155, 156, 162.
Itasca, 118, 120.

James Fisk Jr, 31.
James Melbon, 31.
James Means, 31, 46, 70, 74, 78, 162.
James Raymond, 39, 126.
Jennie Hayes, 27, 32, 45, 65, 66, 134, 157.
Jenny Thornton, 45.

165

Jessie B, 31.
Jessie Bill, 30.
J. G. Chapman, 31, 155.
J. G. Park, 31.
Jim Watson, 31.
J. J. Hill, 31, 53.
J. K. Graves, 30, 134.
J. O. Henning, 34.
John H. Douglas, 30.
Johnnie Smoker, 31.
Jonathan Padelford, 101, 144, 145, 148.
Joseph Long, 53, 88.
Josephine, 31.
Josiah Snelling, 148.
J. S., 8, 122, 141.
J. S. Keaton, 31.
Jubilee, I, v, 114, 115, 145, 146.
Julia B, 12.
Julia Belle Swain, 90.
Julia Hadley, 31.
June Bug, 45, 64.
Juniata, 31, 46, 100, 114, 115.
J. W. Mills, 31.
J. W. Van Sant, 30, 135.

Kabekona, 88.
Kalitan, 116, 140, 141.
Kate Cassel, 41, 155.
Kate Keen, 30.
Kate Waters, 31.
Kit Carson, 30, 50, 153.

La Crosse, 58.
Lady Pike, 159.
Lady Grace, 31.
Lafayette Lamb, 31.
Lake Superior, 32.
Lamertine, 111, 112.
L and M, 57.
Lasing, 160.
Last Chance, 31.
Le Claire Belle, 30.
Le Roy, 57, 159.
Lily Turner, 31, 155.
Little Eagle, 31.
Little Rufus, 88.
Lizzie Gardner, 113, 115, 136.
Lone Star, 160.
Lora, 28, 51, 99, 120, 121, 136.
Lorene, 31, 67, 137.
Lottie Lyon, 41, 153.
Lotus Lily, 113.
Louisville, 30, 49, 50, 136.
Luella, 53, 155.
Luella Alton, 33.
Lumberman, 31.
L. W. Crane, 31.
L. W. Van Sant, 155.
Lydia Van Sant, 32, 81.
Lynn J, 66, 67.
Lynx, 23, 156.

Maggie Reaney, 32, 65, 110, 120, 157.
Markatana, 116, 140, 141.
Mark Bradley, 31, 53, 130.
Mark Painter, 31.
Mary B, 113, 137.
Mary Barnes, 28, 64, 76, 158.

Mayflower, 45, 64.
May Queen, 133.
Menomonie, 134.
Metropolitan, 25, 40.
Mike Davis, 113.
Milwaukee, 161.
Minnesota, 10, 11, 32, 48, 49, 99, 163.
Minnesota Belle, 10, 26, 37.
Minnie Will, 30, 45, 62, 63, 71, 159.
Missouri, 99.
Mollie Mohler, 31, 70.
Mollie Whitmore, 31.
Moline, 31.
Montana, 97, 98.
Montello, 39.
Moonstone, 133.
Morning Star, 32, 154.
Mountain Belle, 31, 121, 161.
Muscatine, 31, 99.

Natrona, 31.
Nellie Kent, 1, 28, 32, 46, 55, 62, 64, 68, 69-77, 106, 130, 157, 160.
Nellie Sheldon, 32.
Netta Durant, 30, 50.
Nettie, 135.
New Brazil, 37.
New Orleans, 3.
New St. Croix, 25.
Nina, 53, 135, 153.
Nominee, 30, 82, 162.
North Star, 30, 141, 145, 159.

Ocean Wave, 33.
Olive S, 24, 28, 29, 31, 59, 60, 122.
Osceola, 32, 47, 61.
Osceola I, 43.
Osceola II, 43.
Osceolin, 47.
Otter, 23, 156.

Palmyra, 16, 19, 20, 101.
Park Bluff, 120.
Pauline, 30, 50, 120, 121, 153.
Pearl, 32.
Penn Wright, 31, 135, 159, 162.
Peoria, 89.
Percy Swain, 53, 85, 86, 90.
Percy Swain II, 89.
Pete Kerns, 31.
Petrel, 156.
Pioneer, 32, 44, 45, 62-64, 69, 71, 130, 133.
Plough Boy, 47, 53, 88.
Polly, 139, 140, 145.
Progress, 86.
Purchase, 18, 28, 113, 121-122, 136, 137, 161.

Queen of the Lakes, 151.
Queen of the Yellow Banks, 37, 39, 155.
Queen Piajuk, 106-108.

Ramora, 50.
Ravenna, 57, 58, 62, 63, 77, 127, 138, 155.
Red Wing, 10, 51, 131.
Reindeer, 31.
Rescue, 86.
R. G. Wheeler, 50, 153.

R. J. Wheeler, 30.
Roamer, 109.
Robert, 57.
Robert Dodds, 31, 50.
Robert Ross, 31.
Robert Semple, 30.
Roosevelt, 90.
Rose Island, 90.

St. Croix, 28, 31, 45, 57, 59, 60, 158.
St. Croix III, 50.
St. Paul, 29.
Sam Atlee, 31.
Satelite, 30.
Saturn, 30.
Sea Wing, 155.
Senator, 106.
Sidney, 31, 123.
Silas Wright, 30.
Silver Crescent, 31.
Silver Wave, 30, 160.
Speed, 86.
Spray, 31, 42, 112.
Staver, 42, 63.
Steamboat Round the Bend, 143.
Sterling, 31.
Stillwater, 30, 31.
Sucker State, 30.
Surveyor, 140.
Swallow, 49, 109, 110.

Taber, 31.
Taylors Falls Princess, 148-150.
Taylors Falls Queen, 149.
Teal, 127.
Ten Broeck, 50, 51.
Tennessee, 21, 22.
Thistle, 31.
Tidal Wave, 31.
Tiger, 46, 160.
Time and Tide, 31.
Tobacco Plant, 33.
Twin Cities, 18, 28, 121.
Two Brothers, 35.

Verne Swain, 14, 31, 53, 86, 88, 90.
Verne Swain II, 88.
Verne Swain III, 89, 90.
Vernie Mac, 26, 38, 135, 157.
Viola, 31, 44, 61, 62, 157, 160.
Volunteer, 31.

Wakerobin, 102, 141.
W. A. Knapp, 41.
Wanderer, 136.
War Eagle, 11, 29, 33, 36, 83, 158, 161, 162.
Western Belle, 33.
Whitmore, 49.
Wild Boy, 31.
William White, 31, 51.
W. W., 36.
Wyman X, 28, 31, 46, 50, 70, 103, 110, 155.

General Index

References to Stillwater, Osceola, Taylors Falls, St. Croix River, Lake St. Croix, Marine, Osceola, and others that are very frequently mentioned in the text are not included in the index.

Afton, 39, 56, 97, 106, 128.
Ainsworth, Juliana, 85.
Albany, Illinois, 80, 82, 84.
Aldrich, Mrs. Paschal, 103.
Aldrich, Dr. Phillip, 34, 103.
Allen, H. S., 41, 157.
Allen, Maj. Charles J., 27, 97, 157.
Amador, Minnesota, 45, 63.
American Fur Company, 158.
American Legion Post 48, 142.
Anderson, Dick, 150.
Anderson, Don, 150.
Anderson & O'Brien Lumber Co., 57, 63, 77, 127.
Anthony, Capt. E. C., 121.
Arcola, Minnesota, 2, 27, 42, 43, 46, 47, 74, 106, 107, 108, 122, 159.
Arcola Sand Bar, 75, 112, 114.
Armson, James G., 89.
Archison, Capt. John, 23, 125.

Baker, Capt. E. L., 78.
Ball, Spencer, 153.
Ballard, Draper & Company, 25.
Barnes, Charles, 53.
Bartlett, Captain, 62.
Batchelder, Josiah Q., 45, 50-52, 88, 89, 153.
Battle of the Piles, 46, 48, 110, 155, 162.
Bayport, Minnesota, (See also South Stillwater), 50, 159.
Bayport Boat Yard, 50.
Baytown, Minn., 34, 53, 57, 153, 159.
Beck, Alfred, 79.
Beef Slough, 97.
Bennett, Emily, 83.
Bennet, William T., 36.
Berkey, Hiram, 21, 22, 35.
Beyle, Gus, 44.
Black Crook, The, 69.
Blair, Capt. Walter A., 51, 84.
Blakeley, Russell, 37.
Boule, Gus, 59.
Bowell, Capt. William, 144, 145, 148.
Bowers, Elizabeth, 153.
Bradley, Capt. Cyrus J., 37, 45, 53, 62, 153.
Brasser, George, 154.
Breckenridge, Minn., 63, 109, 110, 134.
Bronson & Folsom Co, 46, 56-58, 98, 109, 113-115, 127, 134, 137, 154.
Bronson, David, 39.
Brown, Joseph R., 21, 34, 37.
Brunson, B. W., 39.
Brule, Severe, 80.
Bryan, Anthony H., 154.
Bryant, William Jennings, 120.
Buisson, Cypriano, 154.
Burbank, James W., 159.
Burlington Lumber Co., 50.
Burkleo, Sam, 21.
Burkleo, Capt. Henry, 53.
Butler, Charles J., 154.
Butler & Gray, 133.

Cain, John, 78.
Campbell, James, 143.
Campbell, Katie, 143.
Caneday, David A., 42.
Cardiff Giant, 120.
Carli, Lydia Brown, 80.
Carson & Rand Lumber Co., 50.
Cascade Falls, 62.
Catfish Bar, 56, 97, 98, 128, 142.
Cedar Bend, 75, 131.
Cedar Lake, 151.
Champlin, H. D., 154.
Chapin Hall House, 66.
Chicago Northwestern Railroad Ferry, 155.
Chippewa Falls, Wisconsin, 41, 157.
Chippewa Indians, 19, 20, 39, 106, 128.
Chisago Boat Yard, 46.
Chisago Seminary, 13, 41.
Cholera Epidemic, 125.
Christenson, Charles, 140.
Christmas, 65, 110.
Cincinnati, Ohio, 5, 135, 154.
Cincinnati/New Orleans Packet Co., 154.
Circus
  Barnum & Bailey, 120.
  DeHavens Great Union, 69.
  Great Eastern Menagerie and, 70.
  Great Monkey & Burlesque Dramatic Troupe, 126.
  Great New York & New Orleans, 71, 120.
  P. A. Older Museum & Menagerie, 120.
Civil War, 5, 16, 36, 42, 45, 83, 128, 162.
Clark, Matt, 30, 50.
Clemmons, Frank, 135.
Cleveland, Grover, 100.
Clinton, Iowa, 45, 64, 65, 81, 86.
Coca-Cola Bottling, 149.
Collins, Mike, 44, 59.
Combacker, H. C., 131, 135.
Connors, Patsey, 44, 53, 59.
Constaine, Capt. P., 65.
Coon Slough, 109.
Cormack, John W., 154.
Cover, Susan, 159.
Cowan, Capt. Stephen L., 39.
Crane Brothers, 85.
Crosby, Henry W., 45, 102.
Cushing, Capt. Thomas, 36.
Curtis, Fred, 130.
Curtis, Capt. Gold T., 128.

Dakotah, 37.
Dalles House, 27, 143.
Dalles of the St. Croix, 21, 24, 25, 28, 39, 41, 46, 60, 62, 66, 75, 99, 101, 110, 127, 149.
Darrah, L. W., 154.
Davenport, Iowa, 22, 43, 61, 81, 84, 86.
Davidson, William F., 46, 69, 70, 74.
Davis, John B., 97, 98.
Davison, Charles H., 154.
Davison, Daniel D., 154.
DeCamp, Ira, 155.
Deephaven-Wayzata Express, 30.
Delta Queen Steamboat Co., 149.
Densmore, Henry, 42.
Denton, S. S., 129.
Derby, Major, 98, 99.
Diamond Jo Steamer Co., 11, 12, 42, 55, 78, 84, 160, 161.
Dibble, William, 21, 22, 34, 155.
Dickson, Col., 158.
Dotterweich, George, 155.
Doughty, Capt. Henry C., 53, 113, 135, 137.
Dove, Bill, 117.
Dove, Sam, 117.
Dubuque, Iowa, 11, 21, 45, 57, 81, 110, 114, 115, 127, 134, 137.
Dubuque Boat Co., 88, 145, 146.
Dudley, John, 53, 64, 65.
du Luth, Sieur, 19.
Dunn, James Taylor, 17, 22, 39, 108.
Du Pae, Ralph, 36, 135.
Durant, Edward White, 37, 98, 105, 112, 119, 155.
Durant, Wheeler & Co., 49, 50, 51, 53, 119, 121, 135, 136, 153, 156.

Eames, Capt. Albert, 39, 155.
East Side Lumber Co., 134, 136.
Easton, William E., 19.
Ebaugh, Capt. Charles, 86.
Eden, Robert C., 62.
Edwards, Prof. Elijah, 41, 42.
Eller, Elizabeth, 118.
Elliott, William, 155.
Ellison, Smith, 71, 74, 75, 76.
Empire Coal Docks, 51.
Evansville & Bowling Green Packet Co., 86.

Fasiling, H. B., 53.
Farmer, Hazel, 89.
Farquier, Major, 97.
Ferguson, Harvey, 44, 59.
Fey, Mrs. Charles, 90.
Fifield, Sam S., 155.
First Minnesota Regiment, 42, 128.
Fisher, Capt. William, 40.
Fisherman John, 132.
Fitch, Dr., 21.
Fitzgerald, Pat, 58.
Flat Iron Bar, 83.
Flynn, Dan, 44, 59.
Folsom, W. H. C., 19, 23, 33, 36, 46, 97, 155.
Folsom, Wyman X., 46, 110, 155.
Fort Garry, 110, 159.
Fort Snelling, Minn., 19, 21, 23, 24, 33, 37, 42, 125, 158.
Forest Lake, Minnesota, 66.
Foster & Thornton, 45.
Fox, John B., 78.
Fountain City, Wisconsin, 53, 86.
Fourth of July, 75, 118, 120, 133.
Franconia, Minn., 2, 27, 28, 35, 44, 45, 61, 65-67, 108, 110, 135, 157.
Freeland, Isaac, 126.

Frontenac, Minn., 120, 133, 153.
Fuller, Raymond, 58.
Fullerton, Rev. T. M., 126.
Fulton, Robert, 3, 4, 5.
Furber, J. W., 21.

Galena, Ill., 14, 23, 37, 82, 106, 156, 161, 162.
Galena-Minnesota Mail Line, 4.
Galena & Minnesota Packet Co., 40.
Gambling, 117.
Garrison, Lemuel, 155.
German Singing Society, 120.
Gillespie & Harper Co., 51.
Giossi, Frank, 72.
Godfrey, George, 87.
Goff, John, 30.
Goodhue, James W., 111.
Gordon, Captain, 101.
Grady, Asa Barlow, 155.
Grant, Capt. Edward, 37.
Grant, Peter, 47.
Gratz, Anderson, 139, 140.
Gray, Capt. Isaac, 41, 45, 103, 154, 156.
Greeley, Horace, 14.
Green, Capt. Asa B., 41, 126, 127, 130.
Green, Capt. Thomas, 148.
Green, Capt. S. E., 51, 52.
Green Lake, 44, 63.
Green, Sheriff A. B., 130.
Greysolon, Daniel, 19.
Griffith, Capt. A. Carr, v, 115, 139, 145, 146, 151.
Guthrie, Archibald, 88.
Guttenberg, Iowa, 83.

Halleck, Gen. Henry W., 128.
Hanford, John, 156.
Hanks, Capt. David, 42.
Hanks, Nancy, 79.
Hanks, Samuel, 156.
Hanks, Capt. Stephen B., 79-84.
Hanks, Thomas, 79.
Harper & Gillespie Co., 53, 135.
Harriman, Sam, 37.
Harriman's Landing, 14.
Harris, Capt. Smith, 23, 33, 82.
Harrison, Benjamin, 100.
Harrison, Joseph, 78.
Harrison, W. H., 46.
Hastings, Minn., 14, 34, 35, 47, 54, 58, 69, 117, 121, 128, 135, 138, 155.
Haycock & Co., 105.
Hayes, Angeline, 157.
Hayes, Capt. David, 42, 45, 63, 65, 134.
Hayes, George, 86, 100, 113.
Hazzard, George, 156.
Hejland, John, 47.
Heller, Mathias, 35.
Henning, William, 109.
Hermes, Capt. George, 43, 61.
Herrick, Capt. H. M., 112.
Hersey, Bronson, Doe & Folsom, 55.
Hersey, Staples & Co., 155.
Hoey, John, 156.
Holcombe, Gov. Wm. S., 21, 22, 80.
Hole-in-the-Day, Chief, 128.
Holland, Captain, 19, 20.

Hone, David, 20, 21, 22.
Hone, Mrs. David, 21, 22.
Hooper, Capt. William H., 23, 156.
Hotels
    Hudson, 112.
    Michael Marsh's, 66.
    Minnesota House, 112.
    Riverside, 75-76.
Houghton, Capt. George, 70.
Houghton, James, 70.
Houlton, Wisconsin, 35.
Hoy, Capt. John, 57, 127, 138.
Hubbard, Lucius F., 98.
Hudson, Wisconsin, 2, 14, 25, 35, 36, 39-42, 44, 45, 48, 49, 66, 97, 103, 106, 112, 113, 120, 122, 126, 128, 129, 142, 146, 154-156, 158.
Hudson, Edd, 109.
Hugenine, Peter, 72.
Hungerford, W. S., 21, 22.

Iceboats, 106-108.
Immigrants, Swedish, 70.
Interstate Bridge, Stillwater, 35, 145.
Interstate Navigation Co., 26, 57, 135.
Interstate Park, 28, 99, 121, 156.
Irish, John S., 44-47, 49, 106.

Jackins, Miss, 157.
Jackson, Harry, 58.
Jackson, Mrs., 39.
Jacobi, Jacob, 131.
Jenks, A. I., 156.
Jeremy, John, 132.
Jewell, Phillip B., 156.
Johnson, Everett, 94.
Johnson, Frank, 44, 59.
Johnson, George, 44.
Johnson, John, 44, 59.
Judd, Lewis S., 20.
Judd, Sam, 71, 76.
Judd, Walker & Co., 25, 39, 62, 154.

Kahlenberg Company, 145.
Kaiser, William, 136.
Keech, George W., 156.
Kent, Agnes, 126.
Kent, Capt. John A. (Jack), 51, 53, 57, 61, 107, 120, 135, 157.
Kent, Capt. William, 64, 65, 67, 126, 129, 157.
Kent, Robert, 64.
Kidder, Ellen, 126.
Kilty, Michael, 130.
Kirchner, E. H., 86.
Knapp, Ben, 63, 65, 66, 157.
Knapp Bros. & Co., 61, 66.
Knapp, Capt. George B., 63, 64, 66, 100, 157.
Knapp, Capt. Oscar, 27, 42, 44, 61-67, 74, 101, 103, 108, 109, 112, 113, 130, 136, 157.
Knapp, Stout & Co., 65.
Koenig, Edward C., 88.
Krupp Iron Works, 149.
Kutz, Walter, 89.

La Crosse, Wis, 33, 36, 58, 62, 64, 65, 76, 105, 109, 112, 113, 135, 149.

Lakeland, Minn., 25, 34, 35, 39, 45, 47, 61, 102, 161.
Lake Calhoun, 151.
Lake of the Isles, 151.
Lake Minnetonka, 30.
Lake Pepin, 25, 36, 37, 43, 74, 81, 83, 106, 153, 160.
Lake Superior, 19, 158.
Lake Winnebago, 158.
Lamb Lumber Co., 84, 136.
Leach, John, 157.
Leager, Capt. William, 66.
Learned, Rufus F., 88.
Leavitt, William L., 157.
Le Claire, Iowa, 60, 160, 161.
Le Claire Navigation Co., 51.
Lent, Charles, 78.
Libby, W. S., 21.
Lincoln, Abraham, 79.
Lincoln, Thomas, 79.
Liverpool Landing, 38.
Lodwick, Capt. M. W., 37.
Log House Landing, 28, 69, 120, 121.
Losch, J. C., 46.
Louisville-Portland Canal, 90.
Lowell Park, 116, 122.
Lund, August, 35.

McAloon, Thomas, 94.
McCarthy, Nelson, 157.
McDonald, James, 158.
McGlaughlin, Lydia, 161.
McGrath, John, 78.
McKinzie, Capt. Duncan, 135.
McKinley, William, 120.
McKune, Mary, 157.
McKusick & Co., 156.
McKusick, Anderson & Co., 55.
McKusick Mill, 80.
McLagen, Dick, 111.
McLean, Daniel, 21.
McMurchy, Captain, 101.
McPhail, Capt. James (Sandy), 81, 158.

MacCormack, John, 157.
Mackey, John, 44.
Magnuson, Swen, 35.
Maguire, Capt. Frank, 34.
Maguoketa Chute, 57.
Mahoney, W. C., 21.
Maiden Rock, Wisconsin, 45, 153.
Mellon, Bill, 117.
Mann, Horace, Jr., 36.
Marine, Illinois, 20.
Marine Ferry, 35.
Marine Lumber Co., 21.
Marine Mills Cornet Band, 120.
Massy, Louis, 158.
Masterson, S. W., 35.
Matt Clark Co., 30, 50, 134.
Maxwell, C. H., 39.
Mayo Brothers, 145.
Mayo, Dr. Charles, 141.
Mears, Charles E., 107, 158.
Meeds, Capt. Charles H., 51, 158.
Memphis, Indiana, 42, 88, 89, 135.
Merrick, George Byron, 42.

Middleton, Capt. W., 19.
Miller, Jim, 143.
Miller, Regina, 143.
Mills, George T., 35.
Mineral Springs, Wisconsin, 74, 76.
Minneapolis, Minn., 40, 62, 64, 75, 82, 114, 125, 151, 158.
Minnesota Highway Dept., 35.
Minnesota Packet Co., 83.
Minnesota Pioneer, 111.
Monroe Bros., 34.
Monroe, Louisiana, 67, 86.
Morarity, J., 78.
Moses, W. H., 34.
Mount Hope Cemetery Assn., 66.
Mower, Martin, 43, 46, 47, 59, 106- 108, 158.
Mueller, L. W., 71.
Mulberry Point, 35, 60.
Mullen, James W. (Jim), 21, 22, 33, 65, 158.
Muller Boat Works, 8, 53, 55-60, 114.
Muller, Carl, 60, 143.
Muller, Dick, 60.
Muller Family, 149.
Muller, George, 29, 44, 45, 55-60, 64, 98, 115, 118, 122, 127, 134.
Muller, George A. (Mike), 56, 60.
Muller, John, 55, 56.
Muller, Philip, 55.
Muller, Roy (Leroy), 56, 60.
Munch, Adolph, 70.
Munch Bros. Shipyard, 43, 47, 61.
Munson, Dell, 127.
Muntz, Capt. G. A., 66.
Murray, Bill, 60.
Muscatine, Illinois, 43, 81.

Natches, Mississippi, 5, 88, 89.
Ned Davis Minstrels, 126.
Nelson, Rensselaer R., 130.
Nelson, Socrates, 113, 156.
Nelson's Point, 133.
Newcomb, Capt. James, 50, 135.
New Year's Day, 110.
New Orleans, Louisiana, 3, 66, 67, 86, 88, 138, 140, 158.
Northern Lines, 46, 70, 78.
Northern Packet Co., 160.
Northey, A. B., 45.
Northup, Anson, 23, 158.
North Star Iron Works, 46, 62.
Northwest Express Co., 159.
Northwest Lumber Co., 19.

Okey, C. H., 135.
Oakland, California, 146, 147.
O'Brien, James S., 77.
Oliver, Capt. John, 34.
O'Neal, Hugh, 159.
Opsahl, Ole, 131.
Otis, Henry F., 35.
Otisville, Minnesota, 28, 69, 120, 121.
Overseas National Airways, 149.
Owen, David Gale, 94.
Owen, John Philips, 37.

Page, Abigale, 25.
Page, Capt. John, 25.

Page's Slough, 27.
Pankonin, W. H., 122.
Parks, Hi, 78.
Parker, Asa, 21, 22.
Parker, Edwin E., 159.
Parker, Ella, 159.
Parker, John E., 159.
Parmlee Bros., 46.
Peavey, Henry L., 135, 159.
People's Independent Steamboat Line, 74.
Peoria, Illinois, 86-90.
Percey, Will, 17.
Perro, Joseph, 110, 133, 154, 159.
Perro, Sylvester, 159.
Peters, Sam., 40, 135.
Peters, William G., 109.
Peterson, William J., 19.
Phille, E. B., 78.
Pitt, Mr., 19.
Pittsburgh, Penn., 3, 5, 90, 154.
Point Douglas, Minn., 23, 34, 35, 103, 105, 155.
Pole, Gen. John, 128.
Polk County Press, 27, 61, 106, 107, 108.
Pound, Thaddeus C., 97.
Prairie du Chien, Wis., 16, 23, 24, 34, 36, 102, 106, 158.
Pratt, Frank H., 117.
Prescott, Wis., 2, 14, 23, 33-36, 39, 42-44, 46, 47, 53, 59, 64, 69, 70, 74, 99, 102, 103, 113, 117, 128-130, 135, 155, 157, 160.
Prescott Journal, 64.
Prescott Machine Shop, 53.
Prescott, Philander, 23.
Prince, Capt. George, 88, 90.
Princeton, Minnesota, 154, 157.
Puttman, J. D., 112.
Purinton, Eliza, 158.

Quinlan, Capt. John, 60, 159.

Railroads
 Duluth, 66.
 Northern Pacific, 136.
 Omaha, 142.
 St. Paul, Stillwater, Taylors Falls, 48, 65, 109.
 Soo Line, 67, 121, 133.
 Western Wisconsin, 48, 53, 144.
Raiter, Frank M., 160.
Ralphe, F. X., 30.
Raymond, Arthur, 44.
Reaney, Capt. J. H., 65.
Red Wing, Minn., 13, 26, 36, 78, 120, 122, 153, 160.
Reed, Jean, 94.
Reed's Landing, Minnesota, 82, 83, 85.
Register, Capt. Sam, 160.
Retail Grocer's Assn., 121.
Reynolds, Capt. Joseph, 42, 84, 160.
Rhodes, Charles, 160.
Rhodes, Capt. Thomas B., 40.
Rivers
 Apple, 53, 71, 112.
 Arkansas, 88.
 Assiniboine, 161.
 Black, 36, 67.
 Cheyenne, 159.

Chippewa, 41, 65, 81.
Clyde, 146.
Des Moines, 44.
Fox, 41, 62, 158.
Illinois, 38, 46, 86, 88, 89, 90.
Iowa, 88.
Kettle, 53, 192.
Kinnickinnick, 41.
Minnesota, 5, 39, 46, 63, 82, 119, 128, 153.
Missouri, 5, 64, 76, 98, 155.
Monongehela, 3, 90.
Namekagon, 47, 53.
Ohio, 3, 4, 79, 86, 90, 148, 154.
Ouachita, 67, 86.
Red of the North, 63, 85, 110, 134, 158, 159, 161.
Red of the South, 67.
St. Lawrence, 154.
Snake, 20, 53, 80.
Tennessee, 145, 148.
Totogatic, 53.
Totogaticonce, 53.
Wabash, 80.
Willow, 25, 35, 112.
Wisconsin, 155, 158.
Yazoo, 162.
Yellow, 53.
Yellowstone, 43, 61.
Riverside Hotel, 75-76.
Robinson, Danny, 44, 59.
Rock Island, Ill., 40, 43, 44, 61, 86, 160.
Rolling Stone Sand Bar, 97.
Roosevelt, Theodore, 89.
Root, James, 160.
Rose Flour Mill, 72.
Roundy, Mike, 109.
Royal Route, 88, 89.
Ruley, Capt. Russell, 106, 160.

Sachpell, Henry, 109.
St. Anthony, Minn, 39, 46, 82, 125, 158, 162.
St. Croix Boat & Packet Co., 151, 152.
St. Croix Boom, 11, 25, 26, 27, 44, 46, 52, 57, 59, 64, 71, 98, 99, 115, 135, 158.
St. Croix Falls, Wis, 20, 22, 27, 37, 39, 41, 43, 45, 70, 103, 121.
St. Croix Falls Lumber Co., 80.
St. Croix Grasshopper, 108.
St. Croix Lumber Co., 21, 50, 109, 153, 159.
St. Croix & Mississippi Packet Co., 44.
St. Croix Union, 105.
St. Louis, Missouri, 5, 7, 14, 19, 21, 23, 25, 30, 33, 36, 37, 45, 64, 80, 81, 88, 111, 113, 124, 125, 128, 129, 141, 153, 154, 155, 156, 158, 160.
St. Michael's Cemetery, 159.
St. Paul & St. Croix Packet Line, 55.
St. Paul Band, 78, 133.
St. Paul Dispatch, 109.
St. Peter, Minnesota, 37.
St. Petersburgh, Wisconsin, 35.
Saturday Evening Post, 22, 25.
Sauntry, William, 52, 120, 121.
Sawyer House, 120.
Schiffman, Dr. Rudolph J., 109.

Schulenberg & Boeckler Co., 30, 154.
Scully, T., 78.
Shakopee, Minnesota, 82.
Short, Jerome E., 160, 161.
Shreve, Henry, 4, 10.
Sioux Indians, 19, 20, 82, 128.
Smith, Erskine, 108.
Smith, Capt. John T., 138.
Smith, Orrin, 37, 82.
Smith, Capt. W. C., 99.
Somerset, Wisconsin, 14, 37.
Soule, Jesse H., 161.
South Stillwater (See also Bayport), 50, 53, 60, 86, 159, 160, 161.
Sparks, Mel, 44, 59.
Spiller, Felix, 36.
Stack, Ed., 44.
Stambough, 20.
Staples, C. W., 135.
Staples Foundry, 66.
Staples, Isaac, 46, 50, 55, 74, 134, 160.
Staples, Josiah, 110, 161.
Staples, Samuel, 161.
Steamboat Acts, 100, 101.
Steele, Franklin, 19, 20, 80.
Stephen, A. L., 76.
Sterrett, Frank S., 78.
Stickney, G. M., 41.
Stillwater Cornet Band, 66, 69, 110, 129.
Stillwater Dock Co., 44, 50, 53, 59, 153.
Stillwater Gazette, 22, 30, 49, 67, 71, 72, 74, 94, 109, 113, 117, 129, 136.
Stillwater Lumberman, 72, 108.
Stillwater Messenger, 40, 60, 66, 77, 103.
Stillwater Republican, 62.
Stillwater Yacht Club, 60.
Stockholm, Wisconsin, 43.
Storer, Capt. Augustus, 63.
Stover & Barnes, 45.
Stratton, Levi W., 16, 19.
Streif, John, 161.
Strekfus, Capt. John, 86.
Strekfus, Capt. Verne, 142.
Strekfus Line, 124, 141.
Strong, Capt. E. B., 41, 157.
Sturgeon Bend, 83.
Sullivan, Bill, 44, 59.
"Summer Rambles in the West," 118.
Sun Line, 145.
Swain, Arthur, 85.
Swain, Capt. David, 51, 53, 65, 85-90, 122, 129.
Swain, D. M. Marine Engine Works, 85-90.
Swain, Earl, 85.
Swain, Fred, 85, 88, 90.
Swain, Gertrude, 85.
Swain, Maude, 85, 90.
Swain, Verne, 85, 87, 88, 90.
Swede Lake, 42.
Swedish immigrants, 70.

Tannor, Capt. Lewis, 86.
Taylor, Bayard, 128.
Taylor, Dick, 72.
Taylor, Joshua L., 21, 22.
Taube, Count Henning A., 70.
Taylors Falls Journal, 22, 86, 106.
Taylors Falls Reporter, 117.

Teare, Capt. James T. (Jim), 24, 26, 29, 59, 60, 122.
Tennessee Jubilee Singers, 78.
Thing, William, 162.
Thomas, Chet, 60.
Thompson, Capt. Marcus, 65, 131.
Thompson, William, 47.
Thoreau, Henry David, 36.
Thornton, Mr. 44, 45.
Throckmorton, Captain, 20, 23.
Tilton, E. H., 46.
Timmers, Capt. Charles, 43.
Titcomb's Landing, 133.
Torinus, George, 66.
Torinus, L. E., 50.
Tozer, David, 153.
Trader, Napoleon Bonaparte, 117.
Trask, Byron, 57, 127, 138.
Treadwell, Edgar C., 162.
Truax, Mr., 53.
Trumble, Mr., 41.
Tucker Marine Co., 150.
Turner Society, 120.
Tuttle, Calvin A., 19.
Two Rivers, Wisconsin, 145.

Ulrich, Mary, 36.
Upper River Convention, 27.
U.S. Army Engineering Dept., 114, 140, 141.
U.S. Congress, 27, 97, 100, 101, 149.
U.S. General Mail, 39, 71, 88, 102.
U.S. War Department, 64, 100.

Van Hollen, Diedrick, 69.
Van Sant, A. C., 162.
Van Sant, Samuel R., 30, 89, 135.
Vicksburg, Michigan, 88, 89, 90.

Wabasha, Minn., 40, 53, 58, 109, 135, 139, 155.
Wall, Sam, kiln, 74.
Walker, Gilbert, 35.
Walker, Judd & Veazie, 71.
Walker, Louis, 57, 127.
Walker, Orange, 21, 22.
Ward, Ellis, 78.
Ward, John G., 162.
Ward, Thomas E., 162.
Warner, George F., 22, 53.
West, Hamilton, 53.
West Slough, 75.
Westergren, Charles, 35.
Wheeler, R. G., 50.
Wheeler, Capt. R. J., 49.
Wheeler, Ralph, 162.
White Bear Lake, 51.
White, Charles, 53.
White, E., 44, 45.
White, Henry, 162.
Wiard, Norman, 106.
Wilcox, Capt. H. C., 58.
Willow River Sand Bar, 97.
Winch, Capt. Marshall, 45, 46, 62, 64.
Wing, Frank, 122.
Winona, Minn., 36, 37, 44, 59, 114, 115, 155.
Winona Independent, 96.

World War I, 7, 88, 90.
World War II, 141, 146, 147.
World's Fair, 121, 150.
Wright, Norman, 78.

York, Capt. Sol, 86.
Young, Capt. Augustus R., 50, 162.